THE EPIC FILM

Cinema and Society

General Editor

Jeffrey Richards
Department of History
University of Lancaster

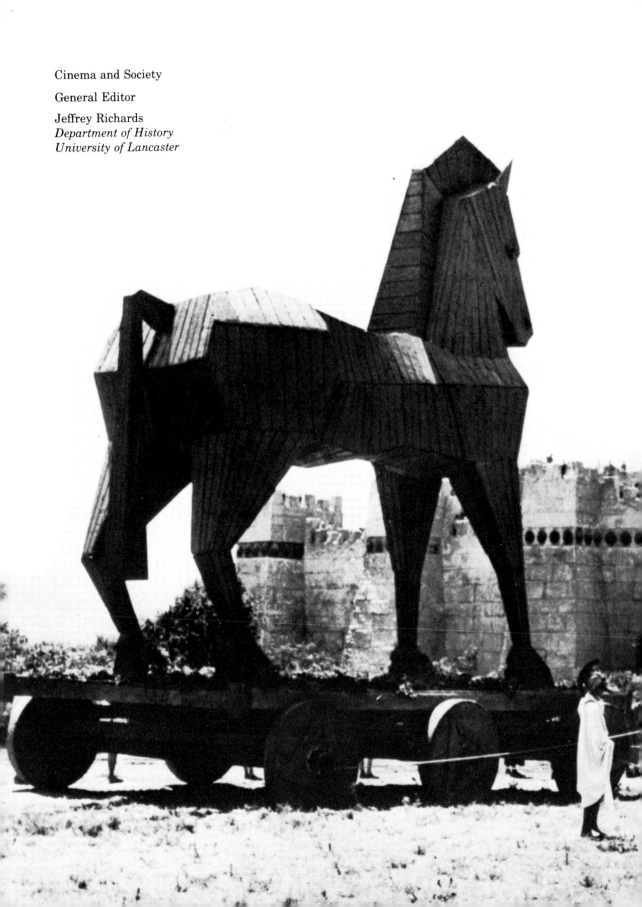

THE EPIC FILM

Myth and History

Derek Elley

Routledge & Kegan Paul

London, Boston, Melbourne and Henley

First published in 1984
by Routledge & Kegan Paul plc
39 Store Street, London WC1E 7DD,
9 Park Street, Boston, Mass. 02108, USA,
464 St Kilda Road, Melbourne,
Victoria 3004, Australia and
Broadway House, Newtown Road,
Henley-on-Thames, Oxon RG9 1EN
First published as a paperback 1985

Set in Century 9/11pt by
Columns, Reading
and printed in Great Britain by
St Edmundsbury Press,
Bury St Edmunds, Suffolk

Library of Congress Cataloging in Publication Data

Elley, Derek.

The epic film.
(Cinema and society)
Filmography: p.
Bibliography: p.
Includes indexes.
1. Historical films – History and criticism. 2. Bible
films – History and criticism. 3. Heroes in motion
pictures. I. Title. II. Series.
PN1995.9.H5E4 1983   791.43'09'09358   83-9535

ISBN 0-7100-9656-9
ISBN 0-7100-9993-2 (pbk.)

To R.G.

qui primus e mea mente
stercus exhausit

There is a time for man when the winds are of
greatest use; a time for waters from the skies,
rain-children of the clouds.
But if someone is successful through endeavour,
  honeyed songs,
source of future fame,
are necessary, a sure guarantee of great respect.
                    Pindar, *Olympian Odes*, 11, 1ff. (476 BC)

I've always thought that *only* the Americans can
do Ancient Rome pictures. Both cultures have the
same kind of relaxed, rangy pomp. Both have
exactly the same kind of bad taste.
                              Peter Ustinov (1977)

Contents

Illustrations

General Editor's Preface

The pre-eminent popular art form of the first half of the twentieth century has been the cinema. Both in Europe and America from the turn of the century to the 1950s cinema-going has been a regular habit and film-making a major industry. The cinema combined all the other art forms – painting, sculpture, music, the word, the dance – and added a new dimension – an illusion of life. Living, breathing people enacted dramas before the gaze of the audience and not, as in the theatre, bounded by the stage, but with the world as their backdrop. Success at the box office was to be obtained by giving the people something to which they could relate and which therefore reflected themselves. Like the other popular art forms, the cinema has much to tell us about people and their beliefs, their assumptions and their attitudes, their hopes and fears and dreams.

This series of books will examine the connection between films and the societies which produced them. Film as straight historical evidence; film as an unconscious reflection of national preoccupations; film as escapist entertainment; film as a weapon of propaganda – these are the aspects of the question that will concern us. We shall seek to examine and delineate individual film *genres*, the cinematic images of particular nations and the work of key directors who have mirrored national concerns and ideals. For we believe that the rich and multifarious products of the cinema constitute a still largely untapped source of knowledge about the ways in which our world and the people in it have changed since the first flickering images were projected on to the silver screen.

Jeffrey Richards

Acknowledgments

Many people have given invaluable assistance during the genesis of this book, either by arranging screenings, reading portions of the manuscript, providing stills or simply sharing their own enthusiasms over the years. I would particularly like to thank the following: first and foremost, general editor Jeffrey Richards (*finis ad Ausonios incolumis accessus*); Adrian Turner (*comes fontis antiqui sitiens*); Barrie Pattison (*nugarum veteranus peritus*); John Baxter (*prima movens, ultima nil praestans*); John Fitzpatrick; Lorenzo Codelli; Barry Edson; Contemporary Films (Charles Hedges); National Film Archive (Jeremy Boulton); and the staff of the British Film Institute's information division, for their always generous access to their resources.

The stills reproduced in this book first appeared in connection with films distributed by the following companies, to whom thanks are due: Archway, British Lion, Columbia, E.J. Fancey, Gala, M-G-M, New Realm, Paramount, Rank, RKO, Supreme, 20th Century-Fox, United Artists, Universal, Warner Bros, Warner-Pathé.

Author's Note

Foreign films are referred to by their UK/US release titles, followed by the original title and year of release in brackets on first mention. Release dates are those in the country (or majority country) of origin. Wherever possible, films are discussed in their most complete, original versions. All translations of literary texts are my own.

Introduction

There's a temptingly simple definition of the epic film: it's the easiest kind of picture to make badly.

Charlton Heston (1961)

This book is not about spectacular films, inordinately long films, heroic films, war films or costume films *per se* – all of which, at one time or another, have been dubbed 'epics'. Rather, it is about epic form in the cinema – specifically in those films dealing with periods up to the end of the Dark Ages, a time when correspondences with literary epic form are greatest. Thus, this book is equally an attempt to redefine the word 'epic' in a filmic context – and, in so doing, to show how closely the cinema is related to the accepted arts. The similarities are far more numerous than the differences: the film epic has taken up one of the most ancient art-forms and propelled it into the present day covered in twentieth-century ambitions, anxieties, hopes and fantasies. The chief feature of the historical epic film is not imitation but *reinterpretation*. It is those works which have carefully respected the legacy received from other art-forms, and adapted and built on it in a thoroughly filmic way, which are the true historical epics of the cinema.

The literary epic was chiefly designed to entertain in a morally uplifting and instructive manner, by trading on the fears and ignorance of its audience. The cinema, as mass entertainer of the twentieth century (a role now being usurped by its bastard child, television), is similarly guided by the expectations and tastes of its audience – tastes which have differed vastly over the years. I trace the development of the historical film throughout this century in Chapter 2, and one can see that its outward face is just as ambiguous as that of the literary epic: different cultures, changing social patterns, various types of audience – all mould the style. And film-makers have an unenviable set of conditions which they must meet if they are to be successful: script, photography, art direction, acting and music must cohere into a satisfactory whole. One or other may divert the attention (Miklós Rózsa's magnificent music to *King of Kings* obscures many of the film's weaknesses; the dazzlingly inventive art direction and visual flair of many pepla compensate for their often unimaginative characterisation) but in the end there should be a fair balance throughout.

Spectacle is the genre's most characteristic trademark. The cinema is an unashamedly commercial medium and historical films have provided ready grist for the publicist's mill: 'They Slashed And Stormed And Sinned Their Way Across Adventure's Most Violent Age!' (*The Vikings*); 'An Epic Film That Sweeps Across The Horizon Of Ancient Times' (*Sodom and Gomorrah*); 'The Mightiest Story of Tyranny And Temptation Ever Written – Ever Lived – Ever Produced!' (*The Silver Chalice*); 'The Glory That Was Egypt! The Grandeur That Was Rome!' (DeMille's *Cleopatra*); or simply, 'The Power The Passion The Greatness The Glory' (*King of Kings*). The ravings of admen should not lead one to despise the films themselves: spectacle is merely the cinema's own transformation of the literary epic's taste for the grandiose, realised on a sufficient scale to impress modern audiences. Dramatically it can work as a resolution of personal tensions (the chariot race in *Ben-Hur*), of monotheism vs idolatory (*Solomon and Sheba*), of national and personal valour (*The 300 Spartans*), of the triumph of a religious code (*The Ten Commandments*), of one man's moral odyssey (*Ulysses*), or even as a point of repose – not merely as a reason for display which is unconnected with the main thread.

Many films, both post-medieval and contemporary, also possess epic qualities equally

1 (*opposite*) Personal tensions: Messala (Stephen Boyd) in *Ben-Hur* (1959)

2 (*right*) Imperial decadence: Commodus (Christopher Plummer) and gladiator friends in *The Fall of the Roman Empire*

3 (*below*) Triumph of a religious code: Moses (Charlton Heston) leads his people from Egypt in *The Ten Commandments* (1956)

4 (*opposite*) Dramatic stages: the frontier fort . . .

5 (*above*) . . . and *forum Romanum* in *The Fall of the Roman Empire* . . .

6 (*below*) . . . and the Antioch circus in *Ben-Hur* (1959)

consonant with those of literature (some of these are briefly discussed in Chapter 12) but it is the romantic possibilities provided by remote historical settings which finally decide the issue. Each period has its own rules and call-signs, and audiences have learnt to recognise these over the years: basic manners, attitudes and speech persist from film to film, the realities of dress, behaviour and make-up in ancient times reflect a film's own era as much as its story's, and history and fact are adapted to accommodate current taste and its receptiveness to allegory. Such traits all find parallels in literature; and the epic film, when used rather than abused, has the same power as the literary epic to express universal concepts of morality.

The form's main aim, however, has been to entertain. I hope I have not buried the sheer fun of the genre beneath too much analysis: for myself it has provided some of the most enjoyable and invigorating hours ever spent in the cinema, from the uplifting qualities of the great masterworks to the raw energy of the most jovially trashy quickies. The 'epics' with which we are concerned, whether true or false, have all worn their label with such glee that their flamboyance has been the main reason for critics' neglect of the genre. I hope to show the many levels on which the films can work, from the most popular to the specialist, each providing a considerable source of enjoyment. It is curious how most critics would never consider discussing a documentary or contemporary work of fiction without reference to the original, but are quite content to dismiss the historical genre glibly and unread: works like *Moby Dick*, *Far from the Madding Crowd*, *War and Peace* and *The Great Gatsby* seem to spawn instant *aficionados* of Melville, Hardy, Tolstoy and Fitzgerald – *aficionados* who would never consider equal familiarity with the works of Tacitus, Pliny, Herodotus, or even the Bible.

The epic genre has seen some of the cinema's greatest stylists and craftsmen working at full stretch, several spending their formative years associated with historical films. In Italy such stylists as Sergio Leone, Vittorio Cottafavi, Mario Bava, Sergio Corbucci and Pietro Francisci developed their skills during the 1950s and 1960s, and many Italian cameramen, set designers, scriptwriters and composers (not to mention actors) cut their teeth on pepla during the same

period. *The Ten Commandments*, *Ben-Hur* and *El Cid* raised Charlton Heston from promising actor to superstar; *Cabiria* shot the beefy Bartolomeo Pagano from docker to contemporary hero; *Hercules* transformed Steve Reeves from physique star to cult symbol. Composers such as Miklós Rózsa, Alfred Newman, Franz Waxman and Alex North have contributed music every bit as evocative of epic emotions and conflict as (for their eras) Bach, Bruckner, Wagner or Richard Strauss. Designers and art directors have expended untold energy (and money) on designs which – generally through a modified reality or, occasionally, sheer stylisation – have provided dramatic stages for the action, stages which often rank as art-works of their own (the frontier fort and *forum Romanum* in *The Fall of the Roman Empire*; the harbour in Joseph L. Mankiewicz's *Cleopatra*; the stadium in William Wyler's *Ben-Hur*; plus countless others, small as well as great). Directors like Wyler, Anthony Mann, Richard Fleischer and Franklin J. Schaffner have had the scope to assimilate the thematic and stylistic threads of their earlier films. And the genre has given two names to cinema history – Samuel Bronston and Cecil B. DeMille.

Thematically, the historical epic film has been dominated by the message of personal and political freedom, more often than not expressed in the form of Christianity (or Zionism) triumphant – often, one feels, by special prerogative rather than any vote of confidence or popularity. Only in the Greek genre – and, to an equally lesser extent, in the secular Roman Imperial genre – has this message of liberty been allowed to emerge untrammelled by religious paraphernalia. The form has, too, been overwhelmingly dominated by two countries: Italy and the United States. Each has remained triumphantly individual, the former displaying flair and self-renewal, the latter pomp and self-importance. The American films have invariably championed a cosy, middle-American groundplan for living, and been inordinately fascinated by the grosser parallels between twentieth-century America and Roman civilisation – even to the extent (most noticeable in Kubrick's *Spartacus*) of grafting 'Roman' characteristics on oppressed parties in a truly Roman attempt to make the enemy worthy of attention, a tendency which grinds uncomfortably alongside the recurrent Jewish propaganda in American historical pictures. Italian productions, free of such self-importance, have been generally less fettered and categorical in their message-making. It cannot be stressed too often how incalculably we are in the debt of the Italian peplum for exploring areas of history with which Hollywood could never have found sympathy. If this book in any way modifies the erroneous equation that Epic Equals Hollywood, then it will have been worth the trouble.

An Epic by
Any Other Name

Then Penelope, in tears, addressed the hallowed
   minstrel:
'Phemius, you know many other tales which
   capture men's imagination,
deeds of both mortals and gods which minstrels
   make famous.
Sit and sing them one of those, and let them
   drink
their wine in silence. Stop this mournful
song which every time distresses the loving
   heart
in my breast; an inconsolable grief lies upon
   me . . .'
Telemachus then prudently spoke up:
'Mother, why do you begrudge the faithful
   minstrel
giving pleasure however his mind takes him?
   Minstrels
are not to blame; the guilty party, rather, is
   Zeus, who gives
to each man who toils for his living as he wants.'

Odyssey, 1, 336ff.

Dictionary definitions of the word 'epic' provide
only a starting-point. The *Oxford English Dictionary* offers: 'Pertaining to that species of
poetical composition, represented typically by the
Iliad and *Odyssey*, which celebrates in the form of
a continuous narrative the achievements of one or
more heroic personages of history or tradition',
noting the word's earliest literary appearance as
1589. The *Oxford Companion to English Literature*
is content to précis its big brother's definition, and
further confuses the issue by stating, under the
heading 'Heroic poetry': '. . . the same as *Epic* (q.v.).'
Far more helpful is the nominally less prestigious
Longman Companion to English Literature (ed. C.
Gillie), which takes the question several steps
further: '(1) A narrative of heroic actions, often
with a principal hero, usually mythical in its

content, offering inspiration and ennoblement
within a particular cultural or national tradition.
(2) The word denotes qualities of heroism and
grandeur, appropriate to epic but present in other
literary or non-literary forms.'

The *Longman Companion* also notes that there
may be Primary Epics ('written for a society still
fairly close to the conditions of society described in
the narrative'), citing the *Iliad*, the *Odyssey* and
Beowulf, and Secondary Epics ('based on the
pattern of primary ones but written for a mater-
ially developed society more or less remote from
the conditions described'), citing Vergil's *Aeneid*.
For further sub-classifications one must turn to the
American *Funk & Wagnalls New Standard
Dictionary*, which opts out of any worthwhile
definition but provides a splendidly detailed list of
classes: epics of growth, or collections of ballads;
epics of art with a single poet concentrating on
some great central figure; mixed epics of growth
and art; heroic poems of medieval knights and
heroes; sacred epics; historical epics; and mock
epics.

The above definitions show that the word 'epic' is
almost exclusively identified with literary works,
and that its application is frighteningly broad.
'Epic' has already joined the long list of words
which are rapidly losing their original meanings.
It may well embody concepts such as 'monumental', 'large-scale', 'far-reaching', 'inspiring',
'awesome' – it is in these senses that it is most used
colloquially – but there is more to the fibre of the
word than that.

Even the terms 'heroic' and 'epic' are frequently
confused. Epic poetry certainly draws its power
from the deeds of heroes, but heroic poetry is
certainly not synonymous with the epic. Heroes
alone do not make an epic unless the other
ingredients are also present: a literary garb which
dresses the action in noble style; the all-important

mythic element which raises the work above mere reportage by the introduction of the irrational, the inexplicable or magical; and the feeling of an overall unity and purpose to the work, of an embodiment of unchangeable ideals, which is frequently national. A similar confusion occurs between 'monumental' and 'epic' – in the same way that the former is present in the latter but does not necessarily receive anything in return.

*   *   *

If we are to redefine the word 'epic' as applied to the cinema, and show the strong correspondences between cinematic and literary epic form, we must first examine the word's genesis. Part of the difficulty in reaching any firm definition of the word lies in its own philological history. The strong literary associations arise from the fact that the earliest surviving examples are naturally in written form. *The Epic of Gilgamesh*, composed in Sumerian from c. 3000 BC onwards and reaching us in its most complete form in an Akkadian Semitic translation of the seventh century BC, is the earliest example known so far. The Sumerians (probably conquerors from the north and east) were the first literate inhabitants of Mesopotamia, and seem to have had an epic tradition of their own; *Gilgamesh*, at any rate, outlived both them and their language.

If not the earliest, Homer's *Iliad* (*Iliados*) and *Odyssey* (*Odusseia*) are nevertheless the prototypes by which all successors have been measured, doubtless because of the greater impact of Greek civilisation. There is no evidence to connect *Gilgamesh* and Homeric traditions, despite the fact that contact was historically feasible and both used central stores of cyclical material. One fact, though, must be borne in mind: all three works started life orally, the *Iliad* and the *Odyssey* as a number of separate tales composed by wandering minstrels during the ninth and eight centuries BC. Their audiences varied from rich noblemen to the larger congregations of religious festivals, and their content, while drawing on a common stock of tales with some foundation in historical fact, could be embellished to suit the particular tastes of the listener: every nobleman would naturally wish his ancestors to be included in a list of brave heroes, and every township would wish its name to be included in a catalogue of those contributing ships, soldiers or money. The Greeks called these professional entertainers *aoidoi*, and they flourished along the western seaboard of Asia Minor.

By the end of the ninth century and during the whole of the eighth, the various songs slowly coalesced into a monumental form of oral composition – perhaps due to the presence of one or more exceptionally gifted *aoidoi* whom for convenience we may call 'Homer' – and with the rise of greater literacy during the seventh century the poems were eventually set down in writing in the form we have them in today. The *aoidos*, accompanying himself on the lyre-like *kitharis* or *phorminx*, was replaced by the *rhapsodos*, a far more organised 'stitcher of songs' (as the word means) whose function was more to recite pre-existing material than to aid the evolution of oral compositions. The spread of writing resulted in poetry as we know it today – composed on paper and imprinted with the personality of its author, and more and more expressing personal emotions rather than recording history and tradition.

The modern view, therefore, of the word 'epic' has little to do with its origins. The term derives from the Greek *epos* (word), which was used by the Greeks themselves in its plural form (*epea*) to describe the oral body of heroic songs of Homer and the like. Pindar, a mainland lyric poet writing in the fifth century, talks of *rhapton epeon aoidoi* (singers of woven words) in an ode composed around 485 BC; Herodotus, a historian writing later in the century, mentions *ta Kupria epea* when referring to the now-lost epic poem *Kypria*. Terms like *epopoios* (literally 'maker of *epea*') and *epikos* are later inventions for a form that had flourished centuries earlier: even to Classical fifth-century Greeks, an 'epic' was an intellectual fabrication which would never have occurred to the original poets. It is from the Greek, however, via the straight Latin loan-word *epicus*, that we have derived our own term, and we are thus forever in their debt.

By the third century BC, Alexandrian Greeks like Apollonius of Rhodes were already faking Homeric epics (e.g. his *Argonautika*) as a purely academic exercise – compare, in the present century, Nikos Kazantzakis' sequel to the *Odyssey* – but the circumstances of their composition, though 'fake' when compared with the Homeric originals, should not detract from their qualification in any epic list. The *aoidoi* of the eighth century were already singing of events and a society long since dead and gone; their purpose, apart from earning a living, was to entertain and inspire, and Apollonius' work does likewise.

The Romans, as in so many fields of creativity, took up the Greek example and modified it to their own tastes, adding a consciously rugged and monumental quality while refining (Homeric) epic language. There is no surviving record of any oral tradition in the Roman culture, though doubtless ballads were sung on celebratory occasions. Livius Andronicus, a captive Greek of the third century BC, is credited with introducing epic form to the Romans, and his translation of the *Odyssey* into Latin was still being taught in schools until the time of the emperor Augustus.

Andronicus' example was swiftly adapted to Roman ends: Gnaeus Naevius, at the end of the second century, wrote his epic *Bellum Punicum* in the native Saturnian metre, and Quintus Ennius, a generation or so later, introduced the crucial dactylic hexameter metre (in imitation of Homeric metres) with his great epic *Annales*, a history of Rome in eighteen books. It was, however, the *Aeneid* (*Aeneis*) of Publius Vergilius Maro (Vergil), written during the last eleven years of his life from 30 to 19 BC, that united the various contrary strands of Roman epic into one cohesive and persuasive whole. The Homeric element is evident in the flashback structure and the escape from Troy, the Roman relevancies in the later books of Aeneas' struggles in Latium, and the all-important Imperial glorification – for Rome was then ruled by the first of its emperors – in the prophetic passages on Rome's future greatness.

No subsequent work quite matched up to Vergil's achievement: during the first and second centuries AD there followed a succession of rhetorical artefacts, of which the most noteworthy was Marcus Lucanus' *Pharsalia* (or *De bello civili*), written under the eagle eye of the emperor Nero and celebrating in ten books of difficult verse the civil war of a century earlier. The work is unfinished – Lucan was forced to commit suicide in AD 65 – but amply demonstrates the Roman propensity for using factual, rather than mythical, material as epic matter. There was no shortage of monumental poems during the following centuries, but their style is generally crabbed and academic, lacking even the sheer imagination that

Apollonius of Rhodes had brought to his earlier scholarship. A significant step was taken by Gaius Iuvencus, a priest in Spain under Constantine the Great (c. 325), who made a metrical version of the four Gospels, but no other poet seems to have taken up the idea of using Christ as a central figure for any epic work.

A last-ditch attempt to revive the spirit of Vergil is evident in the works of Claudius Claudianus, a Greek raised in Alexandria who composed in Latin hexameters at the end of the fourth century AD: using the wars against the Goths and the usurper Gildo in Africa as an excuse to eulogise the powerful general Stilicho, he shows great command of both factual and mythical material, woven in eloquent language of considerable strength. Claudianus was not a confessed Christian, and his poems are thoroughly Roman in viewpoint, but the influence of Christianity can be felt in his and others' works of the period. It is, however, little more than an influence, since right until the end of the Roman Empire there appears no literary epic with any professed Christian message. Many prose treatises were written – by Aurelius Augustinus at the turn of the fourth and fifth centuries AD, and by Anicius Boethius a century later – but it was national rather than religious affairs which remained the focus of the Roman epic.

Curiously it was only *after* the fall of Rome, at the beginning of the fifth century, that Christianity began to make headway as epic material. It was to be several centuries before new literature was to appear, but the troubled years of the Dark Ages (from the Fall of Rome to the eleventh century) provided plenty of orally transmitted tales which later generations wove into epic verse. *Beowulf*, written down in the eighth century in Late West Saxon English, is actually set in Southern Scandinavia of the fifth and sixth centuries and contains no references to either Britain or Christianity; it is, however, the product of a Christian Anglian court and shows the civilising influences of the re-establishment of Christianity in Britain two centuries after the departure of Rome. Similarly, the great Icelandic sagas of the twelfth and thirteenth centuries contain a mixture of the Pagan and Christian: the *Laxdæla Saga* starts in the Age of Settlement and spans the adoption of Christianity in AD 1000; *Njal's Saga* is more directly concerned with the effects of Christianity on its protagonists.

So dim is the boundary between such 'religions' that one is often tempted to spell Christianity with a small *c*. Even in the fourteenth-century *Sir Gawain and the Green Knight* it is more the spirit, rather than the letter, of Christianity which informs the hero's actions, although by now the stark realism of Norse and Anglo-Saxon literature is being tempered by the influence of Romance poetry. The stern heroism of the North, helped by the rise of the feudal system, had for some time been giving way to a new concept, that of 'chivalry', and the Crusades of the eleventh and twelfth centuries against the Saracens in the Near East provided a new source of Christian-oriented epic inspiration. As with *Beowulf*, the present refashioned the past. Of the many French national epics, or *chansons de geste* (originally chanted by *jongleurs*, or minstrels), the *Chanson de Roland* took an incident from the eighth century and refurbished it in eleventh-century terms, and is the finest example of the Charlemagne Cycle. The Breton Cycle, or court epics, dealt (like the English *Sir Gawain*) with Arthurian legend from the early Dark Ages. There also arose an Antique Cycle, or *matière de Rome*, which carried on the Classical spirit by presenting Christian versions of the actions of heroes from the *Iliad*, the *Odyssey*, the *Aeneid*, and the like.

The wheel would seem to have come full circle, and in other countries heroic poetry merely adds national glosses. The *Nibelungenlied*, written for court performance in the thirteenth century, summarises the tradition from which *Beowulf* was derived in Germanic terms. The twelfth-century *Slovo o poly Igoreve* (*The Lay of Igor's Campaign*), though composed in writing, draws strongly on the Russian oral heroic poems (*byliny*) and uses Christianity to draw lessons in national unity against foreign invaders. The thirteenth-century *Cantar de mio Cid* is one of several works springing from the cult of the knight Rodrigo Díaz, who lived in the eleventh century, Spain's Heroic Age. The Finnish *Kalevala* triumphantly sustained the oral tradition until the nineteenth century, when it was finally collected and arranged into its present form of nearly 23,000 lines, while, at the opposite end of the spectrum, Milton's *Paradise Lost* shows how, by the seventeenth century, all that remained was fine scholarship on a technical level with the Alexandrian Greeks or the Roman poets of the Silver Age and beyond.

*   *   *

It is clear from the above that one of the purposes of epic literature is to present a national or religious identity in times of change. It is the peculiar ability of the epic to derive its basis from very real events but to transmute the ingredients into a timeless form; the past has always excited man's imagination more than the tangible present, since it gives him greater scope to dream – the *Iliad*, for example, was a product of real events and an existing social structure, but evolved into a hybrid state to be received by audiences no more in touch with its world than those of the present day.

The message is the important factor, and that remains applicable however distant the setting: it is the latter, however, which provides the all-important mythic ingredient. By 'mythic' I mean not simply 'mythical', although mythology carries its own magic; when dealing with basic moral concepts like heroism, nobility, virtue, bravery, evil, the superhuman is often called into play, and for this reason the true epic form relies on the romantic possibilities of past civilisations rather than the more identifiable settings of recent centuries. The above examination of literary epics has resulted in a stopping-point in the early Medieval period, and history supports this thesis: the accumulation of fact and a more recognisable social structure leads straight to our present century, and in the cinema, which will be our concern from hereon, the post-early medieval period diluted the hero to mere swashbuckler.

Epic into Film

'And what do *you* call an epic?'
'You know, a picture that's real long and has lots of things going on.'

Dixon to Mildred in *In a Lonely Place* (1950)

Defining an epic is only slightly less complicated than making one . . .

Charlton Heston (1961)

As we have seen, the epic form transfigures the accomplishments of the past into an inspirational entertainment for the present, trading on received ideas of a continuing national or cultural consciousness. Myth – the projection of a people's beliefs on a fictional past – allows scope for allegory based on moral, religious or political qualities pertinent to the audience.

There would seem to be no art-form better equipped to handle the epic form than the cinema: its constituent elements of speech, image, sound, music and colour are all present, generally singly, in the other arts. Closer examination reveals even more advantages. Epic literature invariably draws upon history for its source-material, and attains its individual form by progressively colouring real events. Homer's *Iliad* glorifies what was in all probability a trading war based around the Hellespont; the *Chanson de Roland* owes its existence to an attack on Charlemagne's rear-guard in Spain in AD 778 (in which a duke called Roland was killed); Camões' *Lusiads* (*Os Lusiadas*) uses Vasco da Gama's voyage as a springboard to celebrate the history of Portugal. Stock material such as theology and national mythology are frequently called into play but rarely form the actual basis for a work. Cinema has a somewhat freer hand: sources range from literary epics (most of which have been filmed), to historical events which have remained uncelebrated in epic literature, to present-day novels based on history, to vague *mélanges* of mythological shavings (the majority of the Italian peplum cycle).

Cinema thus gains the best of both worlds – it may take a genuine epic like Homer's *Odyssey* or raise totally uncharismatic novels like Howard Fast's *Spartacus* or Lew Wallace's *Ben-Hur* to epic status. This freedom, however, imposes extra responsibilities on the form, for the dividing line between what is merely a historical narrative film and an epic historical film becomes perilously thin. Aristotle made the point over two thousand years ago in his essay *On the Art of Poetry* (*Peri poietikes*):

> . . . [epics] should not be like ordinary histories, in which one deals not with a single affair but with a single period and all that happened to one or more persons during it and all the various consequences.

(23, 2)

elsewhere adding:

> It is clear from the aforesaid also that the poet's job is not to say what *has* happened but what *could* happen. . .

(9, 1)

That is not to say that historical exactitude or period detail are alien to the film epic. Literary epics make much play of the small details of everyday life, and especially the ritual of dress and procedure. Detail in that respect is made to work towards the total design: the description of our hero clothing himself before conflict, for example, not only adds colour but is a suspense device, and very much a part of the epic's regard for panoply. Likewise, because a film is historically accurate it need not fall under the heading of a historical narrative film: a film's accuracy – as we shall see in

7 (*left*) Epic charisma:
Steve Reeves in
Hercules Unchained . . .

8 (*below*) . . . Robert
Taylor in *Quo vadis*
(1951) . . .

9 (*opposite*) . . . and Gina
Lollobrigida and Yul
Brynner in *Solomon and
Sheba*

the following chapters – is more a fascinating sideline than an important qualifier. Many of the greatest film epics take the greatest liberties with history, while many equally great ones manage to reconcile the two sides. It is when narrative or detail become an end in themselves that the epic spirit is found wanting in a film; and as such, the cinema is here in complete agreement with literature.

Cinema is particularly well-endowed in the field of characterisation. The literary epic generally turns on the exploits of a single central character, surrounded by a broad substratum of secondary characters who react upon him morally. This focus, this pyramidal structure, gives epic much of its power – the characters are supra- (sometimes super-) human, waging an allegorical struggle on their own plane. In this respect cinema comes perfectly equipped: the form has its own levels of reality, depending upon its stylisation of 'real life'. Epic cinema is not necessarily reliant upon the artificiality of the studio, but the vast majority of works happily capitalise upon this quality, which provides the all-important distancing from reality that distinguishes epic from historical narrative.

Cinema's star-system, one of its most maligned virtues, also provides invaluable shorthand in epic characterisation. An actor may not necessarily resemble his historical counterpart, but the charisma he brings to a role is a powerful asset. When the poet of the *Cantar de mio Cid* sings passionately that the hero and his wife Ximena

> took leave one from the other   like a claw from flesh
>
> (375)

it is greatly in the film's favour that two superstars, Charlton Heston and Sophia Loren, play the fate-tossed couple. Likewise, an actor such as Charlton Heston, Anthony Quinn, Jack Palance or Steve Reeves is already halfway home thanks to his screen presence when called upon to realise such epic imagery as:

> Achilles approached him
> like the War God in his gleaming helmet,
> shaking over his right shoulder his terrible
>   ash spear
> from Pelium. Around him his bronze shone
>   with the brilliance

of a blazing fire or the rising sun.
Hector trembled as he watched: he no longer dared
to stay there, and left the gate and fled in fear.

> (Homer, *Iliad*, 22, 131ff.)

Yet perhaps the cinema's most obvious debt to literature is in its conscious aping of bardic introductions. Homer's

> Tell me, muse, of the much-talented man who roamed
> so much after sacking the sacred city of Troy
>
> (*Odyssey*, 1, 1)

or Vergil's

> I sing of arms, and the man who, driven by fate, first
> came from the coasts of Troy to Italy and Lavinian shores
>
> (*Aeneid*, 1, 1)

is paralleled time and again in the cinema, nowhere more simply or more eloquently than at the start of *El Cid*:

> This is Spain, one thousand and eighty years after the coming of Christ. It is a war-torn, unhappy land, half-Christian, half-Moor. This is the time and the story of Rodrigo Díaz of Bivar, known to history and to legend as El Cid, the lord. He was a simple man who became Spain's greatest hero. He rose above religious hatred and called upon all Spaniards, whether Christian or Moor, to face a common enemy who threatened to destroy their land of Spain.

*   *   *

In common with many other art-forms, the cinema began to produce large-scale works quite early in its history. As poets had turned to epic verse, painters to murals, and musicians to religious choral works, so film-makers sought to enlarge the range and power of their medium by stretching its technical resources. Early attempts evolved from a natural desire to use the medium's power to evoke past ages – it was, quite simply, fun to re-create Ancient Rome, to go back through the ages by means of this new time machine.

In France, Georges Méliès turned his eye to myth and the past, with shorts like *Pygmalion et Galatée* (1898), *Neptune et Amphitrite* (1899) and *Cléopatre* (1899). But soon Italy, which along with Hollywood would dominate the field throughout the historical epic's history, made its presence felt. Literature was an obvious source for material, and helped to assure a film's popularity. Gustave Flaubert's *Salammbô*, Edward Bulwer Lytton's *The Last Days of Pompeii*, Henryk Sienkiewicz's *Quo vadis*, Lew Wallace's *Ben-Hur*, Shakespeare's tragedies, and the Bible all became grist to the mill, particularly those works which were out of copyright.

Italy's productions, at a time when language was a lesser barrier than now to a film's international acceptance (silent captions were easily replaced by those in another language), were also successful abroad in America. In 1908 Lord Lytton's novel was filmed twice, by Giovanni Vitrotti and Luigi Maggi, and the following year a director from Turin, Giovanni Pastrone, shot *Giulio Cesare e Brutus*. Little did anyone realise that the same man would produce the cinema's first, and still in many ways definitive, screen epic – *Cabiria* (1914), with titles by Gabriele D'Annunzio. During the years prior to the First World War, Italy was in an expansionist mood, especially in regard to North Africa, and the Roman/Carthaginian tale of *Cabiria* excited public imagination. Enrico Guazzoni's *Quo vadis* (1912) set the seal on Italians' interest in their own history, and during those years a flood of historical pictures emerged from Italy. Between 1900 and 1920 most subjects which were to receive fuller treatment in coming years had already been attempted – Pompeii, the Christians, Nero burning Rome, Julius Caesar, Brutus, Mark Antony, Messalina, Cleopatra, Theodora, Spartacus, the Odyssey, Troy, Hercules, the Theban cycle, and so on. Frequently unsatisfactorily but nonetheless attempted.

With the economic collapse of Italy the torch passed to Hollywood. D. W. Griffith had shown that the technical innovations of *Cabiria* were not merely the province of the Italians: in 1913 he had made *Judith of Bethulia*, the longest American film to date, which proved that audiences' attentions could be held over longer periods than simply two- or three-reelers. *The Birth of a Nation* (1915) and *Intolerance* (1916) proved America's technical capabilities and included historical flashbacks to boot. In 1922 Hollywood, looking for more cast-iron successes, started to reconsider Lew Wallace's *Ben-Hur*, and after many travails Metro-Goldwyn-Mayer's version, shot in Rome, emerged at the end of 1925 directed by Fred Niblo. It was a huge commercial success, banned in China and Italy for political reasons (Mussolini was angry that Messala, as the true Roman, was beaten by the Jew Ben-Hur).

Stylistically *Ben-Hur* marked a point of no return for the historical epic. Griffith, for all his spectacular inserts, had been concerned basically with present-day dramas; *Ben-Hur* built more on the tradition of Pastrone's film, remaining wholly within its period and seeing beyond opportunities for mere visual display. Strangely enough, however, the challenge of *Ben-Hur* was not taken up by other filmmakers, and it was to be over twenty years before the genre was to pursue its potential to the full. During the mid-twenties cinema was undergoing giant stylistic and technical upheavals: the development of synchronised sound was only just round the corner (1928), and like a nine-month-old baby which can develop no further in its present environment silent cinema kicked and struggled with a variety of spectacular effects. In the USSR and France, Eisenstein and Abel Gance stretched the medium to its limits, the former in editing and camera positioning, the latter with grand concepts of greater audience involvement (triple-screen Polyvision, etc.).

Such flamboyance, building on the designs of Griffith, did nothing to advance the historical epic along the lines of *Ben-Hur*; for real grist twenties audiences required a contemporary story, and the decade is marked by a whole series of films in which (similar to *Intolerance* and *The Birth of a Nation* ten years earlier) a period story is duplicated later in the film by a contemporary drama, with the same actors in relative roles (Korda's *Samson und Delila*, 1923; DeMille's *The Ten Commandments*, 1923; Curtiz's *Noah's Ark*, 1928). This was something of a stylistic dead-end street, but not without points of recommendation: here was the clearest demonstration of the epic's ability to embody 'message' as much as any other genre, and the greater amount of screen-time allotted to the historical segment meant that some at least attained epic qualities always denied to Griffith.

In 1928 the medium came of age with synchronised sound: the actors gained an extra element of

10 (*opposite above*)   Point of no return: Fred Niblo's production of *Ben-Hur* (1925)

11 (*opposite below*)   Twenties chic: Alexander Korda's *The Private Life of Helen of Troy*

12 (*below*)   Epic flamboyance: Mervyn LeRoy's *Quo vadis* (1951)

conviction and the images were no longer depen-
dent upon the whims of a pianist or *ad hoc*
orchestra. Film-makers eagerly grasped the new
advance and, although for a short while the
camera became tethered by early difficulties of
sound recording, by the mid-thirties it had totally
regained its former freedom. This was, however, a
period of decline for the historical epic, in both
Hollywood and Italy: in 1924 the depressed Italian
industry had produced a vast and expensive
version of *Quo vadis* which, all spectacle and no
comment, had flopped disastrously, and the subsequent years of Fascist rule saw the rise of the
'white telephone' comedy as the prime escapist
genre. It has always been a puzzle why historical
films (specifically Roman) did not undergo a rebirth under Mussolini's rule of Italy during the
twenties and thirties; few genres, one would have
thought, come so ready-made. The answer probably lies in the fact that public taste triumphed
over textbook development: the failure of *Quo
vadis* showed that the Italian public was sated
with the genre that it had helped so much to
spawn. Only one title of interest emerged from
Fascist Italy – Carmine Gallone's *Scipio Africanus*
(*Scipione l'africano*, 1937), blessed by Il Duce's
approval but hardly representative of the decade
cinematically.

The massive switch of taste during the thirties to
contemporary escapism left its mark even on the
few historical pictures which emerged. The new
climate could be seen in the box-office failure of a
re-issue, with sound, of Fred Niblo's *Ben-Hur* in
1931; the film then disappeared virtually without
trace until interest was reawakened in the fifties
by M-G-M's remake. The costume picture took the
side of the musical, with its glossy view of a
privileged society at play. Dialogue and dress
matched the era: Claudette Colbert in DeMille's
The Sign of the Cross (1933) or *Cleopatra* (1934)
might just as well have been cavorting about a
New York hotel suite as a palace or imperial barge;
for the time a work like Ernest Schoedsack's *The
Last Days of Pompeii* (1935) stands out for its
straightforward reflection of Depression hardships.
Even as late as 1945 the chic element still held
sway: Gabriel Pascal's *Caesar and Cleopatra*, with
its witty dialogue and deliberately anachronistic
air, is almost an exact duplicate of Korda's silent
The Private Life of Helen of Troy (1928).

Again, a fresh spur came from Europe, specifically from Italy. Almost in revenge for the long
years under Mussolini, in which the period film
had languished, the late forties saw a familiar
form re-emerge in Goffredo Alessandrini's *L'ebreo
errante* (1947), which featured a prologue set in
ancient Jerusalem before a contemporary story of
Nazi persecution of the Jews. The birth of neo-
realism during the early forties (which would last
until the early fifties) was, in the constructivist
atmosphere of post-war Europe, stimulating the
growth of many opposites, and the flamboyance of
the historical epic fitted the ticket. In 1949
appeared Alessandro Blasetti's *The Fighting
Gladiator* (*Fabiola*), made on a lavish scale hark-
ing back to the silent cinema of the poet
D'Annunzio (one of neo-realism's pet enemies). Its
success started the wheel of fashion turning back,
and the cinema was now even better equipped to
meet the demands, with colour grading and lens
design making great strides forward.

The somewhat effete quality of thirties works
had no place in the post-war era, and historical
films took on a new rigour which reflected the
severity and positiveness of Western society.
Freedom from tyranny and a new life (a reflection
also of fifties Cold War propaganda) became the
genre's dominant themes, and film-makers turned
back to the standards of literature and history.
Americans again came to Italy to film their
projects: the great success of the hardy *Quo vadis*
in 1951 provided the impetus worldwide for a rash
of remakes, with Hollywood giving its blessing to
the genre by choosing *The Robe* (1953) as the first
film to be shot in CinemaScope.

The historical epic certainly provided excellent
opportunities for fifties cinema to show off its
technical prowess, and Hollywood may take the
major credit for the development of the spectacular
side. In Italy, however, a crucial stylistic development was in the making. During the first half of
the fifties the historical film steadily followed
through the impetus given it by *Fabiola* with a
couple of pictures a year (this quite apart from any
American films using Italian facilities): visually
elegant, and treating a variety of subjects, they
lacked the sheer weight and portentousness of
their American counterparts, possessing a vigour
closer to comic-strips or *fumetti*. Riccardo Freda's
Spartacus the Gladiator (*Spartaco*, 1953), Pietro
Francisci's *La regina di Saba* (1952) and *Attila the
Hun* (*Attila*, 1955), Mario Camerini's *Ulysses*

(*Ulisse*, 1954), and Guido Brignone's *Le schiave di Cartagine* (1957) show certain stylistic points emerging: basic concepts expressed in avowedly popular terms, with moral and sexual stereotypes placed in remote historical eras; a move away from the spectacle of Hollywood towards a smaller-scale sensuality, equally positive but less rigorous; and a sheer energy in direction which walked a tightrope between tattiness and vitality.

It was, in retrospect, the sensuality of such films as *Ulysses* and *Attila the Hun* (a sensuality in some ways akin to DeMille's late twenties-early thirties efforts prior to the Hays Office rulings) which provided the biggest area for growth. The mythic possibilities of the former and the enhanced sexuality of dress and manners, brilliantly· evoked by Italy's art directors and cameramen, can also be seen in Robert Wise's *Helen of Troy* (1955) – also shot in Italy – but the American director's shooting style is solidly American. In 1958 appeared *Aphrodite, Goddess of Love* (*La Venere di Cheronea*), which directly pursued the sensual lines of *Ulysses* but lacked some of its mythic content. Finally, Pietro Francisci struck again with the definitive master-stroke – uniting the fifties cycle decisively with *Cabiria*.

In search of a new gimmick, some Italian producers had hired an American bodybuilder, then doing cabaret work in the United States, to star in *Hercules* (*Le fatiche di Ercole*, 1958), another quickie in the Italian cycle to be shot in ten weeks. The American was Steve Reeves, the director Pietro Francisci, and the two co-stars actresses who had made previous appearances in Italian historical pictures, Sylva Koscina and Gianna Maria Canale. The resulting film was bought cheaply by Joe Levine and heavily promoted in the United States, where it took $5 million under the title *Hercules*; Francisci/Reeves/Koscina's follow-up, *Hercules Unchained* (*Ercole e la regina di Lidia*, 1959), also crashed through the British box-office, the first film in Britain to receive nationwide TV advertising. The muscleman, the perfect mythic physical/sexual stereotype complementing the sensually clad, pneumatic heroines of the fifties, had arrived to complete the equation.

The films which followed have since been christened the peplum cycle (from the Latinised version of the Greek word *peplos*, meaning a woman's shawl or long hanging dress); it gained notice with *Hercules* but in fact reaches back to the early fifties (and even *Cabiria*, with its heavily built central character). The majority of pepla are appallingly scripted, hastily shot, and atrociously acted (the stars rarely screen-tested and often working on two or more films simultaneously in a polyglot atmosphere); they are crucial, however, in the development of both the historical epic and the cinema (particularly the Italian cinema). Such stylists as Vittorio Cottafavi, Mario Bava, Sergio Leone, and many others, owe their early development and experience to pepla, and have left the cycle with a collection of masterworks which realised the mythic and epic possibilities of the historical film. Leone later transferred his mythic interests to the Western (the Clint Eastwood 'Dollars' trilogy), showing with *Fistful of Dollars* (*Per un pugno di dollari*, 1964) the new direction that popular Italian cinema was to take after the peplum cycle had all but played itself out. Bava, after rising from cameraman to director (though essentially remaining a supreme visual stylist) went on to horror films, adding a deliberately *fantastique* element which grew from the peplum.

Hollywood never tried to match the muscleman cycle; while the peplum became quicker and cheaper, American-financed works, despite being shot mostly in Europe, became grander. This was as much to promote the most glamorous possibilities of the wide screen, because of the continuing competition with TV, as anything else. And with the increasing budgets came increasing pressures: these expensive films *had* to succeed, had to be pre-sold, and nervous producers were ever-watchful of potential markets which could be offended or needed to be wooed. William Wyler's *Ben-Hur* (1959) marked the zenith of the Hollywood cycle. In Spain, Samuel Bronston continued, almost single-handedly, producing equally inspired works which had showcase runs while the pepla sped through the suburban flea-pits. *King of Kings* (1961) was his slightly uneven calling-card, a mixture of Hollywood guiding talent and Spanish technicians, uniting the peplum's delight in vigorous colour with the American concern for massiveness. His next production, *El Cid* (1961), showed the promise of the earlier work come to resplendent fruition. But early in the sixties, with *The Fall of the Roman Empire* (1964), Bronston was overtaken by inevitable social as well as financial pressures.

13 (*below*) Sensual lines: Iris (Belinda Lee), Lucian (Jacques Sernas) and Praxiteles (Massimo Girotti) in *Aphrodite, Goddess of Love*

14 (*opposite above*) Birth of the peplum: Iole (Sylva Koscina) meets Hercules (Steve Reeves) in *Hercules*

15 (*opposite below*) Resplendent fruition: Chimene (Sophia Loren) in *El Cid*

It was the age in which the youth upswing, set in motion during the fifties by the new post-war prosperity and social readjustment, finally found commercial support, and a market evolved in films just as in music and literature. Also, stylistically, the sixties saw the fragmentation of accepted Hollywood standards of film-making, with Europeans showing alternative forms of cinematic language and a new freedom in examining subjects and taboos. Beside all this the indirect language of the historical epic, allied to its concomitant grossness of budget and scale, seemed slow and outmoded. Also, quite simply, after a decade of success the genre fell from favour.

The prosperity and optimism of the mid-sixties soon petered out and, with the onset of worldwide inflation in the early seventies, both cinema and society began to trim their sails after the reckless careering of the previous decade. As society turned in on itself, in an orgy of doubt and self-questioning, the cinema turned to subjects which reflected this new uncertainty of direction. Horror became the new fashion, expressing the fears of a technological society – whether of Big Brother (government of multinationals), urban violence, the occult or the animal kingdom. Film criticism also turned in on itself, rediscovering vintage areas of cinema in the face of seventies negativism. It was left to the younger generation of Hollywood directors – film-makers imbued with a love of vintage cinema and now with considerable financial power – to turn the tide. George Lucas' *Star Wars* (1977) found a massive audience ready for large-scale escapist fantasy, reinterpreting

ancient myths in space-age terms; and Steven Spielberg's *Close Encounters of the Third Kind* (1977) confirmed this new positivism with a tale in which the 'invader' was shown as a benign rather than destructive force.

With the similar success of *Superman* (1978), *Star Trek – The Motion Picture* (1979), *Flash Gordon* (1980) and *The Empire Strikes Back* (1980), all of which to varying extents turned to myth as a source of inspiration, the stage was once again set for the return of the historical epic. 'Sword and sorcery' replaced the sixties' 'sword and sandal' (peplum), and 70mm showcases again returned to favour. Even as I write, a host of films wait in the wings: Peter Yates' medieval space fantasy *Krull*, Stephen Weeks' new version of the Gawain legend *Sword of the Valiant*, Don Coscarelli's *The Beastmaster*, and a whole range of Dark Age heroes and heroines from Ator the Fighting Eagle to Hundra. Yet the most amazing demonstration that the wheel of cinematic fortune had turned full circle came in mid-1982 with the news that producers Menahem Golan and Yoram Globus were shooting two relatively low-budget spectacles, *The Adventures of Hercules* and *The Seven Magnificent Gladiators*, back-to-back in Italy. The star of both was bodybuilder Lou Ferrigno, with other roles played by original peplumites such as Rossana Podestà, Brad Harris and Dan Vadis. 'The Legend Lives!' cries the poster. 'Courage . . . Virtue . . . Honor . . . Loyalty . . . Power . . . Glory . . . and Magic . . .' For the historical epic film the eighties could be the most interesting decade yet.

Biblical: The Old Testament

And the Egyptians put the children of Israel into harsh service, afflicting their lives with hard labour, making mortar and bricks, and doing all kinds of work in the fields.

Exodus, 1, 13f.

'Why aren't you kneeling at the feet of a princess?'
'I'm afraid the mud-pits have stiffened my knees, royal one.'

Nefretiri to Moses in
The Ten Commandments (1956)

There are two ways of viewing the Old Testament: as a collection of lays and folk-tales expressing aspects of the Hebrew faith, or as a series of historical documents charting the history of the Hebrew people to the second century BC. In epic terms neither view is mutually exclusive: first, the Old Testament presents drama, both human and divine, on a vast scale, reaching back not merely to the age of myth but to the very creation of the world; second, it treats of the foundation and history of a specific race, and its slow evolution into a united nation; third, it is a consistent expression, throughout all its windings and sidetracks, of a people's belief in their destiny, of being the chosen ones and the instruments of a merciful and merciless all-seeing power.

The Old Testament is a selection of thirty-nine Hebraic texts (from a total of nearly two hundred) made by a group of Jewish scholars at Jamnia c. AD 100. It is a motley collection of narrative, prayers, songs, prophecies, laws, genealogies and moral vignettes, stretched over a historical fabric which incorporates events of the Eastern Mediterranean and Near East during the first two millennia BC. It represents a specifically Hebraic view of humanity and human conduct, yet embodies precepts later broadened to include Gentile as well

as Jew. Much of the Old Testament's power, in fact, stems from its inconclusiveness – its promise rather than fulfilment – which emphasises the depth of conviction of the 'hero' (here, of course, the Hebrew people) in much the same way as Odysseus was obsessed with returning to Penelope or Achilles with avenging the death of Patroclus. This, coupled with the historical progression as book succeeds book, gives the Old Testament sufficient unity to call it an epic work: the great individual works (the Books of Genesis, Exodus, Joshua, Judges, Samuel, Kings, Isaiah, Jeremiah) can be considered as narrative, the smaller works (Ruth, Esther, Daniel, Job) as ethical glossaries to the main story-line, and Psalms, Proverbs and the Song of Solomon as celebratory choral interludes. Such content is all basic epic hardcore; and the fact of a body of overlapping works reflecting a national ethos recurs much later with the Nordic saga tradition.

The Old Testament, therefore, can be regarded as a collection of sagas of an itinerant and oppressed people – a collection which incorporates many of the staple folk-tales of the period which, following the epic tradition, generally have some basis in history. The Flood story is found in Sumerian, Assyrian, Old Babylonian and Greek literature, and may well hark back to a Mesopotamian disaster in the third millennium BC. As regards the Exodus, each civilisation finds its own – the Greeks later with the Long March of 401 BC, with Xenophon in the Moses role, and the modern-day Chinese with Mao Tse-tung in 1935. Yet so vast is the Old Testament's historical scope and so central its geographical setting (the Fertile Crescent, scene of man's crucial development from Mesolithic food-gatherer to Neolithic farmer and village-dweller) that a host of other cultures find representation within its pages – Egyptian, Babylonian, Assyrian, Philistine, etc. It is also worth remembering (as a preparation for Chapters 5 and 6) that a few miles to the west Greek civilisation was developing: at about the time of the Exodus (c. 1300 BC), the Greeks were besieging Troy and the Minoan civilisation on Crete was overwhelmed by the volcanic eruption of Thera; as the Philistines conquered the coast of Palestine c. 1100, Mycenae finally fell to invading Dorians from the north and Greece entered its Dark Age (during which time, in Palestine, Saul, David and Solomon reigned, the Two Kingdoms arose, and the exile in Babylon took place); soon after the fall of Nineveh in 612 Solon codified his laws in Athens; as Babylon fell (539) and the two tribes of Judah returned to Jerusalem with Cyrus' blessing, Athens prospered under Peisistratus; and when the walls of Jerusalem were finally completed under Nehemiah in the mid-fifth century BC, Greek culture was at its height.

Much of the Old Testament is thought to have been written (or reworked during the experience of bondage) in the two centuries (721–586) the Hebrews spent in Babylon – hence the 'let my people go' theme of long-suffering innocence which permeates the collection and, given events of the present century, makes this theme so relevant even today. It was, as befits an epic creation, designed as both a record of the past and an inspiration for the future, conceived at a time when the Hebrews lacked identity and any foreseeable future in their own land. The apparent conflict between myth and historical fact, which film-makers have to face to a greater or lesser extent in every historical genre (especially since the cinema is primarily a visual medium), is never more accentuated than in the Old Testament films. As we shall find in the following chapters, the cinema shows no one approach to this problem; success depends more on the consistency of the chosen approach and the extent to which the film mirrors the *spirit* of the original while reinterpreting it in twentieth-century terms. Thus, it may, as in DeMille's *The Ten Commandments* (1956), take note of the Renaissance artistic tradition; or, as in De Bosio's *Moses* (1976), of modern research; or, as in Vidor's *Solomon and Sheba* (1959) or Aldrich's *Sodom and Gomorrah* (1962), of Hollywood star-melodrama conventions or Italian spectacle.

There is one major problem that Old Testament films face. Despite DeMille's famous riposte ('What else has two thousand years' advance publicity?'), the subject-matter is not so familiar as the life of Christ – particularly to non-Jews. The cinema has, therefore, concentrated on the familiar stories which have appealed to the general imagination and are not necessarily the most important in Hebraic or theological terms: Adam and Eve, Noah and the Flood, the Exodus, Samson, David (*pace* Goliath), the Queen of Sheba, etc. Like the ancient rhapsodes, film-makers have seized on already current traditions and perpetuated them for general entertainment and edification.

*　　*　　*

There is no better place to start than with John Huston's *The Bible in the Beginning . . . (La Bibbia*, 1966), which, in just under three hours, takes its audience through the first half of Genesis, up to Abraham's sacrifice of his son Isaac. Producer Dino De Laurentiis' original plan, as befits the promise of the film's title, had been on a somewhat grander scale, but common sense, finance and practicability prevailed. Much of the first twenty-two chapters of Genesis is taken up with genealogies, and there are few extended stories to deal with; Huston's film takes due and faithful account of them – the Creation, Adam and Eve, Cain and Abel, Noah and the Flood, the Tower of Babel, Abraham and Sarah, Abraham and Hagar, Sodom and Gomorrah, Isaac's birth, Isaac's sacrifice. The film has a consequent breadth and spaciousness which is very impressive – a refusal to be hurried or to bow too soon to any of the usual demands of the big-budget picture.

Huston had originally been asked to direct one sequence (at the time when the film was planned as a portmanteau work) and to co-ordinate the others; later he was asked to direct the whole thing, and worked in close collaboration with scriptwriter Christopher Fry (who had worked uncredited on Wyler's *Ben-Hur* and later had written Fleischer's *Barabbas*, the latter produced by De Laurentiis). The film-makers placed no orthodox religious interpretation on the material; Huston treated it as 'the emergence out of myth and legend'.

The film, like Genesis, literally begins from nothing, with the vast D-150 screen empty but for a limitless grey haze; as the image slowly brightens the well-known narration is heard from the back of the theatre in 70mm prints. It is a fine *coup de cinéma*, and the tone of child-like wonder (rather than hammer-and-tongs spectacle) is re-inforced through Toshiro Mayuzumi's uplifting music (tonality from chaos) and through the Creation montage photographed by Ernst Haas, using sites in North and South America, Iceland and the Galapagos Islands – an ingenious idea which stresses the eternity of the Creation in a way which special effects would have over-shadowed. Just as in Genesis 2:7, Man is formed from the dust of the ground (to a stirring musical and visual climax as he walks away to Eden); Eden has a misty naivety (broken by a heavy-breathing serpent); and Noah, in Huston's performance, a deliberate geniality (always part of the original conception – Chaplin, Welles and Guinness had been approached to play the part). The first half of the film ends with a beautiful air of expectation, as the Ark sits on steamy Ararat, its pregnant load of animal and human life finally unloaded.

Part 2 shows the clouds of myth parting ever so slowly: the Sodom and Gomorrah story is treated as straight allegory, Babel word-for-word likewise, and even the Three Angels of the Lord are portrayed by a single actor (Peter O'Toole) – a brave and thoroughly effective decision. With the advent of Abraham one feels the film-maker's first attempts to place the story in some sort of historical perspective, rather than continue the geographically and temporally vague tableau approach. Abraham becomes a simple and devout bedouin, and in George C. Scott's introspective performance contains just the right balance of obeisance and humanity to make the final sacrifice sequence work. There are times during Part 2 when, with the familiar tales over and only specifically Hebraic material left, tension slackens (particularly for non-Jewish viewers) in a deficiency of event. There is nothing wrong structurally: the story of Abraham reworks in more human terms the God/Man relationship of Part 1, and builds towards the new covenant between creator and created; there is only a slight lethargy in Huston's direction which even Mayuzumi's superb score cannot disguise, yet, to the credit of all, the film closes at the actual sacrifice-*manqué* with an imposing simplicity entirely consonant with the picture's English-release subtitle, *In the Beginning* . . .

The Bible is also a superb showcase for the Italians' visual flair and craftsmanship – a skill we shall encounter often throughout this book and which remains vital and inexhaustible even in films in which script, direction and acting plumb new depths of inadequacy. Adam's Creation is told through the clay sculptures of Giacomo Manzu; the final (simple) form of the Tree attributable to the painter Corrado Colliea; the soft photography of the Eden sequences (shot in a zoological garden in Rome) by Lupino Latourno; the Tower of Babel (wisely modelled on the Babylonian ziggurat) and Sodom and Gomorrah (all nooks and crannies of veiled degeneracy) by art director Mario Chiari, previously responsible for *Fabiola* (1949) and *Barabbas* (1962); even the impressive Flood was modelled by Huston on Da Vinci's drawings of water.

One major problem with filming Genesis is that, as soon as its content is translated into images, it begins to lose the innocence of its vision – one may accept an allegory in print but not necessarily when it is thrust before one's eyes with live actors. *The Bible* chooses to present simplicity on a large scale, the stories' clean, simple lines translated faithfully and with due regard for mid-Atlantic audiences (Adam and Eve are blond, clean-cut youths; Robert Bresson, originally hired to direct this segment, wanted darker-skinned actors). Yet each film-maker sees the Creation in his own terms: Alberto Gout's *Adam and Eve* (*Adan y Eva*, 1956) holds to the convention of no dialogue and convenient shrubbery but naturally uses Mexican players, and adds the interesting wrinkle of showing their attempts to stay alive after the Fall. In Marc Connelly and William Keighley's *The Green Pastures* (1936) the Fall, Cain and Abel, and Noah and the Flood are re-enacted in Black American terms ('God appears in many forms to those that believe in him . . .').

The two most awe-inspiring events of early Genesis – the Flood and the destruction of Sodom and Gomorrah – have always remained easy game for cinematic spectacle. Huston is comparatively low-keyed in this respect: his Ark is a *Doctor Dolittle*-like affair and his Cities of the Plain discreet (as is the Bible itself). Michael Curtiz's *Noah's Ark* (1928), subtitled 'The Story of the Deluge', points up the allegory in bolder tones with a story of pure hokum inserted (in the silent tradition) into a modern parallel set during the First World War. The Noah story is told by a

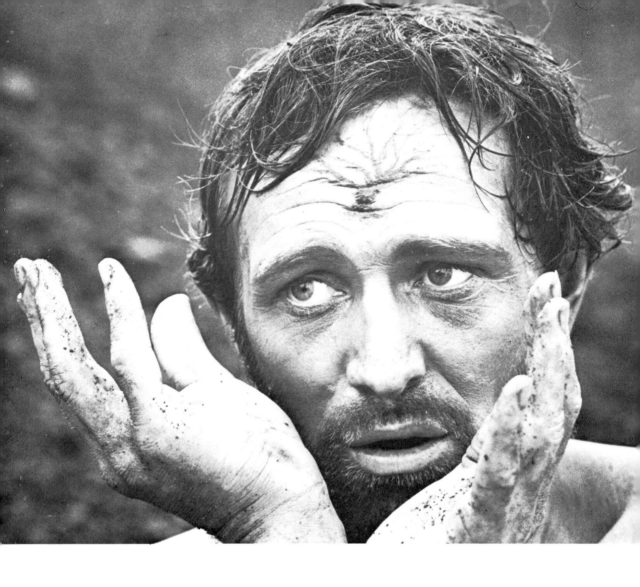

16 The mark of Cain: Richard Harris in *The Bible in the Beginning* . . .

17 (*right*) Ziggurat reborn: The Tower of
Babel in *The Bible in the Beginning* . . .

18 (*below*) . . . and in *Noah's Ark*

minister (Paul McAllister, who also plays Noah) to pass the time when the *dramatis personae* are trapped in an underground vault; parallels between the ancient and modern stories are slim, to say the least, but the Noah flashback is a remarkable demonstration of the epic potential of silent cinema, particularly since the only version of Curtiz's film available now is a sound reissue of 1960, produced and written by Robert Youngson and with an impressive synchronised score (musical supervision by Herman Fuchs and Louis Turchen).

Curtiz's film places the story in Akkad (i.e. mid-third millennium in Northern Mesopotamia) and uses spectacle to tell a tale of idolatory, extravagance and enslavement vs simplicity and freedom: Noah's son Japheth is blinded and chained to a mill, Miriam his future wife is about to be sacrificed before the people of Akkad when a great wind blows open the temple doors to announce Noah, and the Ark is protected against the jeering soldiery by a moat of fire. The script digs even deeper into fantasy and is not content with evoking just the Japheth/Samson parallel: when Noah hears God's warning, he is alerted by a burning bush and sees God's words in the form of a huge flaming book which is set in a mountainside and turns its own pages – a direct crib by Warners from Paramount's *The Ten Commandments* six years earlier (DeMille had also wanted to film the Flood – as *The Deluge* – but had to give up the idea because of Warners' impending release of *Noah's Ark*).

Curtiz's film succeeds simply through its hammer-blow approach. The gritty realism of Japheth toiling at the mill is also found in the muddy rescue scenes after the train crash which opens the modern story, and later in the trench warfare sequences. The spectacle is among the most impressive ever put on film: the destruction of the temple of Akkad, the coming of the rains, the arrival of the animals (realised as a cinematic fugue), and a flood which, in detail and relentlessness (note the desperation of those locked outside the Ark), rates as the most impressive destruction sequence of its kind, even taking into account the disaster cycle of the American cinema of the seventies. Such physical excitement finds spiritual resolution in Japheth's miraculous regaining of his sight as a light shines from heaven – paralleled in the modern story by Mary/Miriam (Dolores Costello) sublimely opening and closing her eyes to heaven as she hears the news of the Armistice after being rescued from the underground vault.

Curtiz's film may be more of a showcase for Hans Koenekamp and Fred Jackman's special effects than anything else, but at least it has point as well as spectacle. Robert Aldrich's *Sodom and Gomorrah* (1962) also invents a full-scale story out of nothing but lacks a sense of purpose beyond its obvious value as spanking entertainment. Aldrich's original, 171-minute cut apparently showed sins worthy of total annihilation; all that remains in his final, 154-minute version are conventional tokens of decadence and a severe queen (Anouk Aimée) who vaguely lusts after her handmaidens. The film sports some colourful art direction (Ken Adam), impressive battle-scenes between Helamites and Hebrews (directed by Sergio Leone), and a powerful and beautiful score by Miklós Rózsa (working in post-*El Cid* vein). All it lacks is an epic rationale to justify the expansion of the story to two and a half hours – a sense of the melding and sundering of cultures (only hinted at in the two love stories of Ildith for Lot and Lot's daughter for Astaroth), or a god-sent hurdle between the Hebrews and their destiny in Canaan. A half-hour early American Underground short, James Sibley Watson's *Lot in Sodom* (1933), hints at the moral complexities of the situation but falls prey to its own camp imagery of young men in bedsheets and Lot in a stylised hairpiece. Again, only Huston's *The Bible* – using an idea by Orson Welles, who was to have directed the Sodom and Gomorrah segment – fully integrates the story by having Abraham walk with the young Isaac through the charred ruins of the cities on his way to the sacrifice – a grim reminder of the Hebrews' ruthless God before the potentially cruellest test of all.

Marcello Baldi's *I patriarchi della Bibbia* (1962) takes in more events than *The Bible* – from the Creation up to Genesis 35 – and makes several advantages of a simplicity imposed by its limited budget (note also the use of animal skins for clothes, as in Curtiz's *Noah's Ark*). However, most of its running-time is spent with the post-Deluge events of Abraham, Esau, Jacob and Rachel, with a crafty coda in which Rachel predicts that one day a virgin will conceive a Messiah. Moshe Mizrahi's *Rachel's Man* (1974) is similarly forward-looking, tracing Jacob's life from birth to when he is named

Israel (or Ish-Rachel, meaning Rachel's man) by a stranger (God) *en route* to his native land; good use is made of a narrator, which reduces the need for spoken dialogue, but the film, though given authenticity by Israeli locations, actors (mostly) and consideration for second-millennium traditions, is little more than a conventional love-story. Similarly lacking in aspirations is Irving Rapper's *Sold into Egypt* (*Giuseppe venduto dai fratelli*, 1961), a straight retelling of the Joseph story distinguished by Belinda Lee's glowering wife of Potiphar and Robert Morley's jarring presence as Potiphar himself.

There are several Old Testament films which deal with such vignettes in a similarly detached way – and not always with as much fidelity to the original as Rapper's. Henry Koster's *The Story of Ruth* (1960) totally misses the warmth and honesty of the original's love between a poor Moabitess and a rich Israelite, and the possibilities of exalting the characters of Ruth (Elana Eden) and Boaz (Stuart Whitman); only Franz Waxman's beautiful archaic/modal music remains. At least Raoul Walsh's *Esther and the King* (*Ester e il re*, 1961) tries to flesh out the characters' motivation while adhering reasonably closely to the fifth-century story of the marriage between a Jewess and a Persian king. In the Old Testament original, Queen Vashti is a marginal character, relieved of her title for a simple act of wifely disobedience; in the film, particularly as played by the sultry Daniella Rocca and photographed by Mario Bava, she is transformed into an unfaithful vamp – a moral counterweight to the righteous Esther (Joan Collins), the new wife of King Ahasuerus/Xerxes (Richard Egan).

Considerably better, however, are the two films based on the Apocrypha story of Judith, the young Judaean widow who helped to stave off the Assyrians' invasion by tricking her way into their general's tent and beheading him as he lay drunk in bed. D.W. Griffith's *Judith of Bethulia* (1914) is famous now more for its pioneering length than anything else, but it is interesting to watch the director at work on epic characterisation before his mammoth efforts to come. Griffith plays up the infatuation side, with Judith (Blanche Sweet) parading before Holofernes (Henry B. Walthall) in clothes more reminiscent of 1914 than the sixth century BC, but deepens the heroine's character by adding occasional doubts as she puts her plan into operation; such human details are also to be glimpsed in the battle-scenes, and show Griffith already appreciating that 'epic' means much more than just 'spectacle'. Fernando Cerchio's *Head of a Tyrant* (*Giuditta e Oloferne*, 1960) takes this idea one step further by having *both* protagonists fall in love, thus emphasising the horror of Judith's plan, the Assyrian general's decision to massacre the people of Bethulia, and the woman's desperate act of hacking off his head. This is a perfectly justifiable tampering with the original (in which Judith never falters), and the film finishes with God-sent lightning and the Assyrians' idol statue crumbling.

Head of a Tyrant is also thoroughly representative of a body of Babylonian and Assyrian pictures – all pepla – which show no consistency towards the relative cultures beyond showing them as a receptacle for ruthless power-politics: Siro Marcellini's *Goliath – King of the Slaves* (*L'eroe di Babilonia*, 1964), Carlo Ludovico Bragaglia's *Queen of Babylon* (*La cortigiana di Babilonia*, 1955), Primo Zeglio's *Io, Semiramide* (1963), Silvio Amadio's *7th Thunderbolt* (*Le sette folgori di Assur*, 1962). There is no attempt to examine Hebraic culture in its Mesopotamian exile, and thus no advance on Griffith's Siege of Babylon and the Feast of Belshazzar episodes in *Intolerance* (1916).

*   *   *

Egypt, to which we now turn with the story of the Exodus, has fared better in the cinema, and three of the best examples will show briefly the range of interpretation. Jerzy Kawalerowicz's *Pharaoh* (*Faraon*, 1966) is in a league of its own, conceived over a period of five years from the classic Polish novel by Bolesław Prus and shot in Uzbekistan, Egypt and the studio at Łódź. It is the only film (apart from the Egyptian scenes in Gianfranco De Bosio's *Moses*) to depict the Egyptian way of life with any historical veracity, from naked breasts to the details of Egypt's imposing and essentially austere architectural beauties. *Pharaoh* concerns the struggle of the young pharaoh Rameses XIII against the entrenched power of the priesthood during the XXth dynasty (1200–1090 BC). The unstated parallels with the conflicts between the individual, religion, socialism and the State in

19 (*opposite above*) Impressive spectacle: Michael Curtiz's *Noah's Ark*

20 (*opposite below*) Token decadence: Queen Bera (Anouk Aimée) and
her latest favourite, Orpha (Mitsuko Takara), in *Sodom and
Gomorrah* (1962)

21 (*above*) A love that asks for nothing: Merit (Jean Simmons) and
Sinuhe (Edmund Purdom) in *The Egyptian*

sixties Poland (plus its anti-Semitism: Rameses takes a Jewish wife, much to the consternation of the high priests) show epic form ever at the service of the present. Kawalerowicz's three-hour 70mm film moves at a baleful tempo characteristic of the director, and despite several powerful visual effects (a subjective battle in which the camera is the victim; the high priest Herhor staking all as he appeals to the people's superstitions from atop the city walls) is a thoughtful and introspective meditation on the loneliness which power brings, particularly within a highly ritualised society such as Ancient Egypt. Kawalerowicz draws sensitive playing from Jerzy Zelnik in the title role, with powerful support from the darkly beautiful Barbara Brylska.

Michael Curtiz's *The Egyptian* (1954), though pervaded by many of the worst Hollywood vulgarities and hampered by the director's lack of interest in realising the full possibilities of the generally literate script and flashy sets, still manages to convey the essence of one character's journey towards an ennobling faith, expressed here in fifties sexual language. The doctor Sinuhe (Edmund Purdom), besieged on one side by ambition and carnality (Bella Darvi's Nefer) and on the other by altruism and spirituality (Jean Simmons' Merit – 'Can't you believe in a love that asks for nothing?'), proceeds to a somewhat embittered state of self-knowledge in old age. Purdom, especially, handles his dialogue with impressive thoughtfulness, more than compensating for the jarring delivery of Victor Mature as the brutish Horamheb.

The film is set during one of the most fascinating periods of the New Kingdom (1567–1085 BC) – the reign of Amenophis IV, later known as Akhenaten, who tried to introduce the religious concept of Aten (a monotheistic idea based on the solar disc). When Akhenaten died c. 1350 BC, the country quickly reverted to the cult of the Theban god Amun, the new pharaoh changing his name from Tutankhaten to Tutankhamun in recognition of this. The film refers to the general opinion that Akhenaten (Michael Wilding) was little more than an eccentric but exalts his ideas further than history can stand (Egyptian monotheism was known long before Akhenaten) and even invokes Christian parallels ('These things happened thirteen centuries before the birth of Jesus Christ'). Sinuhe functions as little more than a device to show court

intrigue and balance the opposing arguments of peace and war, spirituality and carnality. His transformation after the pharaoh's death into some sort of Aten-apostle further enhances the film's Bible-*manqué* atmosphere, signposted at the very start as the baby Sinuhe is rescued Moses-like from the bulrushes. The problem is that Akhenaten's story, more accurately treated, would have made far more interesting viewing than Sinuhe's. A film about Akhenaten's queen, Nefertiti, Fernando Cerchio's *Queen of the Nile* (*Nefertite, regina del Nilo*, 1961), is more interested in the affair between the queen (Jeanne Crain) and a sculptor (Edmund Purdom).

More of a dramatic unity is Howard Hawks' *Land of the Pharaohs* (1955), a visually splendid response by Warners to Fox's CinemaScope showpiece. Here a pyramid and its very construction (by slave labour) provides the epic focus, to which the protagonists, good and bad, react. The massive stone monument causes death, pain, greed, pride, glory and honour, and as the slave-architect Vashtar (James Robertson Justice) leads away his people Moses-like at the end he talks of it as if it were a dead hero ('It will be remembered'). Hawks provides some splendid settings for his central stone hero: the mass scenes of people rallying to start the building and working in the stone quarries (to Dmitri Tiomkin's refreshingly pagan choral music) are directed with impressive sweep, as is the later sealing of the tomb with its creeping sense of claustrophobia. The film goes out of its way to stress its authenticity and evocation of background detail: the opening return of the pharaoh's army (the spectacle balanced with narration about the drug of power), the burial sequence in which the dead are sent off with clapping, and the several details of construction and quarrying. Unfortunately the script does not live up to either the film's visual splendour or its concern for detail. The two leads are uninflected paragons of greed – the pharaoh (Jack Hawkins) for gold, the princess Nellifer (Joan Collins) for almost anything – and there is no genuine interplay between them and the slaves led by Vashtar. However, as a portrait of an age, of an obsession, of a monument which comes to mean different things to different people, it is impressive cinema.

It is important to remember that Egypt and its pharaohs are not always cast as the villains in the Old Testament – relations between the Hebrews and the Egyptians are in permanent flux throughout its pages, recognising the interdependency of nations' fortunes in such a confined part of the world as the Middle East. The migration of the Hebrews to Egypt under the leadership of Joseph, and their subsequent sojourn and Exodus, are not recorded in any of the Egyptians' voluminous records of the period, yet the biblical story can easily be accommodated by the historical facts. The arrival of 'a new king over Egypt, which knew not Joseph' (Exodus 1: 8) is now thought to stand for the new dynasty after the conquest by the Hyksos, Semitic tribes from Canaan and Syria; no Egyptian records have survived for the period during which they ruled (1730–1580 BC), and if one accepts the likely fact that there was a southward migration of Hebrews to the richer lands of the Delta during the time of the Hyksos Kingdom (which stretched from Northern Mesopotamia, right down the Palestinian coast to Egypt), it is understandable that, when the Egyptians rebelled and finally threw off the Hyksos yoke, the new rulers would show no special regard for settlers who had arrived and prospered during foreign domination.

The whole story of Exodus is thus balanced precariously between history and folk-tale. 'Moses' is simply an Egyptian word meaning 'son', and his birth-story strongly parallels the Semitic folk-tale of the third-millennium Akkadian king Sargon. Yet however much that and the Exodus theme itself reflect folk traditions, the details of the journey can be demythified to show probable fact behind the seemingly fanciful happenings. The Red Sea legend stems from a mistranslation of the words *yam suph* ('reed sea', i.e. papyrus-reed marsh); mannah is simply a secretion exuded by the tamarisk bush; migratory quails are known even now over the Sinai peninsula; and the Seven Plagues are merely magnified accounts of various common pestilences. As Moses (Burt Lancaster) says in Gianfranco De Bosio's *Moses* (1976), 'A miracle is simply the right thing happening at the right time.'

Generally, however, film-makers have chosen not to demythologise events, and it is notable that De Bosio's more realistic film (an unsatisfactory theatrical condensation of the fine six-part TV series *Moses the Lawgiver*) appeared during the questioning seventies. However, De Bosio, and scriptwriters Anthony Burgess – also on the team

for Franco Zeffirelli's 'realistic' version of the story of Christ, *Jesus of Nazareth* (1977), a six-hour TV film – and Vittorio Bonicelli, only go part of the way: the Red Sea parts as usual (though somewhat tattily) and the Plagues enter in due succession. Yet such is the depth of the presentation of the opposing cultures, and so convincing the Hebrews' belief in their special destiny (magnificently incarnated in Lancaster's imposing yet deeply human performance), that the film as a whole rises above its halfway-house approach. Particularly memorable are the details of the Hebrews' nomadic existence in the wilderness, their perpetual bickering (which emphasises Moses' stubborn vision), and easy loss of faith; these bring the participants to life without losing sight of the story's epic character. A major bonus is the perfectly attuned music of Ennio Morricone – a moving lament theme for the title character (intoned by solo alto or viola to stress the Hebrews' destiny) and a great paean of praise to Israel as the waters close over the pursuing Egyptians.

The separate tradition of DeMille is basically a refinement of early attempts like *Moses and the Exodus from Egypt* (1907) which, with its confetti mannah, winged angels, flame streamers and God with a paper halo, summed up the reverential Sunday School tradition. DeMille added size, technical virtuosity and showmanship, but the same theatricality and naivety of vision is there. His silent *The Ten Commandments* (1923) is only partly taken up with the biblical story: it forms an extended prologue, running for sixty minutes at modern projection speeds, to a vaguely parallel modern story (with a different cast) almost twice as long and of immeasurably greater tedium. The latter concerns two brothers, John and Dan McTavish (Richard Dix and Rod La Rocque), one good, the other corrupt, and has a measure of suspense at the end as a cathedral, built with suspect materials, threatens to collapse; thankfully, none of the story's long-windedness and flat verbosity is found in the biblical section, which has an impressive urgency and directness, particularly in the frenetic Golden Calf sequence. *The Ten Commandments* shows all DeMille's weaknesses and virtues: it is very impressive technically (quite the equal of the 1956 version); it is closer to the Bible in spirit than the later version; but it lacks a sufficiently imposing presence in Moses to give the pageantry some sort of shape – as much a fault of

DeMille as of the actor Theodore Roberts.

Such a weakness does not mar the 1956 version, DeMille's last film statement before his death on 23 January 1959, peacefully in his sleep (he had already suffered a heart-attack while filming the Exodus). The central performances are of great stature – Charlton Heston (who had distinguished himself in DeMille's *The Greatest Show on Earth*, 1952) as Moses and Yul Brynner as Pharaoh, the latter particularly good in the pivotal scene where he confronts Moses as a Hebrew rather than as an Egyptian. But it is Heston's film – a remarkable transformation of his set-jawed acting style into heroic terms, the eyes blazing with conviction, the frame sufficiently impressive, and the voice taut with emotion (played back slower, his voice also doubles as the Voice of God in the Burning Bush sequence). Heston was to receive more demanding roles in the future – and certainly better scripts – but he fits perfectly here into the theatrical DeMille mould. The Moses who descends from Sinai after receiving God's word has a Michelangelo-like urgency and vigour (stressed in the stormy, grey-streaked hair and different stance) which propels the events of Part 2 with an inevitability only hinted at in Part 1. Much of this is also due to the fact that DeMille is never happier than when dealing with physical drama; Part 1 is often bogged down by unnecessary invention surrounding Queen Nefretiri (Anne Baxter), who is never satisfactorily incorporated into the mainstream of events and is only there to satisfy the DeMille convention of a screen vamp to balance the pious Sephora (Yvonne De Carlo). Lines like 'I'll have you torn into so many pieces even the vultures won't find them' (Nefretiri to her old maid, Memnit) are merely distractions, as is the tedious sub-plot of the love-affair of Joshua (John Derek) in Part 2.

However, the set-pieces are magnificent: the Darkness of Death creeping with green fingers through the night, the glorious chaos of the Exodus (an old man dying; a woman giving birth), the parting of the Red Sea, the Pillar of Fire shooting off small comets to etch the Ten Commandments into the mountainside, and the earthquake as Moses hurls the tablets against the Golden Calf. *The Ten Commandments* is not DeMille's most satisfying film, but it works well as a moving pageant of sharply defined characters against an imposing landscape. From the snatch of Wagner's *Das Rheingold* heard in the bulrushes sequence, through the colourful scene of Moses bringing the Ethiopian tribute to Pharaoh, to Moses' final cry of 'Go! Proclaim liberty throughout all the lands,' we are left in no doubt that this is narrative on a grand scale, faith writ large. Elmer Bernstein's direct, often brash score pays this conception tribute, with free use of the *leitmotif* principle; like the film itself, it is stirring, heart-on-sleeve, with only a suggestion of subtlety unexplored.

DeMille never resolved the struggle in his films between sexual and devout content. *Samson and Delilah* (1949), the best of his historical epics, comes closest to tackling the problem face-to-face. DeMille cast Victor Mature and Hedy Lamarr in the title roles because 'they embody in the public mind the essence of maleness and femininity', but the script expands considerably on this apparently straight sexual confrontation. The opening narration by the director declaims on the freedom of the artist or statesman (at which Victor Young's music obligingly slips into a patriotic march) and ends with the establishment of Samson as a hero with 'a bold dream – liberty for his nation'. The script builds around his character a web of archetypal conflicts – Flesh (Delilah's love) vs Spirit (Miriam's), Money vs Faith, the Sword vs the Hand – and deepens the central portrait by playing on the theme of the humbling of a proud spirit.

Mature, though far from capable of the subtlest acting nuances, is especially good at roles requiring heroic melancholia (as Edgar G. Ulmer's *Hannibal* was later to show) and there is a sadness in the later scenes showing the blinded Samson which is surprisingly moving. The point is well made that Samson's long hair is a symbol of his self-confidence rather than merely physical strength, and the sadness of a simple heroic figure caught up in a web of events beyond his understanding is expressed in the line of an Old Man: 'Why do men always betray the strongest among them?' Hedy Lamarr's glamorous Delilah, all jutting breasts, swaying shoulders and smouldering myopic gaze, is an equally heroic partner, and the sexual tension is finely judged. The pair's final reconciliation in the granary at night, superbly lit by photographer George Barnes, provides an appropriate *piano* resolution of the love theme before the *forte* ending in which Samson meets his destiny.

Despite its several weaknesses (George Sanders'

jokey performance as Saran of Gaza among them), DeMille's film is streets ahead of Alexander Korda's *Samson and Delilah* (*Samson und Delila*, 1923), which features a half-hour biblical section within a modern parallel with the same principal actors. 'The story of Samson and Delilah belongs to an age crammed with lust and Empire,' says an old man when asked by Julia Sorel/Delilah (Maria Corda – Korda's wife) to tell the story. There is little attempt at anything approaching historical veracity – Delilah's palace room is a mixture of biblical and twenties decor, with a gigantic feather over her couch – and the story is denied a fitting climax as the temple set only collapsed when Korda and Co. had given up filming in frustration. Samson (Alfredo Galoar) is introduced as a full-grown man and wades through some interesting spectacle (such as using Gaza's main gate as a shield) but anything deeper is lacking.

The cinema has made generally good capital out of the chapter of Hebrew history which begins with the domination of the Philistines. In several respects the sudden arrival of these 'sea-people' (as the Egyptians named them) parallels the North European experience during the Viking era many centuries later – yet another hindrance to peace and unity in Palestine, again by foreign interference. The Philistines are thought to have been Achaeans and Luvians expanding southwards, and their sudden arrival c. 1180 BC so astounded the native population that it was not until the turn of the millennium that their power was broken by the Hebrews and Phoenicians, with King David finally repelling them in 975. Both Richard Pottier and Ferdinando Baldi's *David and Goliath* (*David e Golia*, 1960), filmed in Rome, Jerusalem and Yugoslavia, with Orson Welles as a tired and brooding Saul, and Marcello Baldi's *Saul and David* (*Saul e David*, 1965), which fills in the earlier years of Saul's nomination by Samuel, take due note of the conflicts, the former pointing up the theme of robbed heritage by showing David bringing back the Ark of the Covenant to Jerusalem after beating the Philistines.

The most thoughtful treatment of some of the problems raised by the period comes in Henry King's *David and Bathsheba* (1951). There is a refreshing dispensing with large-scale set-pieces (even though the sets are spacious they are notably spartan): the couple's wedding is covered in two brief shots, and the flashback to the Goliath fight is

very off-hand. In like manner, Philip Dunne's intelligent screenplay concentrates more on the interior drama of David's kingship, climaxing in a final half-hour dominated by two lengthy scenes – the couple's discussion about whether David should give Bathsheba up to the people and David's prayer at the tabernacle, the latter leading to a reaffirmation of his faith in God after being granted a sign (rain). Alfred Newman's modal score here rises to a full choral setting of Psalm 23 which David had earlier picked out on a harp while musing alone. Gregory Peck's line in bemused integrity makes David a noble, if rightly confused, figure, and the film balances the conflicts of broken friendship (David and Uriah) and the contradictory privileges of power with an impressive simplicity.

The last major cinematic cycle, the Solomon and Sheba films, adds little extra, mostly dwelling on the same problems in the more settled period just prior to the fatal division of Palestine into the Two Kingdoms. The Queen of Sheba, like Bathsheba, is an ephemeral figure to the Bible-writers, and has little more than a footnote to herself; more important is her allegorical role, but, with little material to go on, scriptwriters have been left to their own devices. Whether vamped by Betty Blythe in J. Gordon Edwards' *The Queen of Sheba* (1922), or by Leonora Ruffo in Pietro Francisci's *La regina di Saba* (1952), or by Gina Lollobrigida in King Vidor's *Solomon and Sheba* (1959), she bears little resemblance to the historical figure who came to Solomon more interested in trade-routes and economic deals than in glandular attractions. Francisci's film, with its impressive sets and greater concentration on the queen's activities as a monarch, has at least a slight regard for history, but the plot is otherwise a mixture of cliché (milk baths), familiar stories (the baby and two mothers illustrating the 'wisdom of Solomon'), and uninhibited fantasy.

King Vidor's *Solomon and Sheba* still shows a few signs of the results of Tyrone Power dying halfway through production and having to be replaced by Yul Brynner (Power is still visible in some long shots which were not refilmed). Yet it is still an impressive accomplishment, notwithstanding Vidor's statement that Brynner failed to make as much of Solomon's inner anguish as Power. After a vaguely allusive opening narration ('This is the border between Israel and Egypt. As it is

22 (*left*) Paragon of greed: the pharaoh (Jack Hawkins) in *Land of the Pharaohs*

23 (*opposite below*) Sharply defined characters: Baka (Vincent Price), Seth (Cedric Hardwicke), Moses (Charlton Heston) and Rameses (Yul Brynner) in *The Ten Commandments* (1956)

24 (*above*) A proud spirit: Samson (Victor Mature) in *Samson and Delilah* (1949)

25 (*opposite above*) Bemused integrity: a dancer (Gwyneth Verdon) entertains Uriah (Kieron Moore) and David (Gregory Peck) in *David and Bathsheba*

26 Austerity vs hedonism: Solomon (Yul Brynner) meets Sheba (Gina
Lollobrigida) in *Solomon and Sheba*

today, so it was a thousand years before the birth of Jesus of Nazareth . . .'.) and a clumsy and scrappy frontier battle, the picture settles down into a duet between the leads, the queen introduced in Boadicea style whipping a chariot-team along, and Solomon soon established as a monarch who 'teaches that all men are equal and none are slaves'.

As in *Samson and Delilah* there is a host of thematic contrasts: the hedonism and paganism of Sheba vs the austerity and monotheism of Israel (also reflected in the sensuality of the Sheban settings against the simplicity of the Hebrew ones); Solomon 'the poet' vs his brother Adonijah 'the soldier' (twin aspects of monarchy); the sexuality and guile of the queen vs the spirituality and openness of Abishag (Marisa Pavan), Solomon's Hebrew 'conscience'. Such conflicts are worked out chiefly through the queen rather than Solomon, the former passing through a complex series of quandaries which show considerable inventiveness

if not always natural development. Gina Lollobrigida's electric characterisation more than matches Brynner's wooden acting, and frequently swamps it. Whether indulging in her habit of breaking things when angry, or instilling her lines with a subtle ambiguity ('The way of a woman is truly beyond understanding,' admires Pharaoh. 'The way of a woman,' replies the queen, 'is simple, my lord. It is always to follow the way of a man . . .'), or realising the promise of ten reels in a tempestuous dance in gold and maroon, Lollobrigida dominates the film. The vague conflict between being a woman and a queen – whatever that may mean – is conveniently dropped near the end, and an unconvincing conversion/cure inserted in the final reel when she recognises the power of the Ark of the Covenant. However, the film as a whole works for the same reasons as DeMille's *Samson and Delilah*, and sports better spectacle (especially the final battle) and greater all-round breadth of vision.

Biblical: The New Testament

So the Lord Jesus, after instructing them, was taken up to heaven and sat at God's right hand; and the disciples went out preaching everywhere, the Lord helping them and confirming their message with accompanying miracles.

Mark, 16: 19f.

What else has two thousand years' advance publicity?

Cecil B. DeMille

Whereas with the Old Testament we were concerned with an elaborate mixture of folk-tales and history, in the New Testament we can already feel a new directness in the story of religious beliefs developed against a firm historical backdrop rather than remote folk-tales. To compensate in epic terms for such thinning of the mythic fabric – even though the period is still some two thousand years ago – there is the great central character of Christ, who in the four Gospels moves with varying emphases towards his transfiguration, national concerns metamorphosed into spiritual ones and the specifically Judaic message of the Old Testament broadened to include Gentile as well as Jew.

The cinema has almost exclusively concentrated on the life of Christ when considering the New Testament as source material. (A work like Frank Borzage's *The Big Fisherman* (1959), which uses stories of the disciple Peter as a picturesque backdrop to conventional regal shenanigans, is rare (and best forgotten). Chapter 10 will deal with the theme of Christianity vs Rome.) Thus our focus falls on the Gospels for literary parallels. These are the only reliable sources for the life and teachings of Christ – who only rates a passing mention in Roman sources like Tacitus' *Annals* (*Annales*) – and they are also interesting prose works in their own right.

Like the Old Testament, the New Testament is no epic in literary terms; but amongst the motley collection of works are some individual prose epics – and of the four Gospels Mark, the earliest (written c. AD 65) and probably the most accurate of all, is the best-formed example. Written for non-Jews in unadorned but graceful Greek, and largely based on stories told to Mark by the apostle Peter, it is a gospel of action rather than instruction – a permanent testimony, written after Peter's martyrdom in Rome, to the man who had inspired him. But it is not just a biography, not just a history (the chronology is sometimes confused); it is an epic treatment of the figure of Christ, dominated by the climax of the cross. Mark is interested in the personality of Christ, his influence, the opposition he aroused, the astonishment he caused; and these elements are manipulated with more than chance skill. For Mark, the end of the story – the Passion, Crucifixion and Resurrection – is the most important thing, and it is here that the *dramatis personae* finally assemble to fulfil their destinies. From the actions of a young Jewish 'prophet', who lived and preached with a small band in poverty and enjoyed, first, brief popularity, then general hostility; from what in Roman terms was no more than a local annoyance in an inhospitable and troublesome province – from this comes the Gospel of Mark, the first prose epic in Greek.

The cinema does not measure up to the challenge of filming this material as well as it does in other genres – simply because here myth continues to touch closest on most Western lives, and an excess of reverence has fettered the imaginations of scriptwriters. The four greatest versions, which will be discussed in detail later on, are all, however, marked by an individual intensity and blind purpose which in epic terms manage to transmute the sometimes base material of the scripts into an approximation of gold.

What is of interest in the various film versions of Christ's life is the extent to which each accepts or rejects the 'traditional' concepts of the man, as received by the Church (which incorporates all the medieval and Renaissance embroidery), and looks instead for a fresh view, based on the Gospels considered as literary epics adaptable like any other. On the visual side it is amazing to see how powerful has been the Renaissance artistic legacy: film-makers, presumably to touch an immediately responsive nerve in their audiences, have again and again turned to the Old Masters for style and inspiration. DeMille instructed Peverell Marley, his director of photography on *The King of Kings* (1927), to study paintings in order to formulate a lighting style, and the film reputedly re-creates 298 canvases, with the Crucifixion influenced by both Rubens and Doré. J. Stuart Blackton's *The Way of the Cross* (1909), a series of single-shot tableaux representing incidents in Christ's life, sports the full heavenly paraphernalia in 'Jesus' Sleep' of a choir around the crib with flutes, harps and angels sawing violins. Even Pier Paolo Pasolini's ascetic *The Gospel according to St Matthew* (*Il vangelo secondo Matteo*, 1964) features a Da Vinci-like Christ and Botticelli-haired Angel of the Lord, while the painterly style of George Stevens' *The Greatest Story Ever Told* (1965), like DeMille's film, is saturated by the influence of Renaissance models, most notably Titian and (in the dramatic use of chiaroscuro) Tintoretto.

The dispiriting side of this inclination towards the traditional view of Christ is that film-makers have not looked far for any new language in which to express the message of the Gospels and generally have not, as in other historical genres, gone straight back to the original period for inspiration. There have been very few 'objective' attempts. Pasolini's film is, as we shall see later, only innovative on the surface. Even more disappointing, in the sense of promise unfulfilled, is Michael Campus' *The Passover Plot* (1976), the belated film version of Hugh J. Schonfield's radical sixties reinterpretation, which presented Christ (named Yeshua) as a social and political opportunist who stagecrafted his 'resurrection' from the stone tomb as a deliberate piece of anti-Roman propaganda. Such a thesis is a startling demythification of the Gospel text, robbing it (in epic terms) of the climactic Transfiguration; in human terms, how-

ever, Schonfield's portrayal of Yₑshua is both valid – particularly for our questioning times – and no doubt closer to the truth. Campus' film, however, falls between two stools: there is little attempt to conjure up the realities of the period, and the respectful presentation of the central figure, in combination with the reams of non-dramatic dialogue and plentiful use of close-ups, saps the unconventionality of the approach to such an extent that the final reel seems merely gratuitous radical chic. Alex North's score, in customary Hollywood biblical vein, acknowledges this central failure; only Donald Pleasence's ambiguous Pilate, and the strategy of showing Yeshua in contact with the Jerusalem Jewish underground (which markedly conflicts with the approach of Nicholas Ray's *King of Kings*), are worthwhile.

To date there is no treatment of the Gospels which manages, like De Bosio's *Moses*, to humanise the biblical text yet retain its epic stature. Two Italian productions (the first something of a forerunner of Pasolini's film) have taken a documentary approach: Virgilio Sabel's *Il figlio dell'uomo* (1955) shows a group of Christian believers – drawn from country folk from the Gargano area – re-enacting important scenes from the life of Christ with a Catholic devotion; Roberto Rossellini's *The Messiah* (*Il Messia*, 1975), shot in English and acted by Italian players who understood little of what they were asked to say, draws chiefly on John's Gospel for its material, but curiously omits the Resurrection – it, too, with its close-ups and long takes has a literary feel, with Christ (like Socrates in Rossellini's earlier *Socrate*) a traditionally passive figure, accepting of his fate.

These two films are hardly the norm for the cinema's treatment of the Gospels, but they do show the traditionalism, the respect for all the received paraphernalia about Christ, which forms the basis of filmdom's approach. For whether one approves or not, it is within this framework that one must look for cinematic epic form when considering the New Testament works. Here most of all the cinema shows vivid links with the other arts, consciously respecting the artistic, sculptural and musical legacy of the Middle Ages (Christ as a passive instrument of destiny, seen in pious terms) and presenting it in progressively magnified, though essentially unchanged, dress.

This in-built sense of carrying on a received tradition is evident from the earliest screen portrayals of Christ – from the recordings of various passion plays (including the renowned Oberammergau one) to the earliest major film version, Sidney Olcott's *From the Manger to the Cross* (1913). Olcott had directed the first screen version of *Ben-Hur* four years earlier, and his picture, claiming spurious authenticity from being shot in Egypt and Palestine, was a great success in its time and was even reissued in 1938 with a soundtrack. Its style, informed by a disarming simplicity, lies securely in the Sunday School ambit of cotton-wool beards and ironed bed-sheets. Similar influences are discernible as the years progress: the relevant section on the Nazarene (Howard Gaye) in D. W. Griffith's *Intolerance* (1916) merely shows episodes from the Gospels, but already one can sense a move away from the Olcott representation to one of softer, more pious Renaissance tones. The six episodes from Christ's life shown in *Intolerance* (the original print included a more representational thirty, balancing fairly with the other sections of the film, before the Jewish authorities in Los Angeles ordered the Judean section to be drastically shortened) hardly constitute a film as such, given the interlocking construction of the overall plot, but their style remained the norm for some time. Elsewhere, Robert Wiene's *INRI* (1923) uses passion-play format for its insert of the story of Christ told to an imprisoned murderer; Giulio Antomoro's *Christus* (1915) is modelled, like DeMille's *The King of Kings*, on famous paintings; and Robert Flaherty's *St Matthew Passion* (1952) – the English version of Ernst Marischka's *Matthäus-Passion* (1949) – unites the artistic and musical legacies by setting Bach's choral work to a montage of paintings drawn from wide sources.

Of the four major film versions of Christ's life, undoubtedly the most complex – in the sense of expectations aroused and results offered – is Pier Paolo Pasolini's *The Gospel according to St Matthew* (*Il vangelo secondo Matteo*, 1964). It is not that, for a director with professed Communist sympathies, the work sits uncomfortably within his *œuvre* – on the contrary, his first feature, *Accattone* (1961), features a martyred central figure within its modern neo-realist setting, and there is more than a touch of the Messiah in the later *Theorem* (*Teorema*, 1968) – but rather that Pasolini chooses to adhere rigidly to one particular Gospel, even to the extent of making his decision a

sine qua non of the film's title. There is no reason why Communism should stand in the way of filming a life of Christ – scepticism can only enhance a view of the Gospels as a chronicle of a social reformist working within the constrictions of foreign domination and religious dogma. Pasolini was expected to demythify the figure of Christ; that he did not, shows how dangerous it is to use an artist's stated beliefs as a yardstick for his finished works. Pasolini's Marxism is the *bête noire* in any assessment of his work, and largely spurious beyond emphasising his interest in peasants or under-privileged classes.

Far more important are his views of sexuality (which were to become ever more obsessive during the last decade of his life) and his qualities as a novelist and poet (which preceded his years as a director). Of the four Gospels, Mark is the least adorned by the traditional paraphernalia of Nativity, angels and such stories as the Temptation in the Wilderness: it reads as it was intended to be read, as an urgent record of Christ's teachings, and has the unhoned power of a primitive epic. If Pasolini's political sympathies were uppermost in his filmic intentions, Mark would surely have been his first choice. Instead, he chose Matthew, the most perfectly constructed of the Gospels in literary terms and written in considerably better Greek than Mark; it reads as a conscious attempt to rework Mark in more literary terms, and to this end regurgitates (often verbatim) all but fifty-five verses, adding much more besides (the Nativity, the Sermon on the Mount, several parables, and other incidents). In Matthew, Pasolini found a sufficiently full version of Christ's life which appealed to him as a poet without too much heavenly rigmarole colouring events.

The attraction of Pasolini's film is its marvellous ambiguity: it promises demythification yet adamantly refuses to keep that promise, and it skirts the traditional Hollywood-pious approach but finds its own equivalent. Pasolini was never a fluid film-maker – his pictures proceed in leaps and starts, without any overall sense of rhythm. His poetic interests lie less in metre than in the joy of celebrating the scatology of man's existence in rough yet beautifully composed visuals – a cinematic Henry Miller or Violette Leduc. At the time of making the film, Pasolini was a more disciplined artist than he was to become in the seventies. The film makes no concessions to ordinary entertainment. For almost two and a half hours, in un-compromising monochrome images, frequently of just a face against a clear sky, it batters the audience with Christ's teachings, spoken rapidly and sternly by the young Spanish student Enrique Irazoqui. Non-professional actors and peasants stand in for Hollywood stars; ruined locations in Southern Italy supplant massive sets or colourful art direction.

Yet as Pasolini's film shows, epic form relies on more than awesome surroundings; it is also the examination of people in relation to their period and other people, and simply by instilling his Christ with a human dynamism and anger Pasolini gives him the necessary authority for an epic hero. The surface touches of Neo-Realism and *cinéma-vérité* camera-style only drain the story of traditional piousness; they do not diminish the stature of the central character. And *in toto* such touches are deceptive, for Pasolini is always conscious of that vast legacy before him: his Angel of the Lord reflects that legacy, and the many carefully composed visuals are reminiscent of the fifteenth-century painters Piero della Francesca and Cosimo Tura. Perhaps the musical soundtrack, with its mixture of ethnic (*Missa Luba*), Lutheran (Bach) and modern (Prokofiev, Webern), reflects the film's Janus-like character: a deliberately ingenuous yet straightforward version of Matthew's Gospel, enriched rather than weakened by the film-maker's own confusion – a confusion very much of our own times.

There is a similar sense of disorientation with Cecil B. DeMille's *The King of Kings* (1927), though for very different reasons. DeMille was the complete director-as-*auteur* in an age when neither the term nor the concept existed: his films are personal utterances on a bewildering variety of subjects, marked by a simplicity and ingenuous-ness which borders on simple-mindedness but which is reinforced by a showman's utter convic-tion that he is *right*. The point is worth stressing with regard to *The King of Kings*, for here, of all his films, it is hardest to reconcile DeMille's artistic schizophrenia. The film's beautifully tex-tured visuals, now making dramatic use of chiaroscuro, now saturated in diffused light, pay homage to a thousand years of Christian art; and the picture moves with a measured dignity per-fectly in tune with this reverential style. Yet DeMille the showman interferes: 'I decided to jolt

them all out of their preconceptions with an opening scene that none of them would be expect-ing, a lavish party in the luxurious home of Mary Magdalene.' DeMille, never backward in seizing an opportunity for revelry (even the modern social drama *Manslaughter* (1922) had featured a flash-back to a Fall-of-Rome orgy), is freed by means of this safety-valve to indulge his rococo sensuality – in images every bit as phony as in the later *Cleopatra* (1934) but, as with Lillian Rich cavort-ing in modern splendour through *The Golden Bed* (1925), designed primarily to reach the imagina-tions of his twenties audience instead of presenting them with historically justifiable material. DeMille was the epicist he was for several reasons: he was the master rather than the slave of history, with a supreme gift for reaching an audience in the most direct way, a talent for story-telling, and a convinced naivety which has remained the province of the greatest showmen. That, combined with his taste for moralising on a grand scale and currying his audience's favour directly, marks DeMille as a twentieth-century *aoidos* – and his popularity, if nothing else, attests to his success.

We have already seen these qualities at work in the two versions of *The Ten Commandments*; with *The King of Kings*, however, something more than a 'stitching of songs' is required if the film is to work in epic terms, and DeMille's sexual flam-boyance had to be pressed into wider service. That the film does work is due in no small measure to the impressive naivety (already mentioned) which informs both the exotic and the pious moments: DeMille sweeps the viewer along with the sheer power of his personal vision, impressing him *en route* with images of beauty and extravagance which wheel abruptly from the simple (the blind girl, the Last Supper, the Crucifixion) through the well-laundered theatrical (Christ writing in the sand before the adulteress, and Lazarus' Techni-color sequence) to the ornate (Mary Magdalene's scenes, the set for Pilate's palace). In dramatic terms, DeMille's apparent miscalculation with Mary Magdalene in fact works very well, thanks to Jacqueline Logan's convincing transformation: by expanding the character, DeMille presents a paral-lel story of moral redemption which is all the more powerful for its seeming impossibility (cf. the centurion Lucius in Nicholas Ray's *King of Kings*, or Prince Alfonso in Anthony Mann's *El Cid*).

The King of Kings also broke with the silent

convention of presenting a modern parallel to an ancient tale (DeMille's regular scriptwriter Jeanie MacPherson had originally suggested one but he had overruled her). Though one may take with a pinch of salt DeMille's statement that he wished to break with the Sunday School representation of Christ – H.B. Warner's performance, though soulful, hardly does that, and he again perpetuates the notion that Christ was middle-aged – he clearly wished to treat the story as an epic on its own terms, leaving any modern parallels to be discovered in the story itself rather than serving them up on a plate. In that respect DeMille advanced the historical epic film from adolescence to adulthood, establishing it on a genuine par with the literary epic.

It was little more than the title of DeMille's silent film which producer Samuel Bronston used some thirty years later when he set in motion *King of Kings* (1961), directed by Nicholas Ray. Bronston resurrected some of the publicity humbug with which DeMille had surrounded H.B. Warner (no press interviews, much talk of personal integrity, etc.) but that is of no concern here. Bronston, born in Bessarabia of Russian parents but raised and educated in France, worked as a salesman for M-G-M and United Artists before branching out on his own as a producer with *John Paul Jones* (1959). From his Madrid base, where he made use of American companies' frozen assets for finance, he embarked on a great series of historical spectaculars which built on the Hollywood fifties traditions so perfectly encapsulated by William Wyler's *Ben-Hur*. *El Cid* (1961) and *The Fall of the Roman Empire* (1964) will be discussed in Chapters 11 and 9 respectively; *King of Kings*, though a less perfect work, is nevertheless imprinted with the Bronston style. Unlike DeMille, Bronston was no director; his role was never more than that of producer and promoter, but the high-quality workmanship in all his productions stems directly from his policy of hiring first-class talent in every department, regardless of expense. This is evident even in *King of Kings* (music by Miklós Rózsa; photography by Franz Planer and – when Planer was forced to retire half-way through with heatstroke after shooting the Sermon on the Mount – Milton Krasner); only the script and certain elements of casting are at fault. Bronston's policy was to reach fruition in *El Cid* (already completed by the time *King of Kings* was released)

and become honed to the nth degree by the time of *Fall*.

King of Kings keeps only the well-laundered look of DeMille's film; in all other aspects it is conscious of the great strides forward taken by the historical epic since those days, especially the use of colour during the forties and fifties. To follow Wyler's *Ben-Hur* is a daunting enough prospect for any film-maker in the historical field, and Ray's *King of Kings* sensibly opts for none of that work's heightened realism. Instead, the life of Christ is recounted as a moving picture-book, as a series of pageant-like, celebratory episodes – the whole heightened by voice-over narration (spoken by Orson Welles, written by Ray Bradbury), near-continuous music (including overtures, a total of 130 minutes for a 163-minute film), strong expressionist colours, and a simplicity of texture which marries well with the film's hygienic look (hardly anyone sweats, and when they do – Christ and Herod – it is always decorously). The picture's visual style is perhaps its most impressive achievement, and is evident from the very start: credit titles in gold over a sunset skyscape, and later a crowd scene in which the extras all wear spotless white headshawls in the bright sunshine. Such effects recur throughout the film: the picturesque use of reds, yellows, blacks and whites in the Sermon on the Mount; the warm colours in the Nazareth scenes; the reds and golds in Herod Antipas' palace, with its flimsy curtains and richly patterned floors. It seems entirely consistent that Christ should still be in spotless white when brought before Herod and Pilate, and that the blood from the crown of thorns should run down his face in perfect rivulets. This bold use of colour is inherited as much from the Hollywood glossy comedy tradition, and prefigures its development in the mid-sixties, as from the Sunday School approach and is also discernible in Ray's *Bigger than Life* (1956). It is rarely used in a specific sense, on any *leitmotif* principle, but rather to enhance the general pageantry of Christ's life. Similarly, the famous scenes and quotes are handled with a disarming simplicity: the Temptation as just a voice-over, the Sermon on the Mount as a long series of questions; the choice of Barabbas over Christ as a simple prison- rather than elaborate crowd-scene; the journey to Calvary with just a few women and passers-by in the street; and the Crucifixion with a handful of mourners in black

It is evident from the last two examples that a measure of realism is possible within such a picture-book format. Both Salome and Christ are acted for the first time by people of the right age (the former in her late teens, the latter in his early thirties), and both the disciples and other characters are in the right age-ratios. The accent on youth is more than coincidental, however, for *King of Kings* is consciously angled towards the youth market; and even though the American bias may offend European ears, dramatically it works well. Christ, in the convinced if uninflected performance of Jeffrey Hunter (who died in 1969 aged forty-three), has a wholesome and thoroughly unreal aura which sits well in the atmosphere of Renaissance piety; and Salome, despite embarrassingly bad acting by Brigid Bazlen, emerges as a vicious Lolita-figure manipulating her stepfather's sexual weaknesses. The cinema has already come a long way since the cabaret act of Rita Hayworth in William Dieterle's *Salome* (1953), less important for its preposterous plot than for its portrait of a Bad Woman redeemed by a Good Religion. The Gilda of the mid-forties is transformed by the Puritanism of the fifties into a Good (American) Citizen, just as Lana Turner in Richard Thorpe's *The Prodigal* (1955) is also taught a lesson by religion. Yet by the time of *King of Kings*, the atmosphere had changed: the new threat was from youth, not the mature vamp. Bazlen is but one of a long line of Salomes stretching back to Theda Bara, but hers is probably the most accurate and nastiest to date, if equally a product of her times.

However, *King of Kings* is not ultimately concerned with personalities. There is no individual characterisation of the disciples nor any real concern for Christ as a person: events are presented and the inevitable conclusion arrives. Hunter, capitalising on the beacon qualities of his blue eyes, gives Christ only a magical power of personality rather than any depth of feeling. The drama comes from elsewhere: from the visual style (already discussed), from the story's accentuation of some unfamiliar elements, and from the moving music of Miklós Rózsa.

Rózsa's contribution to the historical film is considerable, his particular modal/archaic language effortlessly derived from his natural Hungarian musical vocabulary. Born in Hungary in 1907, he moved to Hollywood in 1940 after a spell with Korda in Britain during the late thirties; there he has stayed ever since, and we are fortunate indeed that he chose to work on M-G-M's musical staff from 1948 to 1962, golden years for the historical film and the studio which produced *Quo vadis* (1951), *Ivanhoe* (1953), *Plymouth Adventure* (1952), *Julius Caesar* (1953), *Young Bess* (1953), *Knights of the Round Table* (1954), and *Ben-Hur* (1959) – all of which Rózsa scored with distinction. He was assigned to *King of Kings* when M-G-M bought their way into the film in mid-production and his music gives *King of Kings* much of its final cohesion – like the narration, which was also written to that end. Rózsa's plentiful use of the *leitmotif* expresses many a tension or dramatic point which the script scarcely articulates: Christ's entry into Jerusalem and Barabbas' revolt; the glorious melody which sails in as Christ recites the Lord's Prayer (giving the words a poetry not present in Hunter's voice); the copious use of the Virgin Mary's theme as one of redemption (leaving the Christ theme to express the sheer *glory* of god) and, by dint of its shifting harmonic underpinnings, maternal sorrow as well.

However, beneath its pious visual style and exalted music, *King of Kings* conceals some radical reinterpretations of its subject-matter. Instead of opening with the Nativity, the film begins in 63 BC, when Rome first came into contact with the Jews, and the narration begins the first of several elaborate agricultural metaphors which stress the plight of the people. The opening ten minutes are a *tour de force* of narration, visuals and music, building a Zionist fervour which is to inform much of the forthcoming action:

Thus, for more than fifty years after Pompey's invasion, the history of Judaea could be read by the light of burning towns. If gold was not the harvest, there was a richness of people to be gathered. The battalions of Caesar Augustus brought in the crop. Like sheep from their own green fields, the Jews went to the slaughter. They went from the stone quarries to build Rome's triumphal arches. But Caesar could find no Jew to press Rome's laws on this fallen land. So Caesar named one, Herod the Great, an Arab of the Bedouin tribe, as the new, false and maleficent King of the Jews. But from the dust at Herod's feet rebellions of Jews rose up, and Herod in reply planted evil seeds from which forests of Roman crosses grew high on

27 (*left*) Amateur Christ: Enrique Irazoqui in *The Gospel according to St Matthew*

28 (*above*) Reverential Christ: H. B. Warner in *The King of Kings* (1927)

29 (*opposite below*) Polemic Christ: Jeffrey Hunter in *King of Kings* (1961)

30 (*opposite above*) Tragic Christ: Max von Sydow in *The Greatest Story Ever Told*

Jerusalem's hills. And Herod the Great, passing pleased, bade the forest multiply.

King of Kings is the only film version of Christ's life to show the spirit of revolt in Judaea which finally led to the siege and capture of Jerusalem by Titus in AD 70. As a symbol of that revolt it chooses Barabbas, exalting a marginal character in the Gospels to a fully paid-up proto-Zionist. This immediately sets up several interesting resonances. Barabbas and Christ are shown as complementary characters, opposite sides of the Judaean coin, each enhancing the other's moral and historical position. 'We both seek the same thing – freedom!' cries Barabbas (Harry Guardino). 'Only our methods differ.' Thus, Barabbas, rather than Rome, becomes the yang to Christ's yin when dealing with the inevitable argument of violent or peaceful revolt (a recurrent theme in the films of Nicholas Ray). The message of the Gospels is thus played out in purely Judaean terms, with Christ the agent of peace (note his CND-shaped table at the Last Supper – another radical reinterpretation) and Barabbas the agent of aggression. 'I am fire, he is water,' spits Barabbas. 'How can we ever meet?' And elsewhere he adds with prophetic significance, 'If he can free the Jews without spilling blood, he deserves the crown. I'll shape the crown myself and place it on his brow.'

The other marginal character exalted to major status is the centurion at the Crucifixion. Just as the film's prologue goes back further into history than usual, so the character of Lucius (Ron Randell) is established as a full participant in the life of Christ. In a beautifully judged early scene he is shown holding the very future of Christ's life in his hands as he notes, but chooses to overlook, the non-registration of the child's birth. Lucius' awareness that he is witnessing a crucial period of history is seen to grow during such scenes as the Sermon of the Mount, at which he is an official eavesdropper, and the jailing of Christ, during which they meet face to face. In Ron Randell's nicely modulated performance, Lucius emerges as a properly rounded participant in the Christ/Lucius/Barabbas triangle of redeemer/redeemed/unredeemed.

That the Judaean Barabbas should die an unrepentingly violent death and the Roman Lucius end up acknowledging the Judean godhead ('He is truly the Christ') comes as no surprise in the film's Zionist reinterpretation. There are times, in fact, when Harry Guardino's performance as Barabbas is at full throttle, that *King of Kings* diminishes the role of Christ to that of spectator. Unlike Barabbas or Lucius or Pilate or Herod, Christ is not a mover of events, a shaper of history. *King of Kings* is ultimately his film, but beneath its body beautiful runs some dark currents: from Brigid Bazlen's kittenish Salome, to Frank Thring's decadent Herod, to Hurd Hatfield's bored Pilate and Harry Guardino's desperate Barabbas.

There is little similarity, on the face of it, between *King of Kings* and George Stevens' *The Greatest Story Ever Told* (1965). The director had laboured on the film since 1959 with a costly and disputatious meticulousness, and when work fell seriously behind schedule Jean Negulesco and David Lean were called in to direct (uncredited) parts of the Nativity. Where Ray's film presents a polemic message in Sunday School dress, Stevens' looks back to the tragic rather than celebratory tradition of Christ, as shown for instance in Byzantine or sixteenth- and seventeenth-century Spanish art. Stevens' Christ falls midway between the fevered Mannerism of El Greco and Baroque pathos of Gregorio Hernández; and the film's unhurried, measured, Brucknerian rhythm bespeaks solemnity rather than misplaced devotion. After the light and colour of *King of Kings*, Stevens gives us the dark, brooding atmosphere of stylised tragedy: the conspicuous use of cloaked figures placed against sky and landscape invokes the spirit of Aeschylan drama, with its rigid formalism and oppressive sense of human impotence in the face of destiny. Max von Sydow's Christ is perfectly attuned to this conception – a figure journeying towards a known fate, even perhaps (as in the angry temple scene) provoking it.

This is a thoroughly original transformation of the traditional legacy, even if its roots are widespread (Spanish Gothic and Greek tragedy), but Stevens is then able to incorporate a whole host of other traditional paraphernalia simply by processing it through his vision. The composition of the Last Supper is pure Da Vinci but the chiaroscuro, almost monochrome, lighting is Stevens. The script is often a straight unfolding of quotations, but the Temptation is radically reinterpreted as a dialogue between a Dark Hermit (Donald Pleasence) and Christ – workable in human and theatrical terms, since the Hermit/Devil reappears at Judas' betrayal, at Peter's denial, and crying 'Crucify him . . . We have no king but Caesar' in the mob at the end. Even the (historically dubious) act of *nailing* Christ to the cross takes on a grisly, hammer-blow-of-fate quality absent from the same act in either DeMille's or Ray's film (and pointed up by cross-cutting to Judas' self-immolation).

Stevens' film is tragedy writ large. Apart from the film's great length, and its absolute refusal to compromise its standpoint by going faster than *andante maestoso*, there is a sense of amplification, of magnification. In concrete terms there is the detail of Cinerama, the use of spectacular American locations (Death Valley for the Wilderness; John the Baptist in the Colorado River – introduced by a sequence of helicopter shots), and a massiveness in the sets which owes something to DeMille (e.g. the courtyard of Pilate's palace) but has a lugubrious, hopeless quality all its own (Herod's underlit, cracked palace). The choice of Max von Sydow, a Swedish actor then known only in Europe, to play Christ was a bold move; but then to surround him with a gallery of (chiefly American) stars who come and go in an eye-blinking succession of one-line entrances was a serious error, diminishing or accentuating – depending on one's sympathies – von Sydow's magnificent, yet solitary, performance. Many roles were trimmed in the final editing (John Wayne's and Shelley Winters' notably), and centurion Wayne's jarring single line ('Truly this man was the son of God') makes no sense without prior development of his character (cf. *King of Kings*). Ultimately, however, the cameo roles do not harm the picture, since Stevens' Brucknerian construction is more than adequate to swallow up minor vexations – even such dialogue as 'At one time, when you were a little fella, you were always asking questions,' or 'What is *your* name?' 'Jesus.' 'Ah . . . that's a *good* name.'

Stevens' film is blessed with a magnificent score by veteran Alfred Newman. Parts of it, however, were never used in the final picture. Stevens inserted the 'Hallelujah' from Handel's *Messiah* halfway into Newman's own 'Hallelujah' for the Raising of Lazarus sequence which ends Part 1; he later ditched wholesale Newman's final Resurrection and Ascension 'Hallelujah' (which glides in at a breathless pianissimo) for the same piece of Handel, and substituted the first twenty-seven bars of Verdi's *Requiem* for Newman's moving Via Dolorosa music. The long story of cuts, rewrites, directorial interference (Newman by that time was not in good health and tried vainly to have his name removed from the credits) and patchwork editing (when Stevens' final cut of four and a half hours had to be shortened the music was chopped up with the celluloid) makes sorry reading, but such of Newman's music as remains magnificently supports the overall conception. The lost 'Hallelu-jahs' – immensely bracing affairs based on the *alla marcia* transformation of the Faith theme in *The Robe* (used elsewhere to accompany scenes of Christ's teaching) – were points of elation in a melancholic, understated score, full of gentle string and woodwind writing touched by the spirit of the eighteenth-century contrapuntalists but essentially Newman in its high violin-writing, harmonic freedom and inner astringency beneath a seemingly fragile exterior. The great Jesus of Nazareth theme which dominates the score winds chromatically through uneven metres of three and four in partwriting of great intensity; and for John the Baptist Newman provided a modal wind *pastorale* of affecting simplicity – again, though the cadences are traditional, the throbbing under-pulse and vague metre are Newman trademarks.

The Greatest Story Ever Told is a courageous piece of film-making. It neither panders to passing trends nor makes any pretence of telling its story uninflected; it is an interpretation of Christ's life and, thanks to the strengths of its stylistic origins, has weathered the years well. Perhaps its pessimism is too strong – a trait which entered Stevens' work during the fifties and reached its zenith in his last work, *The Only Game in Town* (1970) – and occasionally an American vulgarity jars the otherwise European tone. Yet overall the film has a dignified poetry and feel for the tragic form which is without equal in the genre. Like DeMille or Ray, Stevens shows no special fidelity to any one Gospel, though the Raising of Lazarus (brilliantly shown through the *reactions* of the onlookers) and the opening progression from a star to an oil lamp to a baby's hand shows due notice taken of the simplicity of John's opening verses. Typically, where *King of Kings* ends triumphantly in the manner of Matthew, *The Greatest Story* opts for the matter-of-factness of Mark or Luke – a brief Aeschylan paean, but celebration hard-won, with fate still intransigent.

Greece: Gods and Heroes

'Stop, handmaidens. Why run away at the sight
  of a man?
Surely you do not think he is one of our enemies?
This poor man has wandered here from his
  home;
we must take care of him now, for all strangers
  and beggars
come from Zeus, and the smallest gift is welcome.'

Odyssey, 6, 199ff.

'Be careful, Nausicaa; he might be a god. They
  sometimes take human form.'
'I hope he is not. I want him to be a *man*.'

Ulysses (1954)

The relationship between Ancient Greece and the
cinema has been problematical at best. There
exists a huge body of works dealing with its
mythological age and – as we shall see in Chapter 6
– a mere handful concerned with anything else.
This is a complete inversion of the cinema's
relationship with Ancient Rome (in which myth
suffers badly). The reasons cast much light on
what the cinema has required of epic subject-
matter. First, and foremost, Greece lacks any
immediate rapport with present-day life, its
language and manners being not as far-reaching
as those of Roman civilisation. Second, Greek
history lacks the unity, vastness and ambition of
other civilisations', with no imperial age, no absolute autocrats and no tradition of persecution with
which to appeal to twentieth-century imaginations. Third, it is the only historical period which is
incapable of accepting Christian or Zionist messages, and which must therefore be accepted as
'idolatrous' on its own terms. Fourth, the flowering
of Greek civilisation was a diffuse and complex
affair, a story neither of military conquest nor of a
sudden cultural rise and fall; it is, rather, a tale of
perpetual adaptation.

The first inhabitants of Greece, known as
Pelasgians, were a largely agricultural, non-
Greek-speaking people with a taste for massive,
boulder-like architecture (Cyclopean). Throughout
the second millennium BC Greek-speaking
peoples, known as Achaeans, gradually displaced
the Pelasgians, setting up two areas of prosperity –
one north of the isthmus in Epirus, the other just
south of it at Mycenae. By c. 1600 the Achaeans
were secure in the land; south of them, centred on
the island of Crete, the so-called Minoan civilisation (roughly contemporary with the Egyptian),
then entering its most illustrious phase, acted as a
filter for diverse influences – from Egypt, the East,
and from Achaean Mycenae. This period and the
succeeding centuries are the Heroic Age of Ancient
Greece: here the prototypes arose and the stories
began, to be handed down by word of mouth and
contaminated by anachronisms over the years
until they were assembled on the advent of literacy
around the eighth century BC. This age of flourish-
ing trade in the Aegean was Homer's world,
despite the fact that the tales were not to be
immortalised in writing for over half a millennium; it was also in this age that the first phase of
Greek civilisation reached its peak.

The chronology of this crucial period is still
unsure but around 1470 BC the tiny island of
Thera, seventy-five miles north of Crete, blew its
heart out in a massive volcanic eruption which
overwhelmed the Minoan civilisation centred
around the palace complex at Cnossus. The
Minoans had suffered similar setbacks in their
history (Crete is on an earthquake-line) but this
time they never recovered; the Achaeans, greedy
for plunder, perhaps profited from the disaster. At
any rate, a century later, c. 1380 BC, Cnossus was
destroyed by human hand; and soon afterwards the
Achaeans engaged in a trade-war with the city of
Troy in the north, situated at the entrance to the

Dardanelles. The Achaeans may not, in contrast to the story told in Homer's *Iliad*, have been responsible for Troy's final fall, but their Viking-like taste for aggrandisement characterises the age. Soon, however, they had their own problems: Greek-speaking peoples from the north, known as Dorians, started to move south into Greece, along with those Achaeans who had originally settled in Epirus. The shift was perhaps a response to tribal movements in the Balkans (where the Urnfield culture was getting under way) and these even more warrior-like people profited by the general confusion that the Achaean (Mycenae-centred) world was experiencing. In any event, c. 1250 BC a wave of destruction hit Greece – with settlements abandoned or destroyed – and by the end of the next century Greece's Dark Age had arrived. The Dorians now held Greece (apart from Athens) and Mycenaean civilisation dispersed eastwards to the Aegean islands and the coast of Turkey, where it came to be known as Ionic. From this Dark Age (c. 1100–700 BC) classical Greece was slowly to arise.

* * *

The cinema's treatment of Greek pre- and early history falls roughly into three categories: those films dealing with pure mythology, those revolving around the Trojan cycle, and those based on Greek tragedies. The latter, written during the fifth century BC but reaching back to myth for their subject-matter, do not concern us here: Aristotle, in his treatise *On the Art of Poetry*, clearly distinguished tragedy and epic poetry by noting that the latter was an amplification of technique and content all found in the former, and there is no reason to challenge his distinction.

It should, however, be noted that the cinema has produced some exceptional versions of Greek tragedy: from the charged, oppressive, monochrome world of Michael Cacoyannis' *Electra* (1962; with Irene Papas) and the same director's technically more accomplished if somewhat less 'Greek' *The Trojan Woman* (1971; in English, with Katharine Hepburn, Vanessa Redgrave and Geneviève Bujold), through the equally theatrical and disciplined yet less stylised *Oedipus the King* (Philip Saville, 1968) and Giorgos Tsavellas' *Antigone* (1961), to Pier Paolo Pasolini's Madonna-dominated forays into ethnic myth *Oedipus Rex*

(*Edipo re*, 1967) and *Medea* (1970). Others have adapted, modernised and sponged with varying success: Miklós Jancsó's *Elektreia* (*Szerelmem, Elektra*, 1975) easily absorbs a story as precise as the Atreid myth within a proven flair for ritual; Liliana Cavani's *The Cannibals* (*I cannibali*, 1970), however, is a pretentious, obsessive bore, all inherited kudos from Sophocles' *Antigone* with none of its art.

The other two categories – pure myth and the Trojan cycle – are closely intertwined. Silent cinema possessed a voracious appetite for the myths and heroes of Ancient Greece and – as with biblical stories – essayed the major ones with glee. Where the Bible provided opportunities to play on audiences' religious sympathies, and the Roman world opportunities to play on their taste for cruelty and spectacle, Greece provided fantasy, magic and special effects. Not for nothing was Georges Méliès one of the first to milk the genre.

It is, however, for the mass of Italian pepla in the late fifties and early sixties that the whole genre is best known. In Chapter 2 we traced the rise of the muscleman peplum and its first appearance in full Eastmancolor and Technirama with Pietro Francisci's *Hercules* (*Le fatiche di Ercole*, 1958); such works are not the whole story of the Greek peplum but they are undoubtedly its most famous characteristic. The superhuman hero and voluptuous heroine are sexual stereotypes on a par with Roman or medieval pairings, yet divested of any Christian trappings and with the political chicanery of many Roman films markedly diluted.

The Greek pepla of myths and heroes carry a very physical charge: their language is ingenuous, their imagination unrestrained by the demands of history, and their images a treat for the eye. Yet it is important to remember that their protagonists present more the sexual stereotypes of fifties cinema than those of Ancient Greece. The scantily clad heroes and heroines are based on little more than popular notions of Greek civilisation. Exaggerated musculature is a feature of Hellenistic (and Renaissance) sculpture, not Archaic or Classical Greek; and the Greek ideal of the female physique was considerably less shapely than pepla heroines' hour-glass figures. Small, but crucial, details like hairstyling often have only a token authenticity (an occasional, scanty beard for Hercules) and are more of the twentieth century than any other era. Few films reflect the real

31 The discipline of Greek Tragedy: King Creon (Manos Katrakis)
and Antigone (Irene Papas) in *Antigone*

flavour of the Greek mythological corpus: in the cinema, the ancients' quarrelsome, fornicating and wholly unreliable gods and heroes become the chaste and upright figures of the fifties. Yet to a great extent film-makers have stayed within the epic tradition of old heroes reinterpreted for contemporary audiences. This was the tradition in which Homer forged the *Iliad* and the *Odyssey*, and it also remains valid for the cinema.

The body of pepla is inordinately large, and it is only necessary to examine a few to outline the main characteristics. Pietro Francisci's *Hercules* (*Le fatiche di Ercole*, 1958), besides being the film which started the boom, is a paradigm of the genre. The Greeks were as confused about their own mythology as the ordinary cinemagoer of today, and Francisci's film neatly sums up all the contradictions found in the original sources. Despite the promise of its title, it presents only the First (Nemean lion) and Seventh (Cretan bull) Labours, and then out of context and for the wrong king (Pelias not Eurystheus); in addition, Hercules is thrust into the story of Jason's search for the Golden Fleece, becoming the chief protagonist in the expedition rather than just another crew-member, who is left behind when he goes off in search of his friend Hylas (as in the original myth). But the film has a rationale all its own which makes such inaccuracies unimportant. An opening credit neatly conjures up another world, as we survey a frieze depicting his exploits: 'Huge and immortal was the strength of Hercules, as the world and gods to whom he belonged . . . But one day men crossed his path . . .'

This theme of divine perfection vs human fallibility permeates the film, and a distinct attempt is made to humanise Hercules and his traditional troubleshooter role. 'Enough! I'm tired of doing all these senseless things for the gods! When will I be worthy in the eyes of the gods?' he cries, expressing his (fifties) desire to settle down and have a family. This *Angst* is powerfully summarised in the temple meeting (caught by Mario Bava's pregnant use of reds and purples) between the priestess (Lidia Alfonsi) and Hercules (Steve Reeves) in which the latter begs for a sign from heaven and, like David in *David and Bathsheba*, receives the liberating rains upon his body.

However, to comply with the heroic code, the resolution must come through test and action, the Labours and his struggle against the corrupt King

Pelias forming Hercules' path to Iole (i.e. true love, home and family). Their first meeting – he pulling up a tree to stop her runaway chariot, from which she collapses into his arms – is in *echt*-peplum style, the fact that she is the daughter of Pelias adding the necessary temporary impediment to their happiness. They parade their sexuality before each other, culminating in an extraordinary sequence prior to the Argonauts' expedition in which Hercules, oiled amid his male colleagues, performs photogenically with the discus before the curious and challenging eyes of Iole (Sylva Koscina). The implicit narcissism of the Greek pepla – both male and female – has rarely been more directly expressed, and is the nearest that film-makers have come to tackling the Greeks' own complex attitudes to sexuality.

The end narration ('Hercules and Iole go to happiness, which is the privilege of all mortals when justice and peace are accepted') sums up the properly vague moralising of the genre. The more lighthearted sequel, Francisci's *Hercules Unchained* (*Ercole e la regina di Lidia*, 1959), takes the pair on further adventures, first with King Oedipus' quarrelling sons, Eteocles and Polynices, and then with the rapacious Omphale, Queen of Lydia. In the original myth, which expressed early changes from matriarchy to patriarchy in royal ceremony, Hercules happily sired three sons by her; in the film, Omphale (Sylvia López) becomes a direct sexual challenge to Hercules' fidelity to Iole and domesticity. Backed by Enzo Masetti's lyrical, impressionistic score (from *Hercules*) and spirited playing by a lively teenage Odysseus (Gabriele Antonini) and maniacal Eteocles (Sergio Fantoni in top villainous form), the sequel has a panache and colourful exoticism missing from its predecessor. Only in the over-long final battle for Thebes does it show signs of waning inspiration.

The two Francisci films paved the way for a whole succession of muscular heroes, known variously as Maciste, Ursus, Goliath or Samson, most of whom operated in geographically and historically vague lands somewhere east of Greece. These could vary from thirteenth-century China ('A time of myth and mystery, of conquest and courage,' lies the script) in Riccardo Freda's *Samson and the Seven Miracles of the World* (*Maciste alla corte del gran khan*, 1962) – 'I'm not Chinese . . . but I'll always fight injustice,' states the hero, adding at the end, 'My task is finished.

32 (*left*) Liberating rains: Hercules (Steve Reeves) in *Hercules*

33 (*below left*) Bavaesque imagery: Iole (Sylva Koscina) in *Hercules Unchained*

34 (*below*) Nimble hero: Hercules (Reg Park) in *Hercules Conquers Atlantis*

Destiny brought me here. Now I must go wherever there is a fight between right and wrong' – to a time 'more than a million years before the birth of Christ' in Guido Malatesta's *Colossus of the Stone Age/Land of the Monsters* (*Maciste contro i mostri*, 1962), with its destiny-driven hero caught in a struggle between a black and a white tribe. These films, which have little to do with Ancient Greece, are listed in the Filmography but not discussed here. Whether fighting vampires, moon-men, Saracens, in Baghdad, in Solomon's Mines or in the Valley of the Resounding Echo, the motivation (if not always the characterisation) remains the same.

Greek mythology possesses an ample share of opportunities for the *fantastique* and does not need to stray into other territories for inspiration. Two of the finest examples of this genre-within-a-genre are Vittorio Cottafavi's *Hercules Conquers Atlantis/Hercules and the Captive Women* (*Ercole alla conquista di Atlantide*, 1961) and Mario Bava's *Hercules in the Centre of the Earth/Hercules in the Haunted World* (*Ercole al centro della terra*, 1962), both starring the massive British bodybuilder Reg Park. Bava's film, as befits the ex-cameraman's penchant for horror, is almost a vampire film *manqué*, as Hercules returns from Hades to do battle with a sinister usurper (Christopher Lee) and, in a sublime finale of fire and hurled boulders, his battalions of zombies. The script in part mixes the stories of Theseus and Persephone with Hercules' Eleventh Labour (the Apples of the Hesperides) but finally is unattributable: Hercules must descend to Hades, having first collected the Apple, to retrieve a magical flower which will cure his loved one Deianira's sickness. Bava's visual flair – the lighting all crimsons, purples and greens – and special effects – particularly the duel with the tree in the Garden of the Hesperides and the desperate, muscle-wrenching journey by rope bridge over the lava-lake in Hades – are most impressive and preserve in spirit if not in fact the imaginative world of the Greeks themselves.

Cottafavi's film, shot in lustrous colours on 70mm stock by Carlo Carlini and sharing at least one exterior set (the palace) with Bava's later film, aims higher. There is a sumptuousness in the production, a sheer breadth of imagination, which sets it apart from so many pepla. The pull in *Hercules* between the hero's desire for peaceful domesticity and his obligations as a peripatetic

hero becomes a guiding force in *Hercules Conquers Atlantis*: though Greece is threatened by strange portents, Hercules is extremely loath to desert his wife Deianira to go on yet another expedition to save the country. This becomes a source of humour throughout the action: the hero is as idle as he is muscle-bound, casually going to sleep on ship or shore in the face of imminent danger or, as in the opening tavern brawl, providing a pool of calm amidst total confusion. The joke is that, when roused, he dispatches the enemy with a nimbleness totally at odds with his bulk and demeanour: the script bristles with jocularity, as in the reference to Francisci's *Hercules Unchained* when the hero is asked to prove his strength or the sprightly way in which he spurts out a mouthful of drugged wine when the coast is clear (also neatly turning the tables on us, the audience). Park, in his first and best peplum role, clearly enjoys himself immensely; it is the best-realised portrayal of Hercules in the cinema, perfectly capturing the essence of Greek mythology's most fallible yet constant hero.

The plot is tailored for the Nuclear Age: Antinea (Fay Spain), Queen of Atlantis, possesses a drop of Uranus's blood buried deep in a dark shaft which gives her a terrible power over mankind; Hercules, through superhuman feats, exposes this to the sunlight and causes the destruction of Atlantis. Cottafavi's taste for atmosphere is less striking than Bava's but his vision is wider. The massive world of Atlantis, with its vast temple dominated by an Atlas-figure and colossal gates of entry (art direction by Franco Lolli), its colourfully attired queen (Fay Spain's wardrobe growing progressively more demonic from scene to scene), and sinister phalanx of security guards (the all-enveloping helmets concealing white-haired, slit-eyed features), is all nicely integrated. So, too, the framing of the bizarre world: Hercules' battle with Proteus, who is revealed as a whole island, slowly devouring Antinea's daughter when triumphant, blood pouring from his rocky cliff-face when beaten; and the destruction of Atlantis (*pace* Haroun Terzieff footage and even some from Mario Bonnard's *The Last Days of Pompeii*), in which the massacre of the island's ethnic rejects (herded like radiation victims in a stone quarry) is at last avenged.

There were many paler versions of elements in Cottafavi's and Bava's films. Arthur Lubin's *The*

Thief of Baghdad (*Il ladro di Bagdad*, 1961) is worth mentioning for its introduction of a team of white-faced guards of Pegasus which Karim (Steve Reeves) has to face. Antonio Leonviola's *The Strongest Man in the World* (*Maciste, l'uomo più forte del mondo*, 1961) sports inventive art direction (Franco Lolli again) and a light/darkness theme almost identical to Cottafavi's, but fails to sustain its early promise. The Atomic Age also surfaces in Edgar Ulmer's *The Lost Kingdom/Journey under the Desert* (*Antinea, l'amante della città sepolta*, 1961), one of many versions of Pierre Benoît's 1919 novel. Yet the Lost Kingdom and Atlantis films lie beyond the scope of this book: all feature the twentieth century intruding on the past and are more interested in the incompatibility of the two cultures and the comparative goodness of one over another than in drawing epic resonances from past civilisations on their own terms.

The most significant name on the credits of both the Cottafavi and Bava films is that of scriptwriter Duccio Tessari, to whom one may safely ascribe much of their imaginative flair. His own *Sons of Thunder* (*Arrivano i Titani*, 1962) sends Crios, the youngest of the Titans (primeval children of Uranus and Earth), to overcome the pernicious Cadmus, King of Thebes. Crios (Giuliano Gemma) accomplishes the said task by loving Cadmus' daughter, Antiope (Jacqueline Sassard), kept prisoner due to a prophecy that her love will end Cadmus' reign. *Sons of Thunder* is a rarity among Greek pepla, the hero acrobatic rather than muscular, the script possessing a wit and liveliness in true accord with actual Greek myth, and providing (as one critic aptly stated) a 'Cooks tour of Hades'.

Something of this spirit is also discernible in Roger Corman's *Atlas* (1961), a self-mocking, incredibly small-scale affair in which a Greek athlete frees two cities from a tyrant's rule. The earlier of the two treatments of the Perseus myth is also in similar style: Alberto De Martino's *Perseus against the Monsters* (*Perseo l'invincibile*, 1963) lacks the sheer *brio* of the acting in *Sons of Thunder* but has a field day with reorganising Greek myth, pitting Perseus (minus magic sandals), Andromeda (now a pawn of warring kingdoms), the Monster and Medusa against a host of similarly displaced heroes and villains. The film is notable more for its splendid monster and Medusa than for its dialogue, but it gets by on energy.

The later version of the myth, Desmond Davis' *Clash of the Titans* (1981) sets its sights much higher in both special effects and script. The latter, by Beverley Cross (who also co-wrote *Jason and the Argonauts*), sticks more closely to the original myths, with most of the changes clearly made for dramatic effect and staying within the spirit of the original. Thus, Perseus (Harry Hamlin) gets not magic sandals but Pegasus himself; he meets, falls in love with and battles for Andromeda (Judi Bowker), rather than just seeing her chained to a rock one day; and his progress is helped and hindered by the feuding, selfish gods of Olympus, led by a crusty, paternalistic Zeus (Laurence Olivier) – a device borrowed from *Jason and the Argonauts* and thoroughly in ancient style. Ray Harryhausen's monsters are reasonably convincing (although he does not seem to have technically progressed much since the sixties), and Davis' direction often very perceptive, catching the spirit of dream-like innocence which lies at the heart of Greek myth. And Cross's script ends on a suitably elevated note as the main characters are 'set amongst the stars and constellations . . . Even if we, the gods, are abandoned or forgotten, stars will never fade. Never. They will burn till the end of time.'

The problem of reconciling an expected sense of gravity with a fidelity to the spirit of the original myths is particularly difficult in the case of Greece. The Greeks pictured their gods and heroes like themselves, and this is part and parcel of the great humanity of their art and literature. Works like *Hercules* take a mid-course; *Hercules Conquers Atlantis* has a thematic playfulness. Films like *Goliath and the Dragon* (*La vendetta di Ercole*, 1960), with a bulbous Mark Forest administered various potions by a villainous Broderick Crawford, or Carlo Ludovico Bragaglia's *Loves of Hercules* (*Gli amori di Ercole*, 1960), with Mickey Hargitay fighting wild bulls, a three-headed Hydra and an Amazon queen for the sake of Jayne Mansfield, opt for a Roman humourlessness.

From the small but vital Amazonian corpus, Terence Young's *The Amazons* (*Le guerriere dal seno nudo*, 1974) is the key work: though the actual myth of Theseus and the Amazons is jettisoned in favour of a laboured joke about the warrior-women using the Greeks as breeding-partners, there is an appealing sense of delight in the script's own awfulness and pointed reference to both the Amazons' mythical origins ('Only silly stories and dirty minds,' says Theseus) and that of Greek myth in general (Theseus, when questioned by his wife about the Minotaur, calmly replies, 'My dear, that story is a myth'). The film is appealingly kitted out – the Cnossian design of Queen Antiope's palace is as acceptable as anything else – and surprisingly chooses humour more often than eroticism. When the latter does surface, it does so with a vengeance and appropriateness: the smouldering antagonism between Antiope (Alena Johnston) and her rival Oreitheia (Sabine Sun), both of whom had earlier wrestled for the vacant post of queen, is later transfigured through outright violence into emotional and physical love, with all its paraphernalia of domination and submission.

The only film, however, which convincingly unites disparate cultures and mythologies is Pietro Francisci's *Hercules, Samson and Ulysses* (*Ercole sfida Sansone*, 1964), in which the two itinerant Greek heroes join with Samson to fight the Philistines in Judaea. Though it goes deliriously over the top with the protagonists hurling column-drums at each other, it manages *en route* to make unconscious reference to the modern theory that the Philistines of the Bible may have been of Greek origin.

*　　*　　*

Poised between the films clustered around the Trojan cycle and the aforementioned mythological works comes Don Chaffey's *Jason and the Argonauts* (1963), the first encounter between the cinema and a literary epic we have so far met (*Le fatiche di Ercole* rightly claims that it is only 'freely adapted' from Apollonius' *Argonautika*). There is proof in a passage in Homer's *Odyssey* (12, 40) that there existed an Argo cycle as old as the Trojan; the only extensive written version of this, however, is the four-book epic by the Alexandrian librarian Apollonius of Rhodes, written c. 250 BC in a style consciously aping the balladic-inspired verse of Homer. Apollonius' poem has been sneered at for its misguided scholarship, but judged on content alone it is an impressive, if flawed, work. Jason is as resourceful and nimble-witted a hero as Odysseus (if adopting at times a lower profile) and Apollonius' bickering, partisan

gods are second to none. Chaffey's film, with the help of Ray Harryhausen's special effects, captures the spirit of the original very successfully, even if details do not always tally (Talos, the man of bronze, is on Colossus of Rhodes proportions; Poseidon not Athene, holds the Clashing Rocks apart; Medea is rescued from the sea; etc.) and the script does not quite succeed in conveying Apollonius' Hellenistic romanticism over the love of Jason and Medea (the one aspect which is not authentically Homeric and betrays the poem's age).

The latter is not so much the fault of the actors (an acceptably wooden Todd Armstrong and Nancy Kovack, the latter dubbed by an English actress) as of the script's emphasis on the role of the gods, in particular Zeus (Niall MacGinnis) and Hera (Honor Blackman) perpetually engaged in chess-board tactics to help or hinder the mortals. These scenes have an authentically Greek quality of managed destiny: 'Let Hylas have his moment of triumph while he may,' says Zeus as the young man's brain triumphs over Hercules' brawn at the games (Hylas is later killed by the falling carcass of Talos), and at the end the god's final words ring out resonantly with 'For Jason there are other adventures. I have not yet finished with Jason. Let us continue the game another day.' The mortals' actions are properly dwarfed by such an emphasis – note, too, Jason's journey to Olympus, set to stirring music by Bernard Herrmann. And their quest for the Fleece, which 'has the power to end plague and famine and bring peace', becomes a fitting tribute to human endeavour in the face of impossible odds.

Jason and the Argonauts, despite its often considerable jiggery-pokery with Apollonius' poem, nevertheless has a consistency which quite escapes the only other version, Riccardo Freda's *The Giants of Thessaly* (*I giganti della Tessaglia*, 1961). Despite all the colour filters and an impressive finale in which the Fleece is found atop a giant statue, it is an untidy film (disowned by Freda, who did not finish it) which parades a series of action sequences around a flimsy, and certainly non-Apollonian, central core.

The achievement of Chaffey's film in human terms is all the clearer when one turns to the Trojan cycle. The *Iliad* and the *Odyssey* do not contain every aspect of epic form but they *do*, between them, encapsulate the Greek experience.

The Greeks themselves acknowledged this and frequently used the texts to support this or that historical or philosophical argument throughout their history. The *Iliad*, the older work, shows, through its story of the consequences of Achilles' anger at having his slave-girl requisitioned by Agamemnon, the price to be paid for human *hubris*, for self-interest, for transgressing the heroic mould and the harsh demands required in exchange for its hard-won privileges. The *Odyssey*, the more picturesque of the pair, celebrates the triumph of the *oikos* (home) as Odysseus is tested in every moral, physical, spiritual and intellectual department before he is reunited with Penelope. Homer's world is peopled more by aristocrats than commoners, but this does not restrict his breadth of human vision; the strong and weak men and women who crowd his pages reveal themselves through their *deeds* rather than *words*, and if human life is hard and short and subject to the whims of Olympus it is still to be preferred for its scope, potential and rewards.

Both the *Iliad* and the *Odyssey* are first and foremost exciting narrative works rather than allegorical tracts. Marino Girolami's *Achilles* (*L'ira di Achille*, 1962), the only film with more than a passing interest in the *Iliad*, acknowledges this with some exciting and well-staged battles in the first half but loses momentum when the focus narrows later to the Achilles/Hector conflict. Only when one reaches the *Odyssey*, with the story of the Trojan Horse, the fall of Troy, and the journeys of Odysseus, does the cinema begin to show interest. Piero Fosco's *La caduta di Troia* (1910) is a superior example of the silent cinema's attitude towards Greece: confused, in Roman-*manqué* style (a castellated Troy; Menelaus' court a glorious mixture of Roman, Greek, Egyptian and Renaissance filtered through *fin-de-siècle* eyes; Helen and Paris lying in a Botticelli clam shell, transported by attached nymphs) but with occasionally impressive sequences like that of the Horse being dragged into the city and the inhabitants having to break down part of their main gate to accommodate it.

It is worth remembering that this famous event is dealt with in more detail by Vergil's (Roman) *Aeneid* than Homer's (Greek) *Odyssey*, where it receives only a passing mention. Giorgio Ferroni's *The Wooden Horse of Troy* (*La guerra di Troia*, 1961) is more Vergilian than Homeric, from its exaltation of Aeneas as a major Trojan hero

(fighting Ajax and Achilles *inter alios*) to the final prophecy of Cassandra ('My victory is in your destiny') and the epilogue, both of which look ahead to the founding of Rome. Giorgio Rivalta's *War of the Trojans* (*La leggenda di Enea*, 1962) deals with the latter event (see Chapter 7); *The Wooden Horse* is little more than a prologue. Its main asset is a keen visual design, with impressive Trojan walls amid the plain and a Horse reminiscent of Greek geometric style; its main drawbacks are some dreadfully turgid battles, with lethargic Italian extras, and its garbled version of Graeco-Roman legend. Aeneas (Steve Reeves) is portrayed in overtly pacifist style ('No woman is worth the blood that has been shed in the past nine years'/'Let the gods grant our son will never know the stench of battle – only the joys of life'), his muscular woodenness played off against John Drew Barrymore's wily Odysseus and Hedy Vessel's conventional vamp Helen.

The latter is far from the sympathetic character painted in Homer's *Iliad* and derives from later versions of the story. Film-makers have hardly bothered to challenge this well-accepted characterisation. For instance, Alexander Korda's *The Private Life of Helen of Troy* (1928) falls somewhere between the deliberately anachronistic Shaw/Pascal *Caesar and Cleopatra* (1945) and other jokey conceits such as the visually resplendent (Nazi-architectured) *Amphitryon* (1935) by Reinhold Schünzel. Instead of Hermes on rollerskates, we have a plot in which Achilles, Odysseus and Ajax declare war on Troy because Spartan tailors are heading for bankruptcy due to the fact that all the women are buying their clothes from Troy. The film, free from the usual silent gesticulations and photographed in glistening images, bristles with sophisticated twenties wit. Eteoneus: 'I know you don't like gossip – but your wife eloped with Paris last night'; Menelaus: 'Now we can go fishing!' Or: 'They say the fish are biting so fast you have to stand behind a tree to bait your hook.' Or: 'It takes a long time for a Shipping Board to launch a thousand ships – so for months the two lovers were peacefully happy in Troy.' The end of the film finds Helen back in Sparta still flirting with princes and Menelaus arranging another fishing trip.

Such social banter of the twenties had become the more serious sexual electricity of the fifties by the time of Robert Wise's *Helen of Troy* (1955)

35 (*opposite above*) Chess-board tactics: Zeus (Niall MacGinnis) and Hera (Honor Blackman) in *Jason and the Argonauts*

36 (*opposite below*) Wooden horses: *The Wooden Horse of Troy* . . .

37 (*below*) . . . and *Helen of Troy*

38 (*right*) The love of physical ideals: Paris (Jacques Sernas) and Helen (Rossana Podestà) in *Helen of Troy*

which, though indebted to the *Iliad* for some of its material (mostly at Troy, since Homer hardly mentions the first part of the story), nevertheless diverges from the epic's own presentation of Helen, guilty of the strife she has caused and now despising Paris. Wise's intention was for the film 'to reflect the times and life of the period and to have a better understanding of the people; I wanted it to be modern in terms of the acting and delivery of the scenes' and 'the emphasis in the script to be the story of Helen and Paris'. In so doing he romanticised the love of two 'physically ideal' people, reworked the Spartan end of the story (shipwrecking Paris on his way to talk trade with Menelaus, introducing the lovers on the seashore, and making the satanic Achilles the agent of the lovers' flight to Troy) and resorted to the clichés of Marlowe ('The face that launched a thousand ships') and Vergil ('Beware the Greeks bearing gifts'). Yet despite the frequently appalling dialogue – which ranges from Helen's testy 'Must the Trojans always set their funeral pyres so near this house?' to Paris' first sight of her on the seashore: 'Aphrodite!' 'What?' – the film *does* work on its own terms. First, it is strongly cast in depth, with an array of British talent working at top flight (Stanley Baker, Niall MacGinnis, Harry Andrews, Janette Scott among others). Second, it is splendid to look at, with intelligent production design (by Edward Carrere, with Ken Adam – of future Bond films fame – as his assistant) which posits an early Dorian style for Sparta and Minoan-influenced architecture for Troy, and a Horse which actually looks as if it was built by Greek soldiers rather than a team of twentieth-century joiners. Third, the script is nicely paced and structured, managing to incorporate most of the salient facts without any sense of haste. Fourth, the whole is united by one of Max Steiner's finest scores, which in romantic and triumphal vein complements the lush production, the evocative use of colour, and its cast of beautiful people.

The script ranges Troy ('. . . three thousand years ago, a city of destiny') against Sparta ('A harsh military land where a man will cut off his arm to prove he is brave') and tosses the two lovers between the two as the prototype guardians of correct morality. 'I despise oppression as do many others here,' Helen tells Paris, and the general post-Homeric tone is fortified by an exchange between Pallas and Odysseus when the Greeks decide to wage war on Troy: 'All Greece united in a war of honour!' 'Yes! That's probably what the future will call it.'

Helen of Troy has a heroic language of its own which is not Homeric but is perfect for its time; the film was shot in Italy (with very un-Greek scenery) and stylistically anticipated the pepla soon to come *en masse* (in which Rossana Podestà, the beautiful Helen, was to continue to star). Its intelligent manipulation of cliché completely overshadows the earlier *The Face That Launched a Thousand Ships* (*L'amante di Paride*, 1955), by Marc Allegret, with Hedy Lamarr and Massimo Serato, recounted in a flashback to prove that humanity never learns the lessons of history – in this case, never to say that one woman is more beautiful in the presence of others.

Films like Mario Caiano's *Ulysses against Hercules* (*Ulisse contro Ercole*, 1962), Vittorio Sala's *Love Slaves of the Amazons* (*La regina delle Amazzoni*, 1960) and Giorgio Ferroni's *The Lion of Thebes* (*Il leone di Tebe*, 1965) build up a cinematic Trojan cycle as fanciful as the later Greeks', using characters with free abandon amid troglodytes, bird-men and Egyptians. Apart from a remarkable eight-part Italian TV version (*Odissea*, 1968; directed by Franco Rossi, with Mario Bava doing the Polyphemus episode and Piero Schivazappa the Wooden Horse) and Fritz Lang's non-starter in Jean-Luc Godard's *Contempt* (*Le mépris*, 1963), the cinema has only produced one worthwhile version of the *Odyssey* which combines reasonable authenticity (though not on a par with Rossi's TV version) and the required sense of magic which surrounds the central character's progress.

Mario Camerini's *Ulysses* (*Ulisse*, 1954), with colourful special effects by Eugen Schüfftan, adheres remarkably closely to Homer's original, even including the long flashback while with Nausicaa (Rossana Podestà, pre-dating her *Helen* role) and incorporating the visit to Hades into the Circe episode; and while never forgetting its fifties message, it develops its story in an intelligent, notably urgent style. Odysseus (Kirk Douglas) is drawn authentically as a character torn between his love of the *oikos* (Penelope and Telemachus) and that of adventure and the unknown, and the script shows him progressively resolving this struggle as he nears Ithaca to do battle with his wife's suitors. During the Sirens episode the temptresses – effectively never shown – are given the voices of

39 The glory of being human: Odysseus (Kirk Douglas) and his
former shipmates on Circe's island in *Ulysses*

Odysseus' wife and son (i.e. all he could ever want), and in the long dolly-in on his face as he stands tied to the mast we share his anguish. Later, as Circe conjures up the dead to show him the horrors of death in an attempt to make him stay with her, it is the appearance of Odysseus' mother Anticlea which swings the balance.

However, the most potent device is to have the same actress (Silvana Mangano) portraying both Penelope and Circe, the latter with blonde hair, green lighting and a black veil, thus honouring in totally filmic terms Homer's original intent. It is during the Circe episode, when Odysseus has built a raft to go home and she tempts him with the promise of immortality, that the film reaches its most impressive statement: Odysseus' assertion of the glory of being human, of being born and dying ('There are greater gifts – to be born and to die, and in between to be a man. If it be that in the future men will talk of me, then I hope it will be as one of them'). This message, rather than the more formulary one at the end ('So many years of our youth lost in the savageries of war'), assures Camerini's *Ulysses* of a very special place in the Greek mythic genre, as an entirely satisfying expression in contemporary terms of the ancients' own abiding beliefs.

Greece: From Marathon to Alexander

Going through Greece the Persians were not
 afraid to despoil
the wooden images of gods or burn temples . . .
But mounds of dead, even to three generations
 hence,
will silently demonstrate to people's gaze
that presumption does not become mortal man.
For when arrogance bloomed it bore the fruit
of delusion, from which a tearful harvest is now
 gathered.
Observe all this, then, and the price to be paid,
and remember Greece and the Athenians.

Aeschylus, *The Persians*, 809ff. (472 BC)

The brevity of this chapter is testament enough to
the cinema's lack of interest in Classical and
Hellenistic Greece as opposed to its myth and pre-
history, and the handful of works show an often
uneasy pull between the characteristics of the
mythological peplum and the later Roman works.
There is no shortage of historical subject-matter:
we now enter Greece's most illustrious phase,
when she produced her finest artists, who were to
make an indelible impression upon later European
culture; perhaps only a convenient unity is missing
whereby the modern mythographer may popular-
ise his wares. It remains a sorry tale that hardly
one film exists which exalts Greek thought in the
way that scores of productions have glorified the
Christian or Zionist ideal.

Greece emerged from her Dark Age a quarrelsome and unequal land, split by divisions which
were to shape her history: Ionians (typified by the
Athenians) and Dorians (Spartans), democrats and
oligarchs, freemen and slaves. Solon's reforms in
the early sixth century BC, followed by those of the
benevolent *tyrannos* Peisistratus, thrust Athens to
economic and artistic prominence, while Sparta

developed its closed, militaristic society with
jealous watchfulness. The Persian invasions of 490
and 480–79 showed the kind of unity which Greece
could only muster when under foreign attack. A
confederacy followed, which Athens, as the leader,
turned to her own advantage during the fifth
century, with Sparta finally taking up others'
grievances with a vengeance and engaging Athens
in the mutually exhausting Peloponnesian War
(431–404).

Sparta emerged the technical victor, but the
battle for hegemony in Greece continued throughout the next century, now between Athens, Sparta
and Thebes. As time wore on, however, the
northern state of Macedonia assumed prominence
under its leader Philip, finally demonstrating its
leadership over the rest of the Greeks in the
decisive battle of Chaeronea (338). Philip's son
Alexander took over power after his father's death
in 336 – for which he may even have been
responsible – and in a lightning career of un-
surpassed brilliance took on the might of Persia,
won, and pressed on towards India. He died of a
fever at Babylon on his way home in 323, still only
thirty-two years old.

Alexander's achievement was unique in Greek
history, his vision far beyond the local imaginations of the cluster of small city-states. Greek
culture was spread throughout the Near East on
an unprecedented scale, and the so-called Hellenistic Age traditionally dates from his death. It was
more cosmopolitan than the preceding Classical
Age, certainly less enthusiastic and inspirational
because of the erosion of individuality, but it was
Hellenistic art which was to be absorbed by Rome
and rediscovered during the Renaissance. And it
was the Hellenistic Age which was to see the
Greek cultural centre shift from Athens (which
became little more than a fashionable university
town) to Alexandria, and lead to the Romans'

complete subjugation of Greece by the end of the second century.

*   *   *

Greek history, as far as the cinema is concerned, begins with the Persian Wars in the early fifth century, the traditional end of the Archaic period in which Greece asserted her independence against the might of Persia before entering the Classical Age. The First Persian War had a long gestation throughout the last years of the sixth century and the early ones of the fifth, during which Persia sought to control Asia Minor (modern Turkey) and its Ionian seaboard, finally turning to Greece proper to punish Athens and Eretria for the assistance they had rendered their fellow Ionians. In 490 the Persians landed in Euboea, destroyed Eretria and, with the help of some Athenian traitors, crossed to Marathon on the mainland. The Athenians moved north to meet them, having first sent a professional runner called Phidippides (or Philippides) to Sparta to ask for help. The Spartans said they could not come, because of religious reasons, until the full moon a few days hence; but the Athenians and their allies, through swift and brilliant strategy, managed to beat part of the Persian force at Marathon nevertheless. The rest of the Persians sailed south to attack Athens; the Athenians raced back on foot to fortify the city; and the Persians, seeing it reoccupied, abandoned their plan and sailed back to Asia.

Such are the facts. Jacques Tourneur's *The Giant of Marathon* (*La battaglia di Maratona*, 1960) pays little attention to them, being more concerned with building the peripheral figure of Philippides into a central epic presence. He is thus transformed into the champion athlete of Greece who, under the false impression that his girl-friend Andromeda (Mylène Demongeot) is helping the Persian cause, retires disgusted to the country at the outbreak of the war, finally overcoming his vacillation, asking the Spartans for help, leading them to Marathon and thus helping to win the battle, and only then running back to Athens to organise the battle against the Persian fleet. Apart from transposing Philippides' famous run, making the Spartans take part in Marathon (they actually arrived afterwards, just to look at the bodies), and inventing a final sea-battle (the Persians merely

sailed quietly away), the plot represents reasonably well the political tensions in Athens prior to and during the conflict.

The Giant of Marathon – Tourneur only shot the main dialogue scenes, the rest was finished by cameraman Mario Bava and producer Bruno Vailati, the latter directing the famous run – is most interesting for its transitional approach to the story, told in a style strongly indebted to the mythic peplum. Philippides, as played by Steve Reeves, is in direct line of descent from Francisci's Hercules: the opening shot of him locked in a muscleman pose, javelin in hand, and the subsequent scenes of him winning athletic contests, establish the same sexual ground-plan discussed in Chapter 5. Similarly, his meeting with Andromeda ('You're as beautiful as the statue of a goddess') parallels the hero's meeting with Iole in *Hercules*, with the same displays of physical strength and frailty, Andromeda herself (*oikos*) being contrasted with the more carnal attractions of the splendid Charis (Daniella Rocca, all emotive reds and purples), who offers power and sensuality. 'It would be better if weapons didn't exist,' states Philippides, and the final image of him hurling his sword into the earth and walking off into an agricultural sunset with Andromeda shows domesticity triumphant.

Thanks to its charismatic leads (Reeves, Rocca, Demongeot, and a villainous Sergio Fantoni) and resonant Bava photography, *The Giant of Marathon* is successful with its distortion of history. Despite an occasional paucity in the budget (only one raft for the Persians' crossing, and flimsy battles) and notwithstanding liberties of art direction (Renaissance statues; over-laundered costumes), the film erects a convincing structure of moral choice and intrigue in which the character of Philippides can triumph. It also shows a proper sensibility for things Greek – best seen in the sequence in which Andromeda is tied to the prow of a Persian ship, to be rescued by an oiled Philippides in the nick of time. This neat allusion to the Andromeda myth manages to combine myth and 'history' without straining either.

Ten years later the Persians tried again, this time in earnest under Xerxes: three years of preparations included digging a canal in Chalcidice, building bridges, entering into diplomatic negotiations with various Greek states, and a general policy of scaremongering to pave the way for the actual invasion. This took place in the summer of 480 BC. The Greeks, split over policy, were rallied under the Athenian statesman Themistocles (who since the last war had built Athens into a naval power) and the Spartan king Leonidas (supreme on land and watchful of Athens' growing strength). The latter, when a sacred festival again delayed the main Spartan army, personally led out a force of several thousand Greeks, which included 300 Spartan hoplites (heavy-armed infantry) and their helot batmen to hold a narrow pass between the mountains and the sea called Thermopylae. Leonidas held off the Persians for three days, inflicting heavy losses, until the enemy, shown a secret way round by a Greek named Ephialtes, finally cut them to ribbons.

The Greeks retreated to the Peloponnese and blockaded the isthmus at Corinth as the Persians, checked but far from defeated, advanced south and triumphantly occupied a near-deserted Athens. The war now reached a temporary stalemate: it was already late August, and Xerxes was faced with the unpleasant possibility of being trapped in Greece during the winter (a non-combatant season) unless the deadlock could be broken. Themistocles, convinced that the Greek fleet could defeat the Persians in the right place and at a time of his choosing, manipulated both the enemy and his own anti-war lobby into battle off the island of Salamis, where the Greeks utterly defeated the cocksure Persians in the narrow straits. Xerxes, who had watched the naval battle from a nearby mount, immediately returned to Persia; the following year, the Greeks decisively defeated the enemy on land at Plataea and their fleet at Mycale.

Rudolph Maté's *The 300 Spartans* (1962) is the only cinematic memorial to this historically vital conflict – but what a splendid memorial it is. The script, by Maté's co-producer George St George, based on material by a quartet of Italians, focuses entirely on the Thermopylae incident. The Greeks themselves were quick to realise both the propaganda potential and the inspirational qualities of the event – a typical mixture of valour and good fortune, since Leonidas' delaying action forced the Persians to expose their fleet at anchor off the coast, where it was decimated by a sudden summer storm. But above all, the incident is a tribute to the effectiveness of the Spartan system: a rigid military state of awesome discipline and harshness

which represented an almost complete inversion of the neighbouring Athenians' code of living. A film still remains to be made about Sparta's amazing society, but *The 300 Spartans* conveys something of its spirit – even if, in demonstration of film-makers' preference for *res Romanae*, it is diluted to something approaching a mini-Rome. The film also lacks a proper awareness of the Second Persian War's historical importance: if Xerxes had won, the full flowering of Greek civilisation would never have occurred. There remains, nonetheless, much of the sense of life-and-death conflict which first inspired the historian Herodotus and the tragedian Aeschylus to record the struggle for all time.

Maté's film adheres relatively closely to the facts, expanding such personalities as Ephialtes merely because the stage is smaller. Only an entirely dispensable love-story between a Spartan soldier and Leonidas' niece (Diane Baker miscast and wasted) shows Hollywood formula jarring against the historical ambience. Lines like 'Hey, this is a really good war! They say Xerxes has brought a hundred nations with him. Isn't that marvellous?' (Phylon) cast a shadow over the otherwise sensible dialogue put into the mouths of the leading characters. Of these, Richard Egan's Leonidas and Ralph Richardson's Themistocles form a perfect contrast of body vs mind, Dorian vs Ionian – the twin tensions in Greek life – albeit in Anglo-Saxon terms (Egan's physical American vs Richardson's suave Englishman).

One of the film's greatest strengths is the added atmosphere gained simply by filming in Greek locations, instead of the more usual Spanish or Italian countryside. This compensates for the occasional liberties of art direction and gives the final reels of open conflict a rare authenticity. Maté and his crew convey both the heroic desperation of Leonidas' action and a very real idea of the Spartan military code which the epilogue expresses: 'It was a stirring example to free people throughout the world what a few brave men can do when they refuse to submit to tyranny.'

*   *   *

And then comes a silence without parallel in any other historical genre: Athens' great intellectual flowering during the fifth century, her long war of attrition with Sparta – all are passed over. Just as

40 (*above*) Power and sensuality: Charis (Daniella Rocca) in *The Giant of Marathon*

41 (*left*) Allusory rescue: Andromeda (Mylène Demongeot), Theocritus (Sergio Fantoni) and Philippides (Steve Reeves) in *The Giant of Marathon*

42 (*opposite above*) Heroic desperation: the Spartans pause for breath in *The 300 Spartans*

43 (*opposite below*) Last-ditch defence: Praxiteles (Massimo Girotti) wards off Macedonian soldiers in his studio in *Aphrodite, Goddess of Love*

44 Convinced godhead: Alexander (Richard Burton) in *Alexander the Great*

45 (*right*) Contrasts in style: cramped, low-ceilinged Macedonia . . .

46 (*below*) . . . and spacious, airy Athens in *Alexander the Great*

The 300 Spartans had chosen to treat its story exclusively as an anti-tyranny tract, with Greece somewhat freely described as 'the only stronghold of freedom still remaining in the then-known world', so it is only when another common enemy threatens that film-makers again begin to take interest. Fernando Cerchio and Victor Tourjansky's *Aphrodite, Goddess of Love* (*La Venere di Cheronea*, 1958) shows Greece at war with Philip of Macedonia, and depicts the perils of international relations through a story centred around the sculptor Praxiteles (Massimo Girotti) who shelters the Macedonian soldier Lucian (Jacques Sernas) just prior to the battle of Chaeronea in 338 BC. Lucian falls in love with Praxiteles' model for his Aphrodite of Cnidus, Iris (Belinda Lee), and the humanitarian sculptor's principles begin to come apart at the seams. The art/life motif – also encountered in Mario Bonnard's *Slave Women of Corinth* (*Afrodite dea dell'amore*, 1958) and Victor Saville's *The Silver Chalice* (1954) – is particularly apt in a Greek context, and the fact that Praxiteles' career coincided with the rise of Philip is perceptively brought out by Damiano Damiani's screenplay. We know nothing about the historical Praxiteles' real personality, and Girotti (unlike, for instance, Ralph Richardson's Themistocles in *The 300 Spartans*) is about the right age; Iris and Lucian made an entirely satisfactory pair of doomstruck peplum lovers, but even the spectacular physical presence of Belinda Lee in short *chiton* cannot obscure the fact that the film's ethical centre lies with Praxiteles. His last-ditch defence of the Aphrodite in his studio against Macedonian soldiers is the film's genuine climax, rather than the hasty reunion between the lovers at the end.

Sergio Leone's *The Colossus of Rhodes* (*Il colosso di Rodi*, 1961) makes a work of art carry even greater significance. The statue of Apollo erected in Rhodes harbour (*not* straddling the entrance, incidentally – that is a medieval fiction) in fact had a life of nearly sixty years (c. 280–224 BC) before being toppled by an earthquake. Leone's film, scripted by no fewer than nine writers (including Leone, Tessari, De Martino and De Concini), gives it a much shorter life, its collapse signifying that of the Rhodean tyranny and its interior being used as a secret prison for various rebels. This Greek transformation of elements also encountered in works like Howard Hawks' *Land of the Pharaohs* would have worked better – since the spectacle is

never less than impressive – if the script had not been so hopelessly ill-focused: pagan gods and Christian-*manqué* arena scenes jostle each other for possession of the Greek/Phoenician/Persian storyline.

Alberto De Martino's own *The Spartan Gladiators*/*The Secret Seven* (*La rivolta dei sette*, 1965) also trades on the same device but at the opposite extreme: here a statuette hides an incriminating document against an ambitious Spartan tyrant. An above-average peplum notable for its solid acting and primitive flame-thrower, *The Spartan Gladiators* is set in the period of the Achaean League when Greece's power was declining and Rome's ascending. Started in 275 as a protective measure, this was the nearest Greece as a whole ever came to representative government. De Martino's film establishes it as a peace-giving organisation which must be protected at all costs, and the involvement of the apolitical Keros (Tony Russel) to lead the patriots against Sar (Massimo Serato) is an interesting gloss on the otherwise formulary events, invested with a *brio* thoroughly typical of De Martino's work.

Rome had already intervened to curb the League's power in 168, and when war again broke out in 146 the consul Mummius was sent to teach it a lesson at the request of Sparta – and with typical Roman thoroughness ordered Corinth to be razed to the ground (after first shipping its art treasures back to Italy) and the League dissolved. Mario Costa's *Il conquistatore di Corinto* (1962) deals with this act, though in a confused style not helped by the wooden presence of Jacques Sernas as a Roman centurion torn between love for Rome and love for an equally wooden Greek girl (Geneviève Grad). Its general disarray and blatantly Roman bias could be said to reflect the sad state of affairs of the period, but this is a justification and not an excuse.

As if for solace, one can only turn back to the fourth century, to Robert Rossen's *Alexander the Great* (1956), historically overlapping and following on *Aphrodite, Goddess of Love* but thematically quite separate. Rossen, who wrote, produced and directed the film, sees Alexander as a man who believed he was destined to unite the known world by joining Europe and Asia (thus, by inference, preparing the way for Christianity) but who was caught up in the Machiavellism of power politics and the vortex of success. The theme of good intent gone awry is the dominant one of Rossen's personal *oeuvre* and it marries well with Alexander's story: he is shown dogged by the shade and the guilt of his father, Philip (a studiously vulgar Fredric March), and the film comes a neat full circle at the end when Alexander (a blond Richard Burton) is shown drunk and raving in similar manner. Rossen's original script – reportedly very impressive – expanded much more on this *motif* which, presumably along with the relationship between Alexander and Barsine (Claire Bloom), suffered at the hands of the distributors when the director's version was shortened from three hours to less than two and a half.

Yet even as it stands the film provides an admirable panorama of the period: Alexander's birth and childhood, his crucial tutelage under Aristotle (Barry Jones), the scheming of his mother, Olympias (Danielle Darrieux), against her husband, Philip, on Alexander's behalf, and the anti-Macedonian stand by the Athenian orator Demosthenes (Michael Hordern, splendidly bringing to life actual quotes from his speeches). As Alexander himself, Richard Burton is at his most impressive in an otherwise undistinguished historical epic career. The role of a man who finally united the contradictory intellectual and military strands in Greek life into a satisfying whole fits him far better than the Roman characterisations of Koster's *The Robe* (1953) or Mankiewicz's *Cleopatra* (1963). There is a genuine sense of vision, of convinced godhead, in the portrayal, and Rossen's thoughtful direction supports him well. Yet ultimately, despite the film's effectively spartan art direction (cramped, low-ceilinged Macedonia contrasted with spacious, airy Athens, and Persia deftly drawn with Darius' portable tapestries) and impressive use of colour and wide-open (Spanish) spaces, the film never rises to a sufficiently awesome level, never really takes flight, to match the ambitiousness of its script. This is not simply the fault of Mario Nascimbene's uninspired monodic music; Rossen lacks only the crucial ability to surrender to calculated vulgarity which would have made *Alexander the Great* into *the* showpiece of the Greek historical genre.

Rome: From Myth to Republic

History is allowed to exalt the origins of cities by mixing the human with the divine. And if any nation should immortalise its origins and ascribe them to divine founders, such is the military glory of Rome that, when it claims Mars to be its foremost parent, people should accept the idea with as much equanimity as they accept Roman rule.

Livy, *From the Foundation of Rome*,
Praef. 7f. (c. 26 BC)

The two cultures [Roman and American] are so much alike . . . Even the outlooks are the same: you don't have to be born Roman as long as you accept the Roman way of life, with the flag and the eagle and the Chase National Bank with columns of gorgonzola.

Peter Ustinov (1977)

'Haven't you any manners at all?'
'No, I'm a barbarian.'

Meta to Varius in *Jupiter's Darling* (1955)

If there is one civilisation that has dominated popular ideas of what a historical epic film ought to be, it is Ancient Rome. Part of film-makers' recurrent obsession with Rome stems from the fact that it offers the most versatile parallels for twentieth-century audiences. The West is indebted to no other single civilisation for so many facets of its present life: our law, language, literature, architecture, administration, the problems of empire – all have powerful links with the Roman experience, and many concepts inherited from other civilisations have only reached us through Rome's agency.

There is, too, the vastness of the Roman achievement which appeals to present imaginations. Rome absorbed the quality and depth of Greek thought and added to it her own predilection for size,

replacing the Greeks' disunited, small-scale ambitions with pomp, ruthless conquest and the enforcement of a centralised political and cultural way of thought. Rome's rise and fall accommodates a wide range of developments – from a small warring town ruled by kings, to a more powerful republic which eventually fell after a long civil war, to a virile Imperial power by turns benevolent and despotic, to the centre of a vast and progressively more complex empire which painfully embraced Christianity, to an enfeebled and clumsy bureaucracy which eventually fell prey to warring tribes from the East. It is in the Roman Imperial genre that the American film industry really comes into its own: there is a natural empathy between the two civilisations which is far from fortuitous. This will be discussed in later chapters; once again, however, as with Greek history, we are much in the debt of the peplum.

The early years of Rome's history are first cloaked in vague legends connecting her with Troy and then dominated by the kings (753–510 BC), a period of survival rather than aggression and as rich in mythical opportunities as any period in Greek history. It has, however, been virtually spurned by film-makers, presumably from the notion that Rome did not then measure up to her popular image. The saddest case of all must be the cinema's shabby treatment of Rome's greatest literary epic, Vergil's *Aeneid*. This was a conscious literary creation, based on no oral tradition, and designed to show the triumph of law and civilisation (and by inference, Rome) over the forces of barbarism. Vergil knew the emperor Augustus personally, and the latter not only saw pre-publication instalments but also overruled Vergil's last wish – he died leaving it unrevised – that it should be burnt. The *Aeneid* raises plagiarism (not denigrated in ancient times) to a redeeming level: it trades on the received kudos of Homer and Greek legend, incorporates, often verbatim, excerpts from past Roman epicists (especially Ennius' *Annales*, which for a long time was the Roman schoolboy's source of national pride), and in twelve books of well-turned verse celebrates the thorough absorption and reconciliation of the Greek cultural legacy in the Roman system.

The *Aeneid* can be read simply as a pro-Augustan tract: Aeneas equals the emperor; Turnus, Antony; Dido, Cleopatra; Drances, Cicero; etc. But its wider message, embracing a whole national ethos based on the traditions of the past, assures it of its true title of epic. To the Romans, interestingly, the legend of Aeneas was authoritative: both Sallust and Livy accept the fact that Rome was founded by a conglomeration of resident Latins and a group of Trojan exiles led by Aeneas. It may be true that Aeneas, thanks to Vergil's greater aptitude for lyrical description and passions than for heroism or characterisation, is a far less interesting figure than Odysseus, but then Homer's hero was never meant to be an embodiment of a nation's destiny. The only film to interest itself in the *Aeneid* is Giorgio Rivalta's *War of the Trojans* (*La leggenda di Enea*, 1962), more in the line of a follow-up to Giorgio Ferroni's earlier *The Wooden Horse of Troy* (*La guerra di Troia*, 1961) – see Chapter 5 – than anything else, and sharing Steve Reeves as Aeneas and Ugo Liberatore as scriptwriter.

The film deals with the last six books of Vergil's work (poor Dido is thus missing; only Berlioz has done this most sympathetic of Vergil's characters full justice) and, while simplifying the structure and ditching all the theology, it presents the essentials with fair accuracy, correctly focusing on the Aeneas/Turnus conflict which climaxes in the final hand-to-hand combat. Technically the film shows a measure of craftsmanship, with footage used from *The Wooden Horse of Troy* to show Aeneas' memories as he gazes at a fresco of the fall of Troy. The final combat, between Aeneas (Steve Reeves) and Turnus (Gianni Garko), is also impressive, and the script seizes on a nice female parallel for the two men: Lavinia, Aeneas' betrothed (and symbolic of the strength in union of the Latin and Trojan people), contrasts with the Amazonian *bellatrix* Camilla, splendidly played in best peplum spirit by Liana Orfei.

To fill the gap between the arrival in Italy of Aeneas and his men seven years after the fall of Troy (their wanderings around the Mediterranean in search of a new homeland forming the basis of the first half of Vergil's *Aeneid*) and Romulus' foundation of Rome in the traditional year of 753 BC, the Romans invented the Alban kings, the first the son of Aeneas, the last a usurper who made the true king's daughter a vestal virgin. In true mythic fashion she nonetheless becomes pregnant and her twins, Romulus and Remus, are consigned to the river Tiber (cf. Moses), whence they are rescued and suckled to health by a she-wolf. Again, only Italian film-makers have quarried this period, most recently with Castellacci and Pingitore's ludicrous *Remo e Romolo: Storia di due figli di una lupa* (1976) but most notably with Sergio Corbucci's *Duel of the Titans* (*Romolo e Remo* 1962), an above-average peplum with greater care than usual taken with casting (Steve Reeves and Gordon Scott, the peplum kings of the time, with Virna Lisi and Jacques Sernas) and crew (music by Piero Piccioni, photography by Dario Di Palma, direction by Corbucci). The film adheres fairly closely to accepted legend regarding the foundation of Rome, the major departures being the introduction of Julia (Virna Lisi) for romantic interest, the Sabines for spectacle, and the wholesale elimination of King Numitor to throw the spotlight more on Romulus (Steve Reeves) and Remus (Gordon Scott).

The screenplay (written by Corbucci in collaboration with such other luminaries as Sergio Leone and Duccio Tessari) imaginatively retains the story's legendary character. Remus dies not at Romulus' hands during a quarrel but from a flash of lightning from heaven; and there is a memorable moment (surely ascribable to Tessari) in which Remus and his men are 'attacked' by a shower of red lava as they race against Romulus to found the site of Rome. Visually the film is careful in early Roman period detail (an authentic tang of wool, leather and wooden structures) without diverging at all from the peplum reliance on physical stereotypes for its sexual content. The blonde and physically immaculate Lisi admirably complements the equally immaculate Reeves and Scott.

It is to the peplum cycle also that one must look for subsequent events in Rome's early history. The so-called Rape of the Sabine Women, in which, very soon after the foundation of Rome, Romulus & Co. abducted some neighbouring young blood to

47 Immaculate heroes: Remus (Gordon Scott) and Romulus (Steve
Reeves), with Julia (Virna Lisi) and Curtius (Jacques Sernas), in *Duel
of the Titans*

ensure the city's future, is the subject of Richard Pottier's *Il ratto delle Sabine* (1961), a somewhat sardonic and rather less than serious picture notable only for the presence of a young Roger Moore (as an uncharismatic Romulus) and Mylène Demongeot. The plot follows the traditional story handed down by Livy only in the barest details, playing hardest on the theme of reconciliation instead of war, and that by the women rather than the men. In look the film is careless beside *Duel of the Titans*, more Grecian than early Roman, and the ending, in which Romulus retires as king and spreads a rumour that he has gone to the gods, deliberately contradicts the traditional story and the film's mythic pretensions.

Leaving the eighth century, Ferdinandò Baldi's *Duel of Champions* (*Orazi e Curiazi*, 1962) uses the legend of the Horatii and Curiatii brothers, who decided by single combat the power-struggle between Rome and Alba, to portray the wasting effect of war. The film trades on moral stereotypes: ambitious Romans, wicked Albans (with women wrestlers, and prisoners being thrown to wolves, for entertainment) and a fictitious tribe of Tarpinians ('good, clean, decent people') to represent peace amid the madness of two warring states. Unfortunately, occasional felicities such as the hints of Rome's future greatness and Lavagnino's delicate scoring of the love scenes are negated by Alan Ladd's tired and bewildered central performance as Horatius, too old and lethargic by half for what could have been a simple tale of loss and reacquisition of honour.

Better in that respect, though equally unremarkable, are those films set during the war with Tarquinius Superbus and Lars Porsena at the end of the sixth century, celebrating the two Roman heroes, Mucius Scaevola and Cloelia (strangely, film-makers have never been drawn to the story of Horatius Cocles, immortalised by Livy and Macaulay, who flourished in the same war). Giorgio Ferroni's *Arm of Fire* (*Il colosso di Roma*, 1965) is a tidy Gordon Scott vehicle near the end of the peplum years, a passable historical remix with only the legend of Scaevola (the Roman who failed to assassinate Lars Porsena and who plunged his right hand into a sacrificial fire to show Roman disregard for pain) to give it substance; Cloelia is made Scaevola's fiancée and her own story made to play second fiddle.

Better is the earlier *Amazons of Rome/Warrior Women* (*Le vergini di Roma*, 1961), by Vittorio Cottafavi and Carlo Ludovico Bragaglia, with Sylvia Syms as a somewhat boyish Cloelia amongst a more voluptuous Franco-Italian cast. The film, however, debases the original legend (in which Cloelia, one of a batch of hostages given to Lars Porsena by Rome, escapes, swims the Tiber back to Rome and, when surrendered again to Porsena, is released in admiration of her courage) and turns the Roman story of female courage and selflessness into a glorified Amazonian foray, with Cloelia and the 300 girl hostages routing the Etruscans on horseback. But at the end a moral: Cloelia refuses public honours (contrary to the legend) and devotes herself to chastity, in the form of self-penance for transgressing her role as a woman by causing death rather than life. Such moralising is Catholic rather than Roman but at least shows a final glimmering of realisation as to Cloelia's symbolic role.

*　　*　　*

The Scaevola and Cloelia stories are set during the first years of the foundation of the Roman Republic (after the expulsion of the last king, Tarquinius Superbus, in 510 BC). Myth is already beginning to turn into historical fact, and the Scaevola and Cloelia stories are about Rome's struggles for its own freedom rather than just territorial expansion: early patriotism has also taken on a constitutional tone. As the Roman historian Livy, writing under the emperor Augustus, says when coming to this point in his monumental *From the Foundation of Rome* (*Ab urbe condita*):

> I shall now trace the deeds in peace and war of a henceforth *free* Roman people . . . [But] there is no doubt that Brutus – the same who won so much glory by expelling King Superbus – would have done the state the greatest harm if he had wrested the monarchy from any of the earlier kings in a premature desire for freedom . . . Discord would have broken up the still immature state, which had been held stable by the control of authority and, in so nourished, been brought to bear the good fruit of freedom when in full strength.

(2, 1)

We are exclusively in the debt of the Italian cinema for a record of the major events of the next 300 years. Though the selection is small, and almost entirely attributable to the desperate search of the peplum cycle for new material, it is noteworthy that once again Hollywood has turned its back on the era. Both *Thunder of Battle/Coriolanus, Hero without a Country* (*Coriolano, eroe senza patria*, 1965) and *Battle of the Spartans* (*Brenno il nemico di Roma*, 1963) treat of crucial periods in Rome's Republican history, times when her very existence was threatened, first by one of her most lauded generals and later by migrating Gallic hordes.

Giorgio Ferroni's *Thunder of Battle* claims inspiration from Plutarch and Shakespeare (the script follows Plutarch rather than Livy in the names for Coriolanus' wife and mother, but Livy rather than Plutarch in letting him survive at the end), and in an effort to cast Coriolanus in a positive light plays down the real Coriolanus' arrogance and patrician pride, ditches the class conflict which was ravaging the city at that time, and makes a villain out of Sicinius, the people's tribune. Apart from that the film keeps a fair eye on the facts, and is helped by the casting of Gordon Scott as a physically perfect Coriolanus; the film's original title intelligently sums up the problem of presenting epic material from the story of Coriolanus, but it is a fair stab.

Giacomo Gentilomo's *Battle of the Spartans* is considerably simpler fare. The film drastically simplifies the siege of Rome in 390 BC by the Gaul Brennus, who occupied the city but was prevented from taking the Capitol (to which part of the populace had retreated) when the sacred geese of Juno alerted the Romans to a night attack. In the film the conflict is personalised: Brennus marches on Rome not because some Roman envoys took up arms during a parley but because a beautiful priestess, promised to him by the besieged town of Clusium, has been rescued by a young Roman soldier. The film shows proper respect for the traditional elements, such as the geese of Juno, but misses the epic possibilities in the retreat to the Capitol and the mixture of utter desolation and amazing tenacity later mythologised by Livy.

Next comes the greatest challenge to Rome's authority during the Republic – the three Punic Wars which stretched over a complete century in a bitter trade and political struggle which saw the rise and fall of Hannibal and the total destruction of Carthage (though not without severe losses to the victor). The First Punic War (264–241) has been virtually ignored by the cinema, which passed up the story of the Roman commander Marcus Atilius Regulus (who was sent to Rome to propose peace, proposed a continuation of the war instead, and returned to Carthage to face death by torture) and turned instead to a convenient, ready-made story from literature. Gustave Flaubert's *Salammbô* is in fact set after the defeat of Carthage and deals with the so-called Mercenary War, in which Carthage, battered and bruised, refused to pay its mercenaries; a Libyan-led revolt turned into a full-scale war of unbelievable cruelty, ending in 237 with the total defeat of the mercenaries. Flaubert's novel is a sinister piece of whimsy with little pretension to historical fact or epic stature, focusing on the love story of the Carthaginian priestess Salammbô and the Libyan mercenary Matho. Of the two major film versions, Pierre Marodon's *Salammbô* (1924) is certainly the more spectacular (especially its set for Carthage's great main square) and has a broad, confident pace that equals that of the great fifties historical epics. From its poetic main title, with the sun's rays lighting up the letters of the title, the film shows little of the frantic mugging and hectic action common in silent epics, and goes some way towards developing a parallel in the early stages between Matho's unfulfilled love for Salammbô and Carthage's unfulfilled deal with the mercenaries. Costumes and art direction are strongly Art Deco, but the film is sexually more explicit than Hollywood productions of the time, adding an edge to the lovers' later travails. Sergio Grieco's remake, *Salammbò* (1961) makes the most of its starry cast (Jacques Sernas, Edmund Purdom, Jeanne Valérie) but lacks the barbarity and scope of the silent version.

With the Second Punic War (218–201) we are on safer ground. Hannibal's crossing of the Alps, with an army of 20,000 troops, 6,000 cavalry, nearly forty elephants, and a host of pack-animals (many of whom perished in the crossing), was a source of awe even in ancient times – the first attempt by a civilised army – and centuries later Roman schoolchildren were still being set exercises based on Hannibal's campaign. With the host of attendant stories (the splitting of the rocks with fire and sour wine, the crossing of the Rhône, the battles of Lake

Trasimene, Cannae and Zama), Hannibal still retains his fascination today. Such a fascination is also found in the later story of Spartacus – Rome suddenly shaken to its bowels by an uncontainable force at large within Italy, a force which declined to march straight on the city when at the height of its success (after Cannae in Hannibal's case) and was finally defeated only after appalling losses. Hannibal is a personality of epic stature, a remarkable leader of men by any account (especially considering the disparate nationalities he had under his command), fired by a hatred of Rome inbred from his earliest years. His story is one of history's noblest failures: he died no glorious death on the battlefield of Zama but lived for another twenty years, finally taking poison when vindictively pursued by the Romans to the court of a foreign king. He was the last major threat to Rome in her Republican days; after the Punic Wars Rome started her policy of conscious expansion by conquest which led to the Empire.

The constituent ingredients of this period are neatly satirised in George Sidney's *Jupiter's Darling* (1955), an M-G-M musical spin-off of the fifties' historical fad, reworked into a vehicle for Esther Williams (as a half-Greek heroine of Amazonian stature), Howard Keel (as the Hannibal who falls for her), George Sanders as Fabius Maximus, and the acrobatic pair-dancers Marge and Gower Champion. Only the main characterisation is epic, and Williams and Keel make a worthy pair. Incidental pleasures include a view of the Colosseum, some three hundred years before it was built.

Several other films about this period are of interest, all very different. Luigi Maggi and Roberto Omegna's *Lo schiavo di Cartagine* (1910) is only important as an adjunct to Giovanni Pastrone's *Cabiria* (1914): the sets and backdrops are above-average for the time but the story of a virgin slave-girl sacrificed to the god Baal Molok is pure hokum – human sacrifice was practised by the Carthaginians, but always of male aristocratic children, and their god would be Baal Hammon, not the spurious Molok (Moloch in Pastrone's film). Pastrone's remarkable film is the one really great work from the Punic cycle, and certainly the earliest picture with epic pretensions worthy of serious attention. Ultimately, *Cabiria* fails in epic terms, though visually, stylistically and in the province of spectacle it remains one of the genre's

paradigms. At the time the film capitalised on Italy's expansionist policy in East and North Africa by concocting an elaborate tale around various events of the Second Punic War (including Hannibal's crossing of the Alps, and the siege of Syracuse) and studding the narrative with historical figures (Scipio, Sophonisba, Masinissa, Archimedes, Hasdrubal). The story's kernel – the names and flowery nationalistic captions were the work of the soldier-poet Gabriele D'Annunzio – is the rescue of a young Roman noblewoman, Cabiria, kidnapped by wicked Carthaginians for sacrifice, by the Roman soldier Fulvius Axilla, who is living with his hefty coloured slave Maciste in Carthage. The film's subtitle ('Visione storica del terzo secolo A.C.') immediately establishes its grand claims, and these are at least backed up by its production values: superb spacious sets (Carthage was completely levelled by Scipio Aemilianus in 146 BC, so we possess no records of its architecture; Pastrone's film adopts a massive, geometrical style with Afro-Mesopotamian leanings), precise composition and framing, a vital and exciting use of the tracking camera (the first recorded use at that date), and advanced and alert use of natural (*and* artificial) lighting. There are, too, the great set-pieces: the eruption of Etna, with first the threat to and finally the collapse of Cabiria's house (and the servants grabbing the gold); Hannibal crossing the Alps, with some superb footage in the actual snow-capped mountains, with thronging extras; the rescue of Cabiria from the sacrifice to Moloch, culminating in a great filmic flight of fancy which anticipates Hitchcock's *Saboteur* and *North by Northwest* by several decades – the escape down the side of the temple, built to resemble a massive animal; and the destruction of Fulvius' fleet by means of Archimedes' burning-glass, which focused the sun's rays on the ships' sails and set fire to them.

What fatally flaws *Cabiria* in epic terms, however, is the story's inability to relate the central romance to any larger historical perspective. Matters are not helped by the fact that both protagonists are Roman: the plot boils down to a sophisticated rescue drama, and there is no possibility of exploiting any impossible love between warring nations. The latter was never intended: *Cabiria* sets out to hymn Rome and its conquests, and is not greatly concerned with the subtleties of moral conflict; our hero and heroine suffer merely

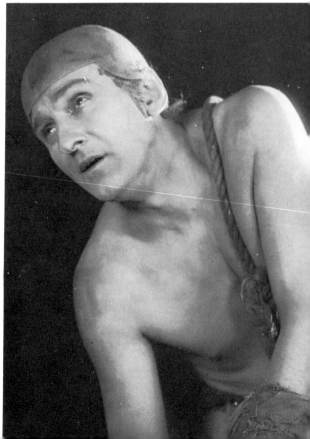

48 (*opposite above*) Symbolic role: Cloelia (Sylvia Syms) in *Amazons of Rome*

49 (*opposite below right*) Sinister whimsy: the Greek slave Spendius (Henri Baudin) in *Salammbô* (1924)

50 (*opposite below left*) Satiric stature: Amytis (Esther Williams) and Hannibal (Howard Keel) in *Jupiter's Darling*

51 (*above*) Brave barbarian: Hannibal (Camillo Pilotto) in *Scipio Africanus*

physical hardship. Pastrone was clearly a pioneer of great vision, but his screenplay let him down; despite that one fatal flaw, however, *Cabiria* was to become a model for the historical epic, an acute remix of established imagery from Flaubert (Carthage), Lord Lytton (the erupting volcano), and Sienkiewicz (strongman Ursus from *Quo vadis*).

When Italy replayed its dreams of empire in Africa during the thirties, the film industry predictably returned to the Punic Wars for its one great foray into historical propaganda, showing the young general Scipio Africanus rising to answer the Roman populace's call to avenge Cannae by taking on the Carthaginians and finally defeating them and Hannibal in Africa at the battle of Zama in 202 BC. The result, Carmine Gallone's *Scipio Africanus* (*Scipione l'africano*, 1937), made with great pomp on a grand scale, was officially blessed by Il Duce, as a special number of the weighty Italian film journal *Bianco e nero* pointed out in its preface:

> In the film theatre of the Ministry of People's Culture, on the 4th of August in the XVth year of the Fascist government, Il Duce saw the film *Scipione l'africano*. He much admired the great historical film, made with exclusively Italian means and manpower, and expressed his deep satisfaction to the film-makers.
>
> (7/8, 1937)

Two years later another special issue of *Bianco e nero* analysed the reactions of Italian children to the film, and the effects it had had on them. The Fascist era may not, contrary to expectations, have thrown up a horde of costume films, but *Scipio Africanus* more than made up for the paucity, and showed epic form more than ever serving national fervour.

The film hardly boxes shy in its allegory: Scipio is shown as the leader of the young and pragmatic party in the Roman Senate, anxious to take the war into Africa; Hannibal is shown as a brave but helpless barbarian, powerless in the face of the inevitable fate which dictates that Rome should henceforth rule the world. The film details with some care the Scipio/Hannibal relationship (finally consummated when the pair have their famous one and only meeting prior to Zama), with the latter being slowly dominated by the former's political

personality. In less pedestrian hands than Gallone's, the film could have mythologised this confrontation across continents of two myths (a theme later explored with great success by John Milius' *The Wind and the Lion*). In the circumstances only Ildebrando Pizzetti's dramatic score shows a real sense of dramatic pacing, with great brass fanfares in parallel fifths topped by a heroic theme (when Scipio first appears at the head of the Roman legions) or an emotive Largo with striding bass. Pizzetti has written that the heroic theme is 'a thematic nucleus representing Scipio himself and his character, his designs, his purpose, and the concept and feeling of being Roman and Italian, and the presentiment of Rome's destiny and its greatness and power'.

There are no films which satisfactorily explore the personality of Hannibal in Carthaginian terms. The closest thing to a sympathetic study came over twenty years after Gallone's picture – Edgar G. Ulmer's *Hannibal* (*Annibale*, 1960), made in Italy during the peplum period with an imported director and two American leads. Ulmer, one of the many Viennese-born directors who later moved to and made a career in Hollywood, was a highly professional and rapid craftsman whose contribution to the quality B-picture has only recently been recognised; his films have a spiritual bleakness and loneliness, often reinforced by a sense of the macabre, which accords well with the story of Hannibal, here shown as a personality bound by the events of history.

In true peplum style the main character's conflict is personalised in a love affair – here between Hannibal and the Roman Silvia, daughter of Fabius Maximus, Hannibal's chief adversary. It is a neat equation, and provides plenty of epic material: Silvia deserts her homeland for Hannibal, and Hannibal forgets his wife and child for her; when Silvia realises she must give up her love for the Carthaginian, she returns to face punishment in Rome; when Hannibal sees the severed head of his brother Hasdrubal, he sets out to face his destiny. The script's structure, then, shows a measure of care, but the large-scale set-pieces and sluggish direction of the film's central section slow down the initial promise. Hannibal's crossing of the Alps is splendidly handled at the outset, with positive use of studio sets, but the later battle of Cannae is such a dim affair that there is no proper sense of climax to mirror the metaphysical struggle of the main characters. Victor Mature's Hannibal is noteworthy: this actor has a sad, stolid quality which accords well with epic characterisation, and it is for his performance that *Hannibal* is best remembered.

In Rudolph Maté's *Revak the Rebel/The Barbarian* (*Revak, lo schiavo di Cartagine*, 1961) Hannibal is spoken of but never appears. The Italian/American co-production is a truly appalling piece of cinema: the script bristles with unspeakable dialogue ('From the moment I saw you, I became a woman' or 'My sword is beginning to breathe again!') and the worst clichés of the historical genre ('You Celtic dog!'; 'Ah! You're truly a barbarian!'), and Maté's direction is formulary and totally uninspired, in complete contrast to his magnificent *The 300 Spartans* made the following year. The story, set during the early years of the Second Punic War, has Revak, a captured Celtic prince, transported to an 'evil and corrupt' Carthage as arena-fodder and freeing a motley group of Roman slaves in between falling in love with the local Princess Taratha. The film is of interest for only two reasons. First, the Romans are portrayed throughout as the good guys, defenders of freedom, stability and honour (one captured Roman noble evokes vague parallels with the historical Marcus Atilius Regulus). Second, the script toys marginally with the theme of misguided nationalism which lies at the heart of many a historical epic film. Unfortunately this latter point is only ever half developed in one speech by Revak (Jack Palance), which raises more questions than it ever has the wit to answer: 'The insanity of it all ... that because one's blood represents a country or a heritage we must ally ourselves with our sworn pledges and hate, even though they themselves are not responsible for being born what they are. When, Varro, will men become of age and not have to hate and destroy only because of a place of birth?' To which Revak gets the cursory reply of 'Noble words, my friend. But for the future, perhaps' before the script resumes its formulary way.

There remain two more works which complete the Punic Wars cycle – Pietro Francisci's *Siege of Syracuse* (*L'assedio di Siracusa*, 1960), which deals with the efforts of the inventor Archimedes to stave off the Roman siege of Syracuse (instigated because the city is sympathetic to Carthage), and Carmine Gallone's *Carthage in Flames* (*Cartagine*

in fiamme, 1960), an accomplished but flawed work by the veteran director which is set at the end of the Third Punic War (151–146) when Carthage was totally destroyed by Scipio Aemilianus. *Siege of Syracuse* is a marginal work by any standard and shows Francisci again working with the actress Sylva Koscina (who had starred in *Hercules* and *Hercules Unchained*); less happily cast are Rossano Brazzi as the inventor and Tina Louise as his pure love Diana. The film signally fails to explore the possibilities of a small island power caught between warring giants, and the character of Archimedes is trivialised by showing him discovering the power of the sun's rays by its effects on Diana's second-century bikini. The picture is attractive fun but no epic. Gallone's *Carthage in Flames*, on the other hand, is more impressive: the script rightly seizes on the fact that Carthage is a doomed and besieged city, and constructs some fanciful but suitably histrionic personal conflicts among the fated inhabitants. Sets (especially the harbour scenes) are well above par; only charisma is missing, and here the Anglo-French leads Anne Heywood, Daniel Gélin and Pierre Brasseur are to blame – their roles require a larger-than-life quality which the likes of Koscina, Reeves and Fantoni (the *echt* villain in films like *The Giant of Marathon*) could have contributed. As the sole representative of the generally ignored Third Punic War, *Carthage in Flames* is not inconsiderable – only, like Ulmer's *Hannibal*, less than it could have been.

And there, for the most part, the matter rests. Following the Third Punic War and the destruction of Carthage, Rome's supremacy in the Mediterranean was unquestioned. Her history now becomes a tale of ambitious expansion abroad – shown in, e.g., Sergio Grieco's *Blood of the Warriors* (*La schiava di Roma*, 1961) and Antonio Margheriti's *Giants of Rome* (*I giganti di Roma*, 1964), both of which show the Roman conquest of Gaul at the time of the chieftain Vercingetorix – and constitutional wrangles at home. The radical political reforms of the Gracchi brothers near the end of the second century have been ignored by film-makers: the Gracchi's redistribution of land and extension of the franchise are laudable social acts but lack the necessary military conflict (civil riots hardly counting). Curiously, the Jugurthine War (111–106) has also been overlooked; this long and laborious struggle by Rome to subdue the troublesome Numidian king Jugurtha is as rich in propaganda material as anything in *Scipio Africanus*. It was used by the Roman writer Sallust in his *The Jugurthine War* (*Bellum Iugurthinum*) to draw lessons for the degenerate present from the past heroism of the populist leader and general Marius. Writing just after the assassination of Caesar, i.e. almost seventy years after the actual events, Sallust explains that one of his reasons for writing the work is

. . . because it was then that the arrogance of the upper classes received its first check – a struggle which threw everything, human and divine, into confusion and reached such a point of senselessness that it took a war and the desolation of Italy to put an end to political passions.

(5, 1)

Imperial Rome: Crisis and Civil War

Have no doubt, then, that everything lies with you and Brutus. You are both awaited – Brutus, indeed, at this very moment. And if, as I hope, you have joined with our defeated enemies, then the republic will recover and return to some sort of good health under your authority – for even if the republic appears to be free of hostile forces, there will still be much that will need curing.

letter from Cicero to Cassius (July 43 BC)

You don't have to lay your story in a meat market to make it true. The Romans had real problems too. History is no fairy tale.

William Wyler (1959)

The Roman Republic officially ended with the accession of the first emperor Augustus (formerly Octavian) in 27 BC, but the last century of the Republic is so rich in qualities traditionally associated with the Imperial period – especially those qualities singled out by the cinema – that it seems sensible to start our examination of the Imperial works somewhat earlier than textbook chronology.

The last century BC was a turbulent period even for Roman history. The Gracchi brothers had earlier paid with their lives for their attempts at radical social reform, but their sacrifice was not forgotten. Rome's Italian allies continued to press for citizenship rights, and only after the assassination of another tribune (Marcus Livius Drusus in 91) and an inconclusive war (the Social War of 90–88) were they granted them by the Senate. Political strife broke out in Rome in earnest: bitter fighting between the aristocratic and democratic factions, led respectively by the generals Sulla and Marius, with proscriptions, gangs roaming the streets and reigns of terror. Sulla and the Senate emerged alive and victorious, but during the seventies democratic forces were again at work, albeit in a different guise.

The age of the all-powerful military leader was already upon Rome, and it now became only a matter of time before successful generals decided *not* to lay down their command before entering political life. Pompey, victorious in Spain, united as consul with Marcus Licinius Crassus (who had rid Rome of the threat of the Spartacus slave revolt) against the Senate. Their so-called democratic faction was later joined by the young and ambitious Gaius Julius Caesar; in 53 Crassus was killed abroad and the triumvirate began to crumble. The Senate allied itself with Pompey; Caesar returned from Gaul, crossed the Rubicon with his armies and civil war broke out. After Pompey's murder in Egypt Caesar installed himself as *dictator* (sole ruler) until his assassination in 44 by republican senators. Antony assumed Caesar's role, Octavian the Senate's. The long and complicated struggle continued throughout the forties and thirties, with Octavian finally left sole ruler of the Roman world after Antony's death in 30.

Thereafter came the Empire proper: its maturation under Augustus, Tiberius, Claudius and Nero, its decline under the later emperors to Marcus Aurelius and Commodus, and its collapse following invasions by warring tribes from the East. The period of the first five emperors is particularly resonant for laymen: Augustus (27 BC – AD 14) immutably changing the constitution and history; Tiberius (14–37), whose reign witnessed the preaching and crucifixion of Christ; Gaius Caligula (37–41), the insane despot whose brief tenure saw the birth-pangs of Christianity in Rome; Claudius (41–54), the scholar-emperor in sheep's clothing; and Nero (54–68), with the Fire of Rome and the first mass persecutions of Christians.

*   *   *

In relative terms the period from the first century

BC onwards is well-documented, hard fact replacing earlier conjecture. There is less of the remoteness which informs other civilisations, no opportunities for the harnessing of mythology or superhuman heroics in the cause of epic scope. Such scope comes from the sheer scale of the civilisation itself, rather than just the characters who inhabit it. The film epic is manacled to the paraphernalia of Roman spectaculars: the vast temples, the marble floors, the Imperial orgies, the thundering chariots, the clattering brass and leather of the Roman soldier, the Christians thrown to the lions, the milling crowds, the huge battles. All these clichés are based on fact; but the demands of spectacle have often tempted film-makers to opt for hyperbole first.

Even the finest epic productions necessarily adopt a stylised reality – a visual equivalent of the stylised language of epic verse. For the most accurate portrait of everyday Roman life one should turn to Richard Lester's *A Funny Thing Happened on the Way to the Forum* (1966), a hilarious parody/pastiche of the archetypal Roman spectacular, based on Stephen Sondheim's stage musical. Lester's subsequent forays into period pieces – *The Three Musketeers (The Queen's Diamonds)* (1974), *The Four Musketeers (The Revenge of Milady)* (1975), and *Robin and Marian* (1976) – have confirmed his uncanny grasp of historical naturalism, the last one being notable for the skill with which myth is finally reaffirmed after so much conscious demythification. *Forum*, thanks to Lester and production designer Tony Walton, is seminal viewing for those interested in the realities of Roman life: the director invited Spanish peasants to live and work in the sets (which were built close to those for Mann's *The Fall of the Roman Empire*), let fruit and vegetables rot for effect, and, through study of Jérôme Carcopino's book *Daily Life in Ancient Rome*, achieved a genuine lived-in feel, heightened by Walton's attention to make-up (excluding the slave-girls!), statuary, and colour design. *Forum* shows Roman life around the time of the late Republic; this is the non-patrician, real Rome, echoed a century later by the poets Martial (see particularly Epigram 12, 57) and Juvenal (his Third Satire). The chariot chase (directed by Bob Simmons) is modelled on Eddie Cantor's in *Roman Scandals* (1933) and the 'Bring Me My Bride' number on Howard Keel's song in *Jupiter's Darling*

(1955), but unlike those two films Lester's picture (in addition to its tremendous entertainment value) is essential reference material for a full appreciation of the extent of epic stylisation. Federico Fellini's *Satyricon* (1969) – see Chapter 10 – is something entirely different.

Few film-makers have used the opportunities available to realise epic form. Imperial Rome, as Vergil realised in the *Aeneid*, is a moral quality in itself, good, bad or indifferent depending upon how and when one looks at it. It can therefore become an active participant in the story, either as something upon which all the other characters react or represented through human characters. Both the tribune Gallio (Richard Burton) in *The Robe* (1953) and Marcus Vinicius (Robert Taylor) in *Quo vadis* (1951) represent moral outlooks specifically Roman which are later qualified as the films progress; Messala (Stephen Boyd) in *Ben-Hur* (1959) stands for the dark (Roman) side of Ben-Hur's make-up that the latter spends the whole film trying to expunge; and in *Cleopatra* (1963) the central character is exposed to two conflicting Roman forces (Caesar and Antony), both of which profoundly and fatally affect her outlook on life. Here is the moral working-out which contributes to the films' epic form, usually (and in literature exclusively) centred on a lone figure.

In films about Imperial Rome the sexual imagery becomes more related to power than is the case in the Greek epics. Rome, like the Viking civilisation, takes on a 'masculine' identity – more specifically, extremes of masculine qualities which find qualification and redemption through 'feminine' contact. There is not so much emphasis, as there is in Grecian films, on sheer sexual electricity: it is no coincidence that Gallio, in *The Robe*, is redeemed through Diana (Jean Simmons), or Marcus, in *Quo vadis*, through Lygia (Deborah Kerr), for here the yin/yang conflict takes on a moral aspect: power, domination, cruelty and lack of understanding vs contentment, equality, tenderness and compassion. Rome's 'masculine' identity is, of course, only metaphorical: Belinda Lee, for example, assumes it in *Messalina (Messalina, venere imperatrice,* 1960) and so, to judge from surviving footage, do Merle Oberon and Flora Robson in *I, Claudius* (1937), in which Charles Laughton, as the emperor, takes on the 'feminine' role; in *Cleopatra* (1963) sexual identities are switched between Antony and the queen; and in

Spartacus (1960) the yin/yang conflict between Crassus (Laurence Olivier) and his slave Antoninus (Tony Curtis) takes on homosexual overtones. What is important is the way in which this essential ingredient of epic form assumes, in a Roman setting, a more political and/or religious role.

It is the religious side – specifically the Judaic or Christian one – which has also branded the Roman spectacular. The popular cliché of lion-fodder Christians pinpoints one of the genre's major obsessions, a convenient and historically justifiable yin to the Imperial yang. The films with an Imperial ethos essentially fall into two categories: those with a Christian backcloth and those purely concerned with Rome – i.e. religious and secular. Both categories emphasise personal freedom; in the religious works this is symbolised by Christianity, and in the secular works by a less escapist resolution. The films made during the fifties and early sixties are deeply impressed by the post-Second World War social and political climate: the feeling of reconstruction, the fear that military and political tyranny might rear its head again, the growing and changed role of youth, and the widespread questioning of automatic and misplaced privilege. The pre-war Roman works, as will be seen, show different emphases. Only the settings remain common to all.

*   *   *

I have sub-divided the secular works into (1) those films concerned with the Civil War, and (2) the rest. This chapter will deal with the first category, Chapter 9 with the second, and Chapter 10 with the religious works. By far the greatest number of secular works revolve around the mid-first-century BC period of civil strife: the dictatorship of Julius Caesar and his (and later Antony's) involvement with the Egyptian queen Cleopatra. It is easy to see why: Shakespeare's two tragedies *Julius Caesar* and *Antony and Cleopatra* are amongst his finest and most popular, and this turbulent era of Roman history, with its mixture of intrigue, violence, sex and politics (satirised in Vittorio Metz and Marcello Marchesi's 1952 *Tizio, Caio e Sempronio*), and its figure of a dominant Egyptian queen changing the face of history, has always titillated public imagination. Despite the fact that Shakespeare is re-

garded as bad box-office in the film industry, several versions of the two plays have reached the screens over the years, Joseph L. Mankiewicz in 1953 and Stuart Burge in 1970 tackling in very different ways *Julius Caesar* (with David Bradley's 1949 16mm version for side reference), and Charlton Heston's 1972 film of *Antony and Cleopatra* the only worthwhile production of the latter tragedy.

The era and its major figures provided plenty of grist for silent cinema. Méliès was among the first in, with *Cléopatre* (1899) and *Shakespeare: La mort du Jules César* (1907), followed in the United States by Charles Kent's *Antony and Cleopatra* (1908), in Britain by F. R. Benson's *Julius Caesar* (1911), the latter a film of the director's production of the play at Stratford; and in Italy by Giovanni Pastrone's *Giulio Cesare e Brutus* (1909) and Enrico Guazzoni's *Marcoantonio e Cleopatra* (1913). Of these, Guazzoni's *Brutus* (1910) is worth more than passing attention, not only for the relative superiority of its sets (though small) and costumes, but also for its balance of spectacle and character. Brutus is perhaps a lesser-known personality than those around him, but he is, as Shakespeare realised, the emotional centre of the early part of that era. A caption in the film neatly, if somewhat incoherently, sums up the issues: 'Brutus surprises the tyrannical aspirations of Julius Caesar his anger for the attempt against the liberty of the republic.'

The opening is set vaguely in 46 or 45 BC, as 'Mark Antony obtains from the Senate the triumph and crowning of Julius Caesar, despite Brutus's opposition' (hopefully this refers to the laurel crown of a *triumphator*, rather than the diadem publicly offered him in 44), and the triumph itself, filmed in a studio set, is reasonably impressive. The dramatic focus veers abruptly to Calpurnia's dream prior to Caesar's assassination – with the assassins superimposed – rather than remaining on Brutus, but after the latter is driven from Rome a scene of his vigil before the battle of Philippi reasserts the emphasis. (The expulsion is dramatic licence: Brutus, with Cassius, actually left Rome peacefully three months after Caesar's death with senatorial commissions abroad.) Brutus' death, a histrionic affair with milling fighters in the background as he stabs himself, is, however, melancholy enough for the Brutus/Republic parallel to find resolution (he in fact committed suicide quietly at night, away from the action). Guazzoni's

52 (*opposite above*) Christian clichés: Alessandro Blasetti's *Fabiola*

53 (*opposite below*) Superior spoof: Cleopatra (Amanda Barrie) receives Caesar (Sidney James) in *Carry On Cleo*

54 (*above*) Extravagant satire: Cleopatra (Vivien Leigh) and Caesar (Claude Rains) in *Caesar and Cleopatra*

film is only a sketch for an epic but it shows more intelligence than the average silent caper.

It is surprising how, despite the mass of material available on the period by ancient writers (Plutarch, Suetonius, Appian, Dio Cassius, Cicero, to name the major ones), few scriptwriters have managed to fashion works which are both literate, accurate, and realise the epic possibilities of the age. No one has yet attempted anything on a par with Lucan's epic literary treatment of the period in his *Pharsalia*. Despite the poem's ill-balance and lack of focus (it was unfinished and only the first three books were revised by the author before his premature death), Julius Caesar emerges as the central epic presence easily enough. All the films dealing with the Caesar/Cleopatra affair miss the epic possibilities inherent in the actual arrival of Caesar in Egypt, so brilliantly conveyed by Lucan at the start of Book 10:

As soon as Caesar, following Pompey's head,
touched land and trod the fatal sands,
the commander's fortune and the destiny of
  guilty Egypt
joined battle whether Ptolemy's kingdom would
  fall
under Roman arms or the Memphian sword tear
  from the world
the head of the victor *and* the vanquished.

The above-mentioned films all rely on Shakespeare; Gabriel Pascal's *Caesar and Cleopatra* (1945) is based on Shaw's play. Of the non-literary versions, only DeMille's *Cleopatra* ('from an adaptation of historical material by Bartlett Cormack') and Mankiewicz's later version ('based upon histories by Plutarch, Suetonius, Appian, and other ancient sources and "The Life and Times of Cleopatra" by C. M. Franzero') have worthwhile screenplays; the remainder – apart from spoofs like the Italian *Totò e Cleopatra* (1963) or the visually superior British *Carry On Cleo* (1964) – come from the peplum cycle. The latter incline towards the hopeless: the early *Due notti con Cleopatra* (1954) is an Alberto Sordi farce revolving around Cleopatra's sexual appetite, and is of interest now only for an early photogenic performance from Sophia Loren; the later *Il figlio di Cleopatra* (1965), a Mark Damon/Scilla Gabel vehicle, fantasises about an Arab freedom-fighting son of Caesar and the queen. Only two pepla are of real interest:

Victor Tourjansky's *Una regina per Cesare* (1963), which sports some colourful sets, an equally colourful Pascale Petit in the role of Cleopatra, and variations on the court intrigues up until the arrival of Caesar and Pompey; and Vittorio Cottafavi's *Legions of the Nile* (*Le legioni di Cleopatra*, 1960), which stars the most authentic-looking Cleopatra yet (Linda Cristal) and posits the degeneracy of the Antony/Cleopatra relationship as the last gasp of a dying Republic, soon to be resurrected in glory under Augustus. Thematically, Cottafavi's film is the most intriguing.

The real nucleus of worthwhile works is typically small. Gabriel Pascal's *Caesar and Cleopatra* and DeMille's *Cleopatra*, while never attaining (or pretending to attain) any epic scope, are nevertheless essential works of reference, self-consciously stylish in their dialogue and visual display, and of more interest here for what they do *not* do rather than for what they do. Pascal's film is a wildly extravagant setting of Shaw's satire on power and statesmanship, the consciously anti-epic bias all the more pointed for the majestic sets and costumes (by John Bryan and Oliver Messel) and luxuriant Technicolor photography (by Freddie Young, Robert Krasker, Jack Hildyard, and Jack Cardiff; camera operator, Ted Scaife). Hungarian-born Pascal produced and/or directed four of Shaw's works between 1938 and 1953 before his death in 1954 at the age of sixty. *Caesar and Cleopatra* (1945) is a consciously ambitious, optimistic work coming at a time of economic and emotional exhaustion in Britain, on a par with Olivier's *Henry V* (1944), Harry Watt's *The Overlanders* (1946), and Michael Powell's *A Matter of Life and Death* (1946), and in its effete chic it looks back to Korda's *The Private Life of Helen of Troy* (1928) and DeMille's *Cleopatra*. The script bristles with Shavian historical wit: 'I shall make a law against all this luxury when I get back to Rome,' says Caesar (Claude Rains) – a reference to his sumptuary law of 46; 'You're bald! So that's why you wear the wreath,' says Cleopatra (Vivien Leigh); or 'A bath? But I had my month's bath the day before yesterday.' More pointedly, Shaw also takes side-swipes at the legends (the carpet containing Cleopatra) and the facts (the age-difference between Caesar and Antony), as well as interweaving a counter-theme of foreign powers' intervention in a country's affairs ('Egypt for the Egyptians!'). The latter, a staple ingredient of the serious epic, here becomes a pointed warning to the age in which the film was made. The whole production is hugely enjoyable, played with utter panache by Rains, Leigh and Stewart Granger.

DeMille's *Cleopatra* (1934) is essentially the same, though tied to the American late twenties/ early thirties glamour tradition and tricked out with more mass spectacle. The tone throughout, as in all DeMille's works, is hectoring, histrionic and visually opulent, with no pretence to anything other than presenting the lives of great ancients in contemporary terms. *Cleopatra* encapsulates many of the director's faults and virtues: a characteristic gift for tersely summing up essentials, for using spectacle at crucial moments, and for always looking beyond the mere presentation of facts vs an equally characteristic failing to *stick* to his facts when a filmic opportunity presents itself, and a one-dimensional use of actors which rarely rises above the cardboard.

Cleopatra starts promisingly, the opening narration ('In the year 48 BC, Julius Caesar, having conquered half the world, turned to . . .') being followed by an equally direct scene which presents the balance of power in Egypt – Cleopatra and her associate Apollodorus the Sicilian being tied up in the desert by Pothinus, chief eunuch of her brother Ptolemy who has ousted her in a power-struggle. Attention, too, is paid to the political side of the Caesar/Cleopatra relationship: the factor which makes him interested in her is the mention of the wealth of India, the path to which lies *through* Egypt (an intelligent idea certainly consistent with Caesar's known character). The promise, however, that their relationship might be extended to embrace its historical perspective – the sense of two characters coming together with an awareness of their positions in history – is ditched soon afterwards. Warren William's characterless, brooding performance as Caesar (despite the occasional good line, like 'For what I have done, Calpurnia, pardon. For what I am about to do, courage') is no help, nor is Claudette Colbert's delightfully racy one as the queen. But the major hurdle lies in the storyline, which fails to solve the problem confronting all Caesar/Cleopatra/Antony productions – how to knit into a dramatic unity two relationships which were historically quite separate. One way is to make Cleopatra the pivot for an epic examination of Rome's destiny; another is to make Cleopatra the central epic character,

upholding her people's independence against two massive political/amorous assaults from a greater nation; a third way, totally unsupported by history, is to somehow forge a relationship between Caesar and Antony which is subject to the dark influence of Cleopatra and which may be used as a collective metaphor for Rome.

The closest one comes to the latter in DeMille's film is when Antony accuses Caesar of changing the Roman calendar to the Egyptian one (in 46) or Caesar's last meeting with Cleopatra on the way to his fateful speech in the Senate on the Ides of March (a dramatically tidy action which never took place: Caesar's house was on the Via Sacra, which led straight to the Senate building, and he was already late when he left it; to see Cleopatra he would have had to make a huge diversion over the river to the Janiculum and back again). Apart from that, DeMille opts for a simple confrontation of life-styles: 'masculine' Rome against 'feminine' Egypt, which is redolent of so many sexual comedies of the thirties, and which takes on a persuasion all its own (though never epic) at the end – a giant dolly-back as Antony and Cleopatra kiss in her barge, with curtains drawn across, followed by garlands, then oars into sight and the *hortator* beating time. DeMille's film once again shows him to be a supreme Paramount stylist, on a par with Ernst Lubitsch or Rouben Mamoulian, a fashioner of grand erotic conceits in which, typically for the decade, technique swallowed up content.

If DeMille's film at least represented an advance over Fox's silent Theda Bara vehicle, one of a host of her pictures directed by J. Gordon Edwards and (to judge by surviving evidence, since the film is now lost) an elaborately theatrical affair, things had much changed by 1963 when Twentieth Century-Fox finally released their much-publicised version, with Taylor, Burton and Harrison. Director Joseph L. Mankiewicz had a chance to re-realise the scope of his earlier *Julius Caesar* (1953) on a grander scale. Fox's original plans for the film had been modest, and only when Elizabeth Taylor fell ill and filming in Britain was abandoned did they call in Mankiewicz and decide to film elsewhere on a vastly bigger budget.

Mankiewicz, who started in Hollywood scripting comedies and only later made his mark as a serious director with a social conscience, imposed his grand concept on the historical facts: 'The *Cleopatra* I have in mind is the story of a remarkably brilliant, ruthless woman who nearly made herself Empress of the then-known world, utilising for her purpose the two strongest men in the world, both of whom failed her.' Of the 'Cleopatra options' mentioned earlier he wisely chose the second: superstar Taylor became the central character, taking on Rex Harrison (Caesar) and Richard Burton (Antony) in what should have been an epic confrontation of charisma. In the event, charisma partially backfired. At the time of release the real-life *affaire* of Burton and Taylor complicated their on-screen activities; viewed more recently, the film still carries lingering associations, and, judged purely on script and performance, the second part is flawed both by weak dialogue and by a lack of the electricity which exists between Harrison and Taylor in the opening half.

The script balances her two relationships well. Caesar is strong and in command, and it is only when a chink appears in the armour of his personality that Cleopatra is drawn to him emotionally: his advances as arrogant ruler are met with iciness ('I promise you will not enjoy me like this') and only when he shares the secret of his epilepsy ('One day it will happen where I cannot hide . . . The mob will laugh and tear me to pieces') does he arouse maternal feelings in her – expressed in a great bedtime speech in which she identifies herself with the fecund and life-giving Nile. Antony, on the other hand, is weaker and prone to envy of Caesar and bouts of self-pity: Cleopatra, in their meeting on the barge, confronts him with this character flaw (by wearing a necklace of coins struck with Caesar's head) and accepts him only when he has shaken himself free of the dead man's shade and merited her love by the strength of his own qualities (partly symbolised by his tearing of the gauze surrounding her bed). Antony's transition from weak to strong is temporary, however, and Alex North's intelligent score underlines Cleopatra's more durable strength: when the pair are reconciled in private after news of Antony's marriage of state, North combines the theme for Cleopatra's ambition with that for the couple's love.

In the eponymous role, Elizabeth Taylor is by turns magnificent and hopeless: her mid-Atlantic accent contrasts pointedly with that of the two Britons, and in sequences of either genuine or petulant regality she is as commanding an epic presence – with a figure to match – as Loren ('The

corridors are dark, gentlemen,' she warns Caesar's guard, 'but you mustn't be afraid – I am with you'). Unlike Loren, however, she is unable to make a satisfying transition to those scenes in which she relaxes her bearing to let genuine emotions come through, scenes which more and more dominate the second half with Burton and which lead to her final suicide. These at times become little more than a constant excuse for wardrobe changes, and it is not by chance that her best moments are with the highly disciplined Harrison, his authoritative yet very human modulation of the lines drawing the best from Taylor (always at her finest when challenged). Burton, a self-indulgent actor at the best of times, only encourages her latent tendency towards lax delivery, and Part 2 would have seemed much the flabbier without the saving grace of Roddy McDowall as Octavian – a splendidly ruthless and accurate performance, with a sure sense of the character's realisation of his own victorious destiny. It is the embodiment of Antony's description, 'It's quite possible, Octavian, that when you die, you will die without ever having been alive.' In any event, Elizabeth Taylor's is a performance of note, never less than charismatic, certainly benefiting from her rapport with Mankiewicz (who had earlier drawn a fine performance from her in *Suddenly, Last Summer*), and generally worthy of the huge responsibility placed on her by the production.

In *Cleopatra* production does dominate. The film is, first and foremost, simply magnificent to look at. No other historical picture – apart from *The Fall of the Roman Empire* – provides such a feast of costuming, art direction and production design. Colours are bold and evocative in the best tradition of Fox films of the time, the sumptuous tones of the Egyptian sets and clothes (based on gold) contrasting with the more sober Roman ones, both informed by an essential massiveness. Details are reasonably authentic yet still recognisably Hollywood in their amplification and adaptation; everything has an unreal, pristine quality which contributes to the film's epic feel. The overall design is the epic framework, its guiding language, from the great set-pieces of the harbour at Alexandria and senate-house entrance at Rome to the cool beauty of Cleopatra's palace and the dark glow of the royal tomb. Over this framework stretches Alex North's impressive musical score, an infinitely superior creation to his earlier work on *Spartacus*, with no

CRISIS AND CIVIL WAR 95

less than three closely interwoven themes for the Caesar/Cleopatra relationship and a quite distinct march-like tune for the latter's ambition which first appears discreetly in the carpet sequence, thunders forth during her entry into Rome, and appears garbed in exotic colours as her barge sails into Tarsus harbour.

North, by giving this melody a portentous, Roman quality, helps to unite the Roman and Egyptian ends of the story – and mirrors the script's careful construction. Mankiewicz fell on an ingenious solution to the problem of knitting his central trio together, choosing to make Cleopatra the epic figure and the plot spin around her desire for recognition of her son Caesarion. All roads thus run through her. Caesar is attracted first by the lure of cheap corn ('Roman greatness built upon Egyptian riches,' as Cleopatra says) but finally through his desire to have a son, since his wife Calpurnia is barren. Cleopatra is also a physical manifestation of Caesar's desire for autocracy over his own people, through her quite open demand that she be recognised as a queen:

> Caesar: The time has come, I think, for us to understand each other. Whatever else I may be in your opinion, first of all I am Caesar.
> Cleopatra: And *I* am Cleopatra, queen, daughter of Isis.
> Caesar: If I say so, and when I say so, you are what I say you are. Nothing more.
> Cleopatra: Hail, Caesar!

Antony, who first sees her during her entry (with child) into Rome, is attracted for further political reasons, for by supporting her claims for Caesarion he can foil the claims of his enemy Octavian (Caesar's adopted son and the future emperor Augustus) to being Caesar's official heir. And Cleopatra is drawn to Antony at the end of Part 1 (which prepares us for the *grand amour* of the second half) through her ambition to rule the Roman world through him.

Mankiewicz skilfully capitalises on unproven facts. The entry into Rome is a grand cinematic conceit, presumably inspired by the real-life Donations of Alexandria pageant celebrated with Antony over ten years later in 34 BC, which works in epic terms as a resolution of the kingship theme. It cannot be conclusively proven, either, that Cleopatra desired world domination (this was probably propaganda by Octavian) or that Caesar fathered Caesarion. Only the dialogue and the weakly scripted Antony/Cleopatra relationship let Mankiewicz's concept down. For the majority of the time the dialogue is literate, sensible, yet amazingly dull, with a static quality which rarely realises the epic potential of the characters and settings; at other times there are jarring injections of Shavian wit (Cleopatra to Caesar in bed: 'I've been reading in your *Commentaries* about your campaigns in Gaul'; or, Antony: 'Fabulous feast!' Cleopatra: 'One is always so limited when one travels by ship'). Otherwise, however, *Cleopatra* stands as a remarkably bold, and frequently successful, attempt to hew epic form from one of history's most thankless characters.

For the rest, film-makers have relied on Shakespeare for their inspiration. Despite the playwright's essentially non-epic approach to his characters, there is an underlying romanticism in his works which chimes well with epic form. Shakespeare's main (perhaps only) source for events in *Julius Caesar* and *Antony and Cleopatra* was the collection of *Parallel Lives* (*Bioi paralleloi*) by the late first-century AD philosopher Plutarch, a Greek writing several centuries after some of the events he describes. Plutarch is more a moralist than a factual historian, drawing elaborate parallels between his pairs of Greek and Roman personalities, and concerned with bringing out the moral characters of each through his achievements. Shakespeare inherits some of this approach but his slant is often different. Regarding Antony and Cleopatra, Plutarch sees the love affair as the infatuation of a great soldier, while Shakespeare sees it as embodying the double pull in life between sexual and political ambition. The cinema, however, can work epic form from any source, and for their versions of *Antony and Cleopatra* and *Julius Caesar* director Charlton Heston and Mankiewicz came up with very different results.

For *Antony and Cleopatra* (1972), Heston took the popular line that 'Shakespeare was a born screenwriter. The stage he wrote for was far more fluid than any we know, but only film can provide the total freedom he yearned for. He is our greatest asset, and the best service I can offer him, both as director and actor, is simply to provide him with a camera before which his magnificent work can flourish.' But Heston did more than that: he reworked the play with intelligence and respect in

55 Brooding histrionics: Caesar (Warren William) in *Cleopatra* (1934)

56 (*right*) Genuine regality: Cleopatra (Elizabeth Taylor), with maids Charmian (Isabelle Cooley) and Eiras (Francesca Annis) in *Cleopatra* (1963)

57 (*below*) A strumpet's fool: Antony (Charlton Heston) and Cleopatra (Hildegard Neil) in *Antony and Cleopatra*

order to meet the demands of cinematic epic form. The opening credit-title sequence at once announces great things to come: a boat sweeps into Alexandria harbour carrying Proculeius with urgent news, and over a suitably Oriental-sounding ostinato the long-breathed main melody of John Scott's score steals in on lower strings – a wide-ranging tune in A minor, full of resonant fourths and sixths, which dies away, passion spent, in a reluctant downward tumble of thirds. This is music of great calibre, one of the seminal film scores of the seventies, from an unexpected source. In succeeding scenes Scott continues to back up Heston's conception with music which characterises the enervation behind the more epic qualities of the love affair: the couple's first appearance, with Antony half-naked in beads and earrings and Cleopatra tousled but vampiric, is suffused with a strange post-coital languor which marks them as doomed lovers, an acute cinematic translation of Philo's opening speech in Shakespeare's original:

Take but good note, and you shall see in him
The triple pillar of the world transformed
Into a strumpet's fool; behold and see.

(1, 1, 11)

Examples of Heston's acute grasp of the form are legion. He is afraid neither to transpose passages of the original nor to change settings, if it adds to the overall design. Pompey, in his opening scene, is identified with the sea and consistently (and unhistorically) made a figure of fun, unshaven, generally drunk, and prone to all of actor Freddie Jones' customary eccentricities. This works, however, in the epic design, for Pompey is essentially a marginal figure in the power-game being waged over the dying Roman Republic, a great man now in decline (and a potent warning to Antony). The Act II Scene 2 meeting of the Antony/Octavian/Lepidus triumvirate is transposed to a small gladiatorial arena, in which the privately arranged combat below provides a visual metaphor for the verbal cut-and-thrust above, nicely driven home by the shock effect as a contestant's arm is pinned to the arena floor by a trident. Such effects are spread throughout the film (a severed arm in the Actium battle which ends Part 1; Enobarbus' suicide off a cliff; Antony and his horse rolling in slow-motion down a slope as he escapes from the final battle) and remind us that this is not just a literary filmicisation. Despite budget limitations (smoke and swift editing, plus some footage from Ben-Hur, used in the sea battle) Heston gives the film a sumptuous look, with solid and colourful sets by Maurice Pelling and photography of much brilliance and clarity by Rafael Pacheco.

Yet it is Heston's awareness of how to transform his material into epic cinema which impresses at every turn. There is a magical feel to Antony's last hours as he and Eros escape by boat at night ('... the long day's task is done, And we must sleep'), climaxing in the appearance of the soothsayer as Antony undergoes a suitably slow and agonising suicide; the use of the soothsayer as a Wagnerian Erda-figure who appears at crucial moments (an example of Heston's compression of characters to tighten the film's focus); and finest of all, the sequence in which Antony, overhearing Enobarbus' eulogy on Cleopatra,

Age cannot wither her, nor custom stale
Her infinite variety; other women cloy
The appetites they feed, but she makes hungry
Where most she satisfies;

hurls down a cup and sails into the arms of his lover in Egypt, leaving Octavia sitting alone in her chaste bedroom. Over the breathless images, John Scott's music reprises in full orchestral and choral dress the film's main melody, and the effect is both powerful and tragic.

Heston, who carries epic resonances over from his earlier films, surrounds himself with a gallery of renowned English actors. John Castle is a splendidly ambitious Octavian (compare Roddy McDowall in Cleopatra); Eric Porter a solid Enobarbus. It is, then, a pity that Hildegard Neil's shortcomings as Cleopatra should be such that the couple's passion hardly equals, in epic scope, the political aspect of the story. Radiantly beautiful yet over-cool and clumsy in her delivery, she possesses insufficient charisma to match Heston's, and thus the film turns more on Antony alone than on the two of them together. The death scene of Jane Lapotaire's Charmian completely eclipses Neil's, and Heston's final efforts find no fitting complement. Antony and Cleopatra remains a remarkable achievement, nonetheless – a genuine epic creation.

Heston had played the same role two years earlier in Stuart Burge's Julius Caesar (1970), also produced by the young Canadian Peter Snell, but far more literary in conception. Heston is known to have had a strong hand in its making, but this was far from the total control he exercised over *Antony and Cleopatra*. The mixed cast of English and American players chimes ill, and a half-hearted attempt to forge some sort of parallel between the assassinations of Caesar and John F. Kennedy further obscures the drama. *Julius Caesar* is well-mounted, though never far from just filmed theatre, and it is fatally flawed by a dithering, inept performance by Jason Robards as Brutus – in any production of *Julius Caesar* the pivotal character. Burge's earlier directorial credits included the Laurence Olivier *Othello* (1966), and in considerations of epic form his film has little to offer except a gallery of well-drawn individuals, John Gielgud's Caesar and Richard Johnson's Cassius in particular, with Heston performing on a entirely separate plane. More integrated is David Bradley's renowned 16mm amateur production, *Julius Caesar* (1949), starring an over-young but forceful Charlton Heston in his first screen portrayal of Antony, with Bradley himself as a noble yet unself-confident Brutus. The director had earlier worked with Heston on *Peer Gynt* (1941) while both were still at high school, and he at least imparts a conscious visual drama to his subject: an opening featuring a track-in to the soothsayer's face as he exclaims, 'The Ides have come!' and plentiful use of low-angle shots to give his characters stature and added resonance. The script, however, departs little from the original, so the achievement remains heightened Shakespeare (despite accurate settings like Chicago's Senate building) rather than any epic transformation.

For such a transformation within a theatrical/literary approach (i.e. unlike Heston's *Antony and Cleopatra*), one must turn to Joseph L. Mankiewicz's 1953 *Julius Caesar*. This is an uneven work, yet it manages to conjure up considerable epic atmosphere whilst always seeming to remain a filmed play. The dramatically clean-lined monochrome photography, and the by turns naturalistic (street-traders at the beginning; running drains in the night meeting of Casca and Cassius) and stylised (the Capitol) sets – most of which, like the costumes, came from M-G-M's earlier *Quo vadis* – give the film an ambivalent feel, strengthened by the fact that the whole work is studio-filmed apart from a shot of a sentry at Brutus' camp and a

subsequent attack in a narrow defile. This neither wholly stylised nor wholly naturalistic approach does not work to the film's advantage (nor do such bloomers as Brutus holding a book a couple of centuries before they were introduced in Rome), and it is finally left to the acting and music to make the work cohere.

A fake quote from Plutarch opens the picture after credits over a 'Roman' eagle:

> Upon Caesar's return to Rome, after defeating Pompey in the Civil War, his countrymen chose him a fourth time consul and then dictator for life. Thus he became odious to moderate men through the extravagance of the titles and powers that were heaped upon him.

A suitably portentous introduction, yet Miklós Rózsa's title music, featuring Caesar's stern yet doomed theme (based on the incomplete-sounding chord of the seventh) only as punctuation to Brutus' sad, brooding melody (also based on a chord of the seventh, but with the minor third now diminished), has already warned us that the latter is to be the major focus of the drama. After Caesar's death Mark Antony musically assumes his theme, and for the final section Rózsa pits the Brutus and Antony themes against one another, the former having the last tragic word. Antony's theme is transformed into a *Marcia Romana* on brass, woodwind and percussion, Brutus' on strings alone. The score here is in two parts, and for the original stereo soundtrack the halves were recorded separately, with the Antony march placed in the right-hand channel and Brutus' music coming from the centre and left-hand channels – a perfectly integrated musical/visual conception, as Antony's army approaches and overwhelms his adversary. The music in *Julius Caesar*, which Rózsa, feeling he was being typecast at that time with period pictures, only wrote under protest, is infrequent but developed with great insight; the assassination scene and the subsequent two great orations are left mute.

On the acting side, James Mason and John Gielgud are fully able to bear the dramatic burden. The film's emotional strength lies in the development of the relationship between Brutus and Cassius, fired by the polarisation of interests after Caesar's murder –

58 (*opposite above*) Lend me your ears: Antony (Charlton Heston) in
Julius Caesar (1970) . . .

59 (*opposite below*) . . . and Antony (Marlon Brando) in *Julius
Caesar* (1953)

60 (*below*) Noble and epic: Brutus (James Mason) and Portia (Deborah Kerr)
in *Julius Caesar* (1953)

The conspirators having fled, there came to
Rome the young Octavius whom Caesar had
adopted as his son. So did he and Antony
divide the power between themselves and pre-
pare to make war against Brutus and Cassius
for the empire of the Romans

(caption following the riot after
Antony's oration)

– and transfigured by their double suicide. Mason's
delivery of the lines on seeing Cassius' body ('O
Julius Caesar! thou art mighty yet! / Thy spirit
walks abroad, and turns our swords / In our own
proper entrails') and his own death-scene are both
magisterial, giving the character a full realisation
of his own historical significance. Other players –

ignoring a variable Caesar and a dreadfully histrionic Calpurnia – never quite attain this level.
Marlon Brando, who makes Antony (then almost
forty) seem little more than a beardless youth,
presumably to help strengthen the Caesar/Antony
father/son relationship (reinforced by Rózsa's
music), makes wondrously free with Shakespeare's
verse rhythms. He shares a fine scene with
Mason's Brutus as he carries out Caesar's body
midway through the latter's speech, and brings
much guile to Antony's famous funeral oration, but
otherwise acts in a Method vacuum. *Julius Caesar*
is without doubt James Mason's film: forty years
after Enrico Guazzoni's hero sought a showy
suicide on the screen, the cinema finally found a
noble and epic Brutus.

Imperial Rome: Slaves and Barbarians

For slaves a household provides a sort of mini-constitution with its own form of citizenship. But, although I find relief in such solace, I feel crushed and broken by that very compassion which led me to allow my slaves privileges. Yet that does not mean I would want to become more unfeeling. I am well aware that others regard the death of a slave as no more than a business loss – and think themselves great and wise human beings for doing so. Whether they are great and wise, I don't know; they are certainly not human beings. A human being should be moved by grief, have feelings, resist yet admit to solace – not deny it.

> letter from Pliny the Younger to a friend
> (c. AD 108)

'There's more slaves in Rome than Romans.'

> senator in *Spartacus* (1960)

'We have reached the point where there are more slaves in Rome than citizens.'

> Gallio in *The Robe* (1953)

The other secular Imperial works are few but highly significant, figureheaded by a remarkable pair of Romanian films, plus Anthony Mann's *The Fall of the Roman Empire* (1964) and Stanley Kubrick's *Spartacus* (1960). Around these giants scurry a group of peplum works which fight over droppings from the thematic table, chiefly divisible into the 'revolting gladiator' category and the 'Roman vs Roman' school, both treated on a monumental scale in the Kubrick and Mann pictures.

Vittorio Cottafavi's *The Warrior and the Slave Girl* (*La rivolta dei gladiatori*, 1958), Giuseppe Vari's *Revenge of the Barbarians* (*La vendetta dei barbari*, 1961), Mario Caiano's *Fight or Die/The Two Gladiators* (*I due gladiatori*, 1965), Alfonso Brescia's *La rivolta dei pretoriani* (1964), Michele

Lupo's linked *Seven Slaves against Rome* (*Gli schiavi più forti del mondo*, 1964) and *Sette contro tutti* (1966), plus Piero Pierotti's *Hercules against Rome* (*Ercole contro Roma*, 1965), all show Roman fighting corrupt Roman (generally a provincial governor or leader of the Praetorian Guard), with help from slaves or gladiators. Connoisseurs of female gladiators are well catered for by Steve Carver's *The Arena* (1973), an American-produced romp shot at Cinecittà with Italian personnel. The *gladiatrix* did not actually appear on the scene until the first century AD, but *The Arena*, set quite soon after the Spartacus revolt (73–71 BC), is excused this trifling inaccuracy: spirited playing, realistic touches like the *lanista* in search of a gimmick, highly authentic sets, and a very fine score by Francesco De Masi more than compensate. Both Pam Grier (as the Nubian slave Mamawi) and Margaret Markov (as the Briton Bodicia) bestride the screen with a gutsy sexuality, and promising Corman alumnus Steve Carver directs the formulary escape-to-freedom story with considerable panache.

All the above works are simple expressions of honesty and freedom, with the social undertow of salvation lying in solidarity with one's *déclassé* brothers. Though often set in late Imperial times, in remote provinces, and with minimal attention to history, the films preserve their message; indeed, the vagueness in historical detail can even enhance any allegorical pretensions (Pierotti's film even introduces a mythic and muscular Hercules-figure). Yet, as so often in the peplum cycle, tatty production makes many a film interesting only thematically.

Already, however, after leaving the Civil War works and the Italian offerings just mentioned, one can already start to feel the pull towards the more conventional theme of blighted Christianity. Even in *The Fall of the Roman Empire* the altruistic figure of Timonides (James Mason) is made a

103

Christian (and, to complete the minority syndrome, a Greek and former slave also), and there is a brief, but resonant moment when Lucilla (Sophia Loren) fingers his *chi-rho* over his dead body. Spartacus, a freedom-fighter open to any number of interpretations, is construed in Stanley Kubrick's film as a Moses-figure, with strong overtones of twentieth-century Zionism. Of the monumental works in an Imperial setting, only a pair of films shot in Romania during the late sixties can be classified as completely non-Christian.

The large-scale historical spectaculars produced by the film industries of Eastern Europe (notably Poland and Romania) and the USSR show the closest possible parallels to the epic literary tradition – one of whose purposes is to kindle national identity by drawing lessons from the past. Sergiu Nicolaescu's *The Dacians/The Warriors (Dacii,* 1967) and Mircea Drăgan's *The Column (Columnă,* 1968) are overtly designed to propagandise Romanian valour in the face of foreign interference (as much a warning to Moscow as to Washington, one would have thought, especially since both pictures were co-productions with Western Europe), by detailing the victories and subsequent courage in defeat of the Dacians (Romania's topographical forebears) against invading Romans between AD 86 and 106. This Roman push beyond the Danube spanned the reigns of three emperors (Domitian, Nerva and Trajan) and excited writers' imaginations at the time. Soon after the end of the Second Dacian War in 106 we find Pliny the Younger writing to his friend the poet Caninius Rufus:

> What an excellent idea to write about the Dacian War. What other subject-matter is so fresh, so rich, so elevated; what, in short, is so poetic and (though hard fact) so fabulous? You will picture new rivers let loose at the land, new bridges flung over rivers, mountain gorges occupied by camps, and a brave king driven first from his palace then from life itself; and, in addition, a double triumph – one the first over an invincible people, the other the last.
>
> (8, 4, 1f.)

Rufus's work, if it was ever written, has not survived, but something of the spirit described by Pliny (so typically Roman in its concentration on the practical, military aspects of the campaign)

survives in the Romanian films. Both have scripts by the novelist and scriptwriter Titus Popovici, and the few fictional additions are dramatically justified; since hardly anything remains of the Dacian civilisation, the costumiers and set designers have tried for a simple stylisation of old peasant clothes found near the Haţeg mountains in Romania.

The story of *The Dacians* works in two massive blocks which finally confront one another near the end: on the one hand, the Roman troops massed on the southern bank of the Danube, awaiting the order to cross into unknown territory (and one of the generals, Severus, having discovered that his father was by birth a Dacian chieftain); on the other, the court life of the Dacian king Decebal and the sylvan wanderings of his soon-to-be parted son and daughter, Cotyso and Meda. The Dacians are given darker, more reserved colours, in contrast to the Romans' glittering whites and silvers and flaming red cloaks; and there is a massiveness not only in the set-piece battles (the siege of the fortress of Argidava) but in the overall design (the Cyclopean architecture of Decebal's palace, the mountain-top sacrifice of Cotyso). The eventual military confrontation of Roman and Dacian troops, of Severus and Decebal, is the dramatic framework, and the filling is imbued with mythic elements: the passing of an uncomplicated way of life (expressed by the forest horse-rides of Cotyso and Meda), Cotyso's initiation into adulthood and the ranks of the warriors, his self-sacrifice to Zamolxes the god of war, the divided patriotism of the half-Dacian general Severus, and the symbolic margin of the Danube which divides the two civilisations.

Amazingly, *The Dacians* was Nicolaescu's first feature, and he had to set up his country's first team of stuntmen to handle the action sequences. He has since become one of Romania's premier directors, and was to work even more assuredly with writer Popovici on the epic *The Last Crusade/ Michael the Brave (Mihai viteazul, 1970),* but *The Dacians* evinces a natural grasp of epic form. The sequel, *The Column* (the title of which refers to the Column of Trajan, during whose reign the first serious inroads into Dacia were successfully made), was entrusted to the more experienced Mircea Drăgan, the cast this time being Anglo-Italo-Germano-Romanian instead of Franco-Romanian. In scale, design and scripting, the picture is equally impressive, with more time given to exploring the mechanics of the Dacians' 'national unity'.

The egalitarianism of the Romanian films, expressing the Roman/barbarian struggle in necessarily atheistic terms and finding Communist propaganda in a monarchical age, is very different from that of Anthony Mann's *The Fall of the Roman Empire* (1964), which also opens on the Danube frontier but confines its debate chiefly to Roman circles. Mann's film is the finest product of the secular school. Its relative box-office failure also signalled the imminent fall of the empire of producer Samuel Bronston, an acute and generous businessman whose belief in quality spectaculars led to the engagement of the finest talents for each of his enterprises. Anthony Mann (who had directed Bronston's earlier *El Cid* so successfully) and his various collaborators have set on record their intention not to make just another epic in which Christianity was shown as the sole exponent of the social message of racial harmony and freedom from persecution but, instead, to examine Roman thought at its most civilised peak, at a time when the Empire was a still manageable instrument for the dissemination of ideas, rather than dwelling solely on its violent, oppressive and supposedly antipathetic qualities. By thus making Rome the 'hero' rather than the traditional 'villain' – and in a Christian rather than a pre-Christian age – Mann and Bronston were breaking new ground.

Spectacle, always geared to show Rome in the guise of imperialistic oppressor, was consequently to play a different role: this was to be a discussion on power and corruption swathed in traditional epic clothes. By basing the title on Edward Gibbon's six-volume *The History of the Decline and Fall of the Roman Empire*, the film-makers found a suitable soulmate: Gibbon also placed little importance on Christianity, preferring a broader view of the reasons for the collapse of the Empire, and he too was apt to let strict chronology fall victim to his overall plan. Any expectations aroused by the swaggering title of Mann's film are thus rarely gratified and, even had the makers wished for merely a blood-and-thunder period piece, the facts of the 'collapse' of the Roman Empire would never have provided them with subject-matter. The film's impressive prologue-narration, written by historian Will Durant, gets its facts right about the time-span but obfuscates a perfectly clear question: 'Two

of the greatest problems in history are how to account for her rise and how to account for her fall. The process was spread over three hundred years.' The effect, however, is what counts. Gibbon himself started his *Decline and Fall* with the death of Marcus Aurelius Antoninus (AD 121–180), and the film does likewise. The juxtaposition of a humane, cultured and philosophical emperor with a young, irresponsible and dissolute one (his successor Commodus, who ruled 180–192) provides a ready-made – and historically accurate – metaphor for the film's design.

The Fall of the Roman Empire makes quite clear that it does not lay claim to any great exactitude, though while fashioning epic form from the stuff of history it manages to avoid any anachronisms or unconscious blunders. The majority of the divergencies are founded sensibly on the invent-and-destroy principle. There is no hard proof that Aurelius was *not* poisoned – he died of an infection contracted in Vindobona (Vienna), or perhaps Sirmium (in present-day Yugoslavia) – and the means chosen for the film (a knife with poison on one side of the blade which cuts an apple for him in full view of everyone) ensures that the crime is undetectable. There is also no hard proof that Aurelius did not nominate on his death-bed someone other than Commodus to succeed him, and in the event Livius tacitly refuses the honour. History thus remains undisturbed. Only Commodus's filmic death jars a little (he was, in fact, quietly strangled on the orders of his mistress by a young wrestler while drunk in bed), but the sequence is fine cinema, is in tune with the real character's liking for bravado and display, and in epic terms resolves the long-simmering Livius/Commodus conflict in suitably public language. Likewise, Cleander, Aurelius' assassin, was certainly not blind, but his infirmity is put to good dramatic use (the real Cleander later rose to great power under Commodus but was publicly decapitated in 189). Above all, since *The Fall of the Roman Empire* is, of all epics, the least concerned with plot or specific events, such licence is understandable.

Character stereotypes loom large throughout the picture, and the scriptwriters have sought their own solutions for each person's make-up. The change in Commodus (only nineteen when he ascended the throne) from libertine to cruel despot is hard to account for in concrete terms. Gibbon focused on the muffed assassination attempt of 183

61 (*opposite above*)
Revolting gladiators:
Vittorio Cottafavi's *The
Warrior and the Slave Girl*

62 (*opposite below*)
Gutsy sexuality: Deirdre
(Lucretia Love), Bodicia
(Margaret Markov),
Mamawi (Pam Grier)
and Livia (Marie Louise)
in *The Arena*

63 (*right*) National
unity: Andrada
(Antonella Lualdi) and
Gerula (Ilarion
Ciobanu) in *The Column*

64 (*below*) *Pax Romana*:
Timonides (James
Mason) and Livius
(Stephen Boyd) in *The
Fall of the Roman
Empire*

to explain the transformation; the film, following the line that the son of a 'good' emperor cannot be all bad, introduces a *deus ex machina* to account for both Aurelius' dislike of his son while still alive and Commodus' own divergent personality – he was, we are told, a bastard, his real father being his gladiatorial tutor Verules (Anthony Quayle). Again, history remains mute and undisturbed over this effective device which adds instant motivation to several characters.

The film is structured in two huge, paragraph-like sections. Part 1 starts with a lengthy introduction set in the bleak Danube frontier army camp where Aurelius (Alec Guinness) is wasting away his time, and ends with a brief respite in sunny Rome as Commodus returns to the capital in triumph. Part 2, for which we have already been prepared, is set almost entirely in Rome – some years having elapsed in the meantime – and proceeds to develop the subjects raised in the earlier exposition. The structure is simple. Aurelius, the Stoic philosopher-ruler, explains his concept of the *pax Romana* to an assembly of governors and chieftains from all over the Empire; Commodus, in Part 2, does his best to destroy it.

The theme of racial unity is thus wrapped in Roman rather than Christian clothes. Aurelius speaks of the 'unity that is Rome', adding the despairing aside 'May the gods hasten the day.' The speech is an expansion of an earlier scene in which Lucilla prays before an altar of Vesta for her father's health and for peace in the Empire, and is developed in more pragmatic terms by Aurelius' war against the Germanic tribes. The scene in which Timonides (James Mason), the humanitarian Greek, enters the cavernous cell of the German captives in an attempt to make them relinquish their god of war for the *pax Romana* concept of united peace is the first testing-point of the film's main theme. Timonides assumes Aurelius' role in Part 2, championing resettlement as a tool towards understanding and taking part in the long Senate debate which is the moral core of the film. The three themes of equality, freedom and peace (argued *pro* by Timonides and Caecina, and *contra* by Julianus) are discussed at elaborate length, in one of the most thoughtful sequences ever placed on 70mm. The argument of Caecina (Finlay Currie) cleverly unites the trio of themes with the film's other interest in the effects of power: an empire begins to die when people no longer believe

in it, he says, comparing the golden days under Trajan, Hadrian, Antoninus Pius and Aurelius with the present Commodus regime.

This message is very different from the positive, reconstructivist tone of the fifties epics; already the atmosphere of the sixties, with its obsession with the generation gap and the questioning voice of youth, has begun to make its mark on the historical film. The important issue is raised of how far imperialism (to the young sixties filmgoer synonymous with paternalism) conflicts with personal liberties – earlier mused on by Aurelius as he lies dying ('Is it not in the nature of the fig-tree to give figs, as for the honey-bee to give honey?'). And in all these discussions runs a recognisable thread of impending doom: the seeds of decay are *within* the Empire, perhaps within the Roman system. Aurelius, for all his philosophy, upheld specifically Roman virtues in the guise of Stoicism; his reign saw the most serious persecution of the Christians during the second century, and (as the film shows) decimation was still employed as a military punishment for disobedience or cowardice. As Caecina observes, 'We have changed the world. Can we not change ourselves?'

The Fall of the Roman Empire was a trail-blazer in several ways, but it was also one of the last of its kind. Specifically, it could only have been made when it was, since it presumes an extensive knowledge on the part of its audience of the conventions of the genre. It is this which makes the film a connoisseur's piece, since it consciously pares down the requirements of the historical epic to the bare essentials. The start is quiet and mysterious, Brucknerian in its pregnant calm – the hour before dawn, Bergman's 'Hour of the Wolf'. Spectacle is kept firmly at bay until the magnificent scene of the assembling governors and princes, and it is over an hour before the film opens up with the familiar sight of temples and thronging extras in the *forum Romanum*. Even that splendid set, in true Mann style, is introduced casually, almost incidentally at the end of a wide panning shot, and it is not used again in full until the finale.

The first seventy-five minutes are visually bleak but have a restrained power and beauty thanks to Veniero Colasanti and John Moore's solid designs. The requisite battle is handled in fitting style: set in a claustrophobic German forest rather than a spectacular sun-baked plain (that is held back until Part 2) as Commodus and his men ride through the still and eerie trees, the atmosphere underlined by Tiomkin's music of bird-like woodwind over a threatening bass. The requisite chariot-race likewise feeds off the clichés of the epic (as in *Ben-Hur* it is a metaphor for male antagonism) but is almost off-hand in its dramatic effects. A fallen tree parallels the crashed chariot in the Wyler film, and a log fence on a bridge stands in for the circus *spina* in *Ben-Hur*; the three-minute race has no accompanying music (until the end) and in the film's 70mm version makes thrilling use of stereo sound.

Fall also shares with *Ben-Hur* the theme of male friendship split by broader issues. The meeting of Commodus and Livius, and their subsequent carousing with wine-skins, recalls the other film's 'Down Eros, Up Mars!' sequence. The rupture in *Fall* is caused not by one character's Judaism but by Livius' news that *he* is to be Aurelius' successor and not Commodus – a Roman power conflict rather than one of opposing faiths. Feminine interest is pared down to essentials, concentrated in the epic presence of Sophia Loren's Lucilla. Male rivalry is confined to career and ambition rather than the promise of her hand. This is perfectly consistent with epic form: Livius is Lucilla's clear partner from the very beginning (an arranged marriage of state constituting no real challenge), and the script – as in *El Cid*, *Ben-Hur*, *Spartacus* – capitalises on their separation and eventual reunion. The latter, like Rodrigo and Chimene's in *El Cid*, takes place in a circular room, accompanied by a stunning overhead shot of Lucilla lounging in a flimsy pink outfit. The scene, typically, is understated (as is Lucilla's final rescue from the pyre); its failure to exert a really strong emotional pull is because the script, in seeking to refine epic conventions, sends romance to the wall.

From here on the pull towards Christianity becomes ever more insistent, the conflict being at its most complex in Stanley Kubrick's *Spartacus* (1960). The story of *Spartacus* is in fact set in the Republic, but in theme, ambition and outlook it belongs very much to the Imperial collection. The historical facts are as follows. In 73 BC some fifty or so gladiators escaped from a training school at Capua; mostly composed of Gauls and Thracians – and with three leaders, Spartacus, Crixus and Oenomaus – their numbers were soon swollen by other runaway slaves, and they successfully re-

pulsed almost all the forces the Romans were able to throw at them. After trying to push north back to their homelands, the various groups became trapped in the toe of Italy around Rhegium, and soon after breaking out, Spartacus (the only surviving leader) and his men were defeated by Marcus Licinius Crassus in 71, with Pompey wiping out the remaining slaves. Spartacus was killed on the field of battle; his surviving supporters were crucified along the Via Appia. The rebellion, which had shaken Rome for two years, was not the first of its kind – there had been the Great Slave War in Sicily from 134 to 131, and a second uprising there c. 104–100, plus many smaller affairs elsewhere – but it was the biggest and the last. Its moral and sociological lessons are obvious, and in the present century Spartacus has been canonised by Marxist ideology: a fine example of political mythologisation is Yuri Grigorovich's Bolshoi ballet *Spartacus* (*Spartak*) (filmed effectively but with little extra inspiration by him and Vadim Derbenyov in 1975), which extracts the figures of Spartacus and Crassus, twins them with female counterparts, and, working with only the merest glance at history, polarises the story into a simple conflict of tyranny and revolt, the whole stirringly set to a score of true epic breadth by Aram Khachaturyan.

The ballet was first produced in Leningrad by the Kirov Ballet in 1956; five years earlier the American novelist Howard Fast finished his novel *Spartacus*, a brave and polemical novelisation of history written when his country's anti-Communist witch-hunt was at its height. Fast gives the novel an epic preface: 'It is a story of brave men and women who lived long ago, and whose names have never been forgotten. The heroes of this story cherished freedom and human dignity, and lived nobly and well. I wrote it so that those who read it ... may take strength for our own troubled future and that they may struggle against oppression and wrong – so that the dream of Spartacus may come to be in our own time.' But the novel's structure hardly lives up to its fanfare; its focus is too diffuse, its flashback structure clumsy, the dialogue veering wildly between colloquialisms and rodomontade with epic pretensions. Only occasionally, as in Varinia's speech to Crassus near the end, does one catch a glimpse of the book that might have been, rather than the misty meditation on freedom that resulted.

When in the late fifties Kirk Douglas, through his company Bryna Productions, decided to film Fast's novel with the help of Universal Pictures, an extra gloss was added to the story. Douglas, riding high on the success of *The Vikings* (also a Bryna production), saw *Spartacus* as an opportunity to make a large-scale Zionist statement – Otto Preminger's *Exodus* (1960) also dates from this period – and reinterpreted the slave-rebel's story as a Roman variation on the let-my-people-go theme. What to Fast was a parable on equality became to Douglas one with specific Zionist leanings, with Spartacus a Moses-figure attempting to lead his brothers and sisters out of a repressive Italy (with Crassus its Pharaoh) to an unspecified Promised Land. It is a perfect example of epic transformation of material to suit contemporary taste, and Douglas should take full credit. Equally brave was his choice of Dalton Trumbo to write the screenplay (his first screen credit, along with *Exodus*, since being blacklisted in 1947), although Douglas' guiding hand is clear throughout. Universal wanted Anthony Mann to direct, but after a few days' work (it is thought on the scenes of Crassus' arrival at the training school) Douglas persuaded Universal to replace him with the young Stanley Kubrick, with whom the actor had worked successfully on *Paths of Glory* (1957).

Spartacus' production history makes it difficult to decide whom to ascribe the film to. Trumbo is the official scriptwriter but clearly had trouble meeting Douglas' brief (the script ran to seven versions); Kubrick is the official director but his every decision was subject to Douglas' ratification. Nevertheless, the picture should be ascribed to Kubrick: when he arrived the script was finished and the cast chosen, but he was still able to effect certain changes. The first meeting in the cell between Spartacus and Varinia originally had full dialogue, but Kubrick insisted on shooting it more visually, to greater mythic effect. And in its visceral reality and ultimate pessimism, *Spartacus*, by coincidence or not, fits effortlessly into Kubrick's *œuvre*.

Spartacus is, first of all, an extremely tough film. From the very first, starting with the opening titles showing clenched fists, hands and Roman faces, which finally crack before our eyes, and Alex North's unyielding music, heavy on brass and woodwind (even when the love theme finally appears in the cell scene it is handled not by the strings but by the reedy oboe and cor anglais), it is an aggressive and pessimistic picture. The opening narration ('In the last century before [Christ], the Roman republic stood at the very centre of the civilised world . . .') immediately sets up the slavery/freedom polarity, and for about fifty minutes the film simmers until the revolt – which is shown to be spontaneous, arising from an insult to Spartacus – bursts forth with an exhilarating and cathartic energy.

From here on the film divides, and much of the dramatic motion comes from observing groups on both sides who are bound by the events of history but never meet. Crassus' desire to see Spartacus in the flesh, a desire which grows to an obsession and extends logically to wanting to possess him by proxy through Varinia, is one of the strongest dramatic threads. The screenplay here makes a small but vital change to the original novel: it is for Crassus that Spartacus is ordered to fight at the gladiatorial school, rather than the insignificant Bracus; thus, later, when Crassus seizes on the *lanista* Batiatus to identify the slave's body, Batiatus can say, 'But you saw him . . . In the ring . . .' It is but one example of the way in which the film tightens and sharpens the novel, imposes dramatic shape, and thus quarries epic form from lacklustre material. The most major change, apart from the rejection of the flashback structure, is the addition of details of everyday life and training at the gladiatorial school (emphasising the life/death no-man's-land of a gladiator) and comradeship amongst the gladiators (essential for the later scenes stressing universal brotherhood).

However, although the major part of the film's moral message resides in the slaves' story, most of the film's political debate is found among the Roman characters. *Spartacus*, despite its title, is as much a study of Crassus as it is of the eponymous hero and, like Homer's *Iliad* with Achilles and Hector, has a dual epic focus. With such a towering performance of restrained power as Laurence Olivier gives, Crassus soon begins to dominate the film: where Douglas, as Spartacus, is like a perpetually coiled spring, asserting a continual physical presence, Olivier is watchful and assured, a human embodiment of patrician right to power. It is a fine contrast, impeccably cast, but Crassus emerges as the more complex and fascinating character: 'One day I shall cleanse this Rome which my fathers bequeathed me,' and later, in response to a statement that 'Rome is the mob,' 'No, Rome is an eternal thought in the mind of God' – words which combine a Brutus-like respect for traditional Republican virtues with a naked and total thirst for patrician power.

This is some way from the historical Crassus, who, though a patrician and having suffered for it during Marius' reign of terror, had become wealthy by unscrupulous profiteering under the counter-reign of the dictator Sulla, hardly a Republican paragon. Otherwise, however, the cinematic and historical Crassuses tally well: the film shows guarded friendship with the young and ambitious Julius Caesar (though no mention of Pompey again – surely the most neglected Roman figure in the cinema), and a desire for military honour to match his political and financial powers.

To Crassus, Spartacus is first an annoyance, then a threat, and finally an unattainable myth. ('I'm not after glory,' he says before the final battle. 'I'm after Spartacus. And I mean to have him.') In the final reels the pull towards their 'reunion' is very strong, the more so for having obtained a complex sexual gloss. The most direct expression of this is Crassus' desire to possess Varinia, 'Spartacus' woman', if he cannot have the man himself, and the final scene between these two, with superlative understated playing from Jean Simmons to match Olivier's, shows Crassus starting to crumble before Varinia's unbreachable faith. Crassus' sexuality had earlier been shown to be inextricably combined with his lust for power: for the film he is made bisexual, and after trying to seduce the Greek slave Antoninus rails at him in a speech in which Crassus and Rome, lover and victim, become interchangeable, telling Antoninus that he must abase himself, grovel, and love her (Rome) – 'No man can withstand Rome. No nation. How much less . . . a boy?' When Antoninus flees to join Spartacus and is discovered with him by Crassus at the end, Crassus has thus been doubly emasculated by Spartacus – rejected by both Varinia and Antoninus for a slave-leader. When the pair come face to face ('Spartacus. You are he, aren't you?'), Crassus' behaviour is as much that of a cuckolded lover as a frustrated general, his scream a terrifying expression of inadequacy.

Antoninus is an invention for the film, weak on anything other than a symbolic level thanks to Tony Curtis' acting. The oblique seduction scene prior to Crassus' speech was cut by Universal from all prints before general release (in Britain between press previews and the first public opening), under an 'agreement' with the American League of Decency. The British censor had already passed the full version but UK prints had to accord with those in the United States; Crassus, who now appears suddenly fully dressed, seems to enter into his tirade for little reason. Other deletions, which totalled some twelve minutes, included 'excessively violent' passages from the final battle, and a scene in which Gracchus and Caesar stroll through the back alleys of Rome, the former explaining the realities of Roman political life to the younger man. Both that and the Antoninus deletion severely weaken the film's political content.

The other Romans are mere adjuncts of Crassus, as the slaves are of Spartacus; the two characters are the film's dual pivot, and thus it stays. Peter Ustinov's portrait of the venal Batiatus is more than simply light relief: Batiatus is an example of the *nouveau riche* class of *lanista* (the owner of a gladiator school – gladiators at that time were only just beginning to develop into a full-scale industry), a class naturally abhorrent to Crassus but a necessary evil on which he must depend. Charles Laughton's Gracchus (for whom 'hatred of the patrician class is a profession') fills the social gap between Batiatus and Crassus as the *lanista* does between slave and Roman. Gracchus, like Batiatus, is of little importance in determining the film's epic structure, and must not be considered as some form of Ciceronian counterweight to the corrupt Crassus (for he is equally ambitious, only more cynical), but both of them, like the underdrawn Caesar (John Gavin), flesh out the Roman political spectrum of the time.

When considering the side of the slaves, the main problem, and indeed that of the film, is how to make the message hopeful in the knowledge that Spartacus' rebellion failed and did nothing to help the situation of slaves in Roman times. The religious/Zionist approach succinctly solves this, by setting up Spartacus as a vague Moses/Christ figure (his filmic crucifixion at the end invokes Christian parallels, but the rest of the story is pure Old Testament) who recognises but never enjoys the Promised Land. There are several scenes which are openly optimistic: the reconstructive aspect of the gladiators bringing their various trades to bear, and the detail of slave life, especially shots of the children. But overall *Spartacus* is an extremely pessimistic picture, and it is to its credit that it achieves epic scope within such dispiriting confines.

It does so by looking beyond its own era and drawing moral lessons which are shown to be true by their very ineffectualness in a corrupt and unjust age. In contrast to the tangled skein of good and evil on the Roman side, Spartacus states his messages loud and clear: 'As long as we live we must stay true to ourselves. I do know that we're brothers, and I know that we're free'; 'A free man dies, he loses the pleasure of life; a slave dies, he loses the pain. That's why we'll win'; and to Antoninus' final question whether it was all worth it, 'When just one man says "No, I won't" – and we were tens of thousands who said no – that was the wonder of it.' In contrast to the divisions in Roman society, with the Republic still weak from twenty years of civil strife, with wars in Spain and Asia, and pirates threatening the grain supply from overseas (viz. Gracchus' speech), the slaves show an uncomplicated solidarity, movingly expressed in the mass declaration of 'I am Spartacus' when Crassus tries to identify their leader. And in contrast to the Roman disregard for human dignity, a simple concern for the sanctity of life: 'Who wants to fight? An animal can learn to fight'; Spartacus to Batiatus, 'I'm not an animal'; and Spartacus to his warring fellow-gladiators, 'What are we becoming – Romans?'

Douglas and Kubrick had already made a strong pacifist statement in *Paths of Glory*; but in *Spartacus* it is harder to ascribe pacifist feelings to the leading character, except by justifying his actions as force demands force. Perhaps this is why we never see any of the slaves' actual victories against Roman troops (of which there were many), only their final defeat. It is a dramatic weakness of the film, to be sure, but helps to maintain the oppressive, hopeless backcloth against which Spartacus' vision operates. Here the historical facts have been simplified or changed in the cause of epic structure, and with complete justification. No mention is made of the push northwards to Cisalpine Gaul, nor of the various breakaway groups which went it alone; and Spartacus in fact tried to cross from the toe of Italy rather than the heel at Brundisium (erroneously called Brundusium in the film).

To enrich further the character of Spartacus, the film charts his relationship with Varinia in four idyllic scenes which are set in suitably unrealistic studio sets apart from the main action – points of repose which tell of Spartacus the man rather than Spartacus the symbol: their first reunion after the escape from Capua; a scene in which Spartacus says he is free, but knows nothing (a pivotal remark which establishes him as an unwitting puppet of history); a pool scene in which Varinia announces her pregnancy (the child is used at the end as a symbol of hope for future generations); and the vital eve-of-battle scene in which Spartacus tells of his dreams for their coming child. These interludes of Middle American domesticity, though providing splendid platforms for the lustrous Douglas/Simmons chemistry to shine, push *Spartacus* dangerously close to the American Western ethos; Alex North's *Big Country*-like, Coplandesque music for the framing shots of the gladiators riding shores up this feeling. Kirk Douglas' inclinations towards such clichés are apparent in his career – and in his own directorial effort *Posse* (1975), which used the Western for contemporary political comment – but fortunately they reinforce the epic structure of *Spartacus* rather than undermine it.

It is interesting in the religious regard to compare Kubrick's film with Riccardo Freda's *Spartacus the Gladiator/Sins of Rome* (*Spartaco*, 1953), one of the progenitors of the mature peplum and now often forgotten. Freda, along with Pietro Francisci, was there in the very beginning, and both directors made further contributions when the cycle was fully under way. Nicely photographed by Gábor Pogány and cast in strength with a positive Massimo Girotti, a beautifully villainous Gianna Maria Canale, and a rather old-fashioned Ludmilla Tcherina, *Spartacus the Gladiator* also opts for a child as a symbol of hope, with Spartacus' wife (here a Thracian called Amytis) declaring she is pregnant after her husband has been killed in battle. Spartacus' death, and the film's opening in which he is captured in Thrace and taken to Rome to be sold, are almost the only things which are historically accurate, however. Jean Ferry's script naturally rejects any Zionist approach, preferring to establish the story on a truly secular basis, though the arena scene, with Amytis tied to a ship's mast surrounded by (real) lions and Spartacus literally leaping to her rescue, invoked uncomfortable memories of the far from secular *Quo vadis* shot in Italy fractionally

65 (*right*) Theatre of cruelty:
Spartacus (Kirk Douglas) takes on
Draba (Woody Strode), watched by
Varinia (Jean Simmons), Helena
(Nina Foch), Crassus (Laurence
Olivier), Glabrus (John Dall)
and Claudia (Joanna
Barnes) in *Spartacus*

66 (*below*) Moody heroism: Amytis
(Ludmilla Tcherina) and
Spartacus (Massimo Girotti) in
Spartacus the Gladiator

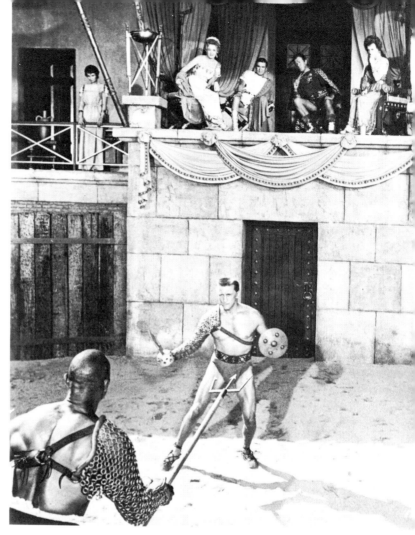

earlier. Nevertheless, the film emerges more as a heightened tale of one man's heroism than one of epic implications like the Hollywood version. It is the brilliantly handled large-scale sequences which stick in the mind, well-designed (often using genuine locations and buildings) and revealing Freda as a top-class action director, whose potent use of tracking and crane shots (notably in the arena scene and the night attack on the Roman camp) is as emotive as anything by Delmer Daves or Anthony Mann.

There exist no other comparable sound versions of the Spartacus story. Nick Nostro's *Day of Vengeance* (*Spartacus e i dieci gladiatori*, 1965) is more concerned with the Ten Gladiators of the title than the slave-leader. The film is a tired novelty in the peplum cycle, and one of a short series which also featured Nostro's *Triumph of the Ten Gladiators* (*Il trionfo dei dieci gladiatori*, 1965). *Day of Vengeance*'s only concession to history is a fight in a ring at Capua; its only concession to any moral message is a victory celebration of Spartacus' freedom when the Ten have had their escapade. *The Revenge of Spartacus* (*La vendetta di Spartacus*, 1965), directed by (Michele Lupo) and starring (Scilla Gabel, Giacomo Rossi Stuart, Gordon Mitchell and Daniele Vargas) regular peplumites, is even flimsier, with Spartacus already dead by the start and the rest of the film featuring a laboured vengeance plot set amongst Roman commanders. Only Scilla Gabel, as in so many of these films, emerges with any mystery.

Characteristically, it was Sergio Corbucci who contributed the best of the Spartacus sub-works: *The Son of Spartacus* (*Il figlio di Spartacus*, 1962) seized on the last reel of Kubrick's film for inspiration, showing the babe-in-arms now grown to the prime of manhood and risen to become a Roman centurion sent on a secret mission by Julius Caesar to Lydia, where he is captured, enslaved, and leads a successful revolt. The plot cleverly reverses the anti-Roman bias of *Spartacus* and runs the gamut of mythic devices (Randus is recognised as Spartacus' son by an amulet he wears, and vows to continue his father's challenge). The film is neatly stitched together by Corbucci, who directs fluidly throughout, but is too small-scale by half. Steve Reeves, despite having reached the covered-chest stage of his career, still shows presence, and Gianna Maria Canale is a sexually electric foil, but the overall tone is too pinched to realise fully the implications of the parent film's ending. *Son of Spartacus* works best as an escapist adventure film with derivative nods towards its more mythic progenitor, and does not measure up to the earlier Corbucci/Reeves product, *Duel of the Titans* (*Romolo e Remo*, 1962).

Imperial Rome: Christian Conflicts

'Man's desire to be free – the greatest madness.'

Tiberius in *The Robe* (1953)

So when people hate something through ignorance of what they are hating, why should it necessarily be worthy of hate at all?

Tertullian, *Apologeticus*, 1, 5 (AD 197)

'Be wise, Judah. It's a Roman world. If you want to live in it you must become part of it . . . I tell you, Judah, it is no accident that one small village on the Tiber was chosen to rule the world . . . It wasn't just our legions . . . No, it was fate that chose us to civilise the world – and we have. Our roads and our ships connect every corner of the earth; Roman law, architecture, literature are the glory of the human race.'

'I believe in the future of *my* people.'

'Of course you do.'

Messala to Ben-Hur in *Ben-Hur* (1959)

There is a highly resonant moment in Vergil's *Aeneid* when Aeneas, visiting his dead father, Anchises, in the Underworld, receives a glimpse of the future greatness of the race he is to found:

Others will forge softer, more life-like bronzes
(I have no doubt), draw living features from
  marble,
plead cases better, and chart the movements
of the heavenly bodies and predict the risings of
  stars.
But you, Roman, remember, will rule over
  nations
(these will be *your* skills) and impose order on
  peace,
spare the defeated and crush the proud.

(6, 847ff.)

It is a fine piece of poetic rhetoric, written with Augustan foresight for a people dedicated to empire as an end in itself, as an amplification of Rome, and as a desirable moral quality. Such concepts are specifically Roman (Vergil's 'others' are the Greeks) and carry little of the ill odour associated with the word 'empire' today. In the simplest terms, the Roman saw his role as imposing order on disorder, on demonstrating the inherent superiority of his system through conquest rather than culture.

The concept of Christianity was slow to grow – the Christian apologists of the second and third centuries gave a romanticised view of its spread during the first, when it was chiefly confined to the poorer classes of Asia and Africa. It first rose to Imperial attention in AD 64 when Nero, seeking a scapegoat for public dissatisfaction after the Great Fire of Rome, pandered to popular superstition and persecuted the small Christian sect – to such a gross degree, however, that he almost invited general sympathy for the scapegoats. Organised Imperial persecution of Christianity only began during the brief reign of Decius (AD 249–51); until then provincial governors were allowed considerable latitude in dealing with 'offenders.' It should be remembered that there was considerable hostility felt towards Christians by non-Roman locals, and, as in the case of Christ, Roman governors were more concerned with general civil order than with persecuting any one faith. When the emperor Constantine converted to Christianity in AD 312, it is thought that about one-tenth of the Empire was of the faith; paganism was not officially abolished until 395, by the emperor Theodosius.

The Rome vs Christianity formula is the most commonly accepted form, in general filmgoers' eyes, of the historical epic. Martyrs hurled before lions or roasted in the arena *are* attested to by history, and film-makers are merely perpetuating a romantic tradition begun by the early Christian writers and more recently picked up by novelists like Lytton and Sienkiewicz. At its most basic the conflict attains a theatricality earnestly seized upon by silent film-makers: J. H. Perry's *Soldiers of the Cross* (1900), instigated by William Booth, founder of the Salvation Army, presented short film sequences interspersed with slides of passive martyrs, children inside dummy lions and fantastically arrayed Romans – all conceived as a lecture/entertainment for Australian audiences. European works like *Marcus Lycinious* (*sic*) (c. 1910), with its dreadful histrionics, are little better.

The problems of maintaining some kind of balance when using Imperial Rome as a metaphor for moral degeneracy have led to film-makers recognising their own clichés and often creating new ones by satirising the old. Federico Fellini's *Satyricon* (1969) is a sumptuous mish-mash of several traditions, thinly based – on the director's confession – on the mid-first-century AD scatalogical novel by Titus Petronius. Though hyperbolic, it is the first extended work which gives us any idea about Roman slang and the tiny details of life amongst the lower levels of Roman society, with its Till Eulenspiegel-like anti-hero Encolpius constantly besieged on his travels by the wrath of the god Priapus and jealousy for his young friend Giton. Fellini plays up the original's *Odyssey* satire, his tracking camera roaming inquisitively as Encolpius (Martin Potter) proceeds from situation to situation with a detached concern. However, he rejects the original's Rabelaisian energy in favour of emphasising – with the ease of the exoticist of *8½* (*Otto e mezzo*, 1963), *Juliet of the Spirits* (*Giulietta degli spiriti*, 1965) and *Toby Dammit* (1968) – a grotesque realism which, though faithful in its colourful vulgarity, is no more true a picture of Roman habits than his homage to early Italian spectaculars in *Roma* (1972).

The rash of recent Caligula pictures, from Tinto Brass's *Caligula* (1979) to Antonio Passalia's *Caligula and Messalina* (*Caligula et Messalina*, 1982), thrive on the simple equation that absolute power equals moral degeneracy, the wages of which in Brass's film are a pathetic and bloody death. The latter sequence, played out in a courtyard with a nice sense of cumulative unease, is the only part of Brass's priapic farrago to show any genuine feeling for its characters. Other studies of the Caligula/Messalina/Claudius period have also been so dazzled by its mixture of court intrigue and moral anarchy that they have been unable to treat the characters in properly human terms. Of the various Messalina works, Vittorio Cottafavi's *Messalina* (*Messalina, venere imperatrice*, 1960) is the best. Though small beer compared with more liberal later versions, the film has a charismatic lead in Belinda Lee, who is a distinct improvement on Maria Félix in Carmine Gallone's *The Affairs of Messalina* (*Messalina*, 1951). As a whole, however, it is more successful when concentrating on either the battles or her lovers: the sequence in which the Praetorian Guard relentlessly hammer their shields on the way to arrest Messalina at a bacchanalia is a nice metaphor for one form of Roman ruthlessness confronting another. Such scenes completely overpower the formulary sub-plot of a Roman soldier rejecting military honours for a young Christian's love.

The biggest tragedy is that the cinema has yet to produce a balanced portrait of the emperor Claudius, except as a harmless spectator to Caligulan court intrigue. Josef von Sternberg's unfinished *I, Claudius* (1937), the only attempt so far to film Robert Graves' two-part novel, is very thirties in its visual design but features a splendid line-up of acting talent to breathe life into its portrait of the Caligulan and Claudian eras. Of the major sequences which have been pieced together from the month's shooting, such as Claudius being summoned from his farm to meet Caligula in Rome, Caligula, Livia and Claudius meeting during a public ceremony ('You take your uncle for a fool,' Livia tells Caligula. 'But he's not. I sometimes think he pretends to be one so as to make fools of us'), and Caligula's introduction of his horse Incitatus to the senate, one can see a remarkably perceptive film in the making. But the finest bleeding chunk of all is the five-and-a-half-minute speech Claudius (Charles Laughton) gives to the Senate on accepting the emperorship. It incarnates the very spirit of Claudius as a leader who identifies his own misfortunes with Rome's:

Since no one else seems eager to show his eloquence, I will inform you of the conditions upon which I will accept your support. I, Claudius, will tell you how to frame your laws. Profiteering and bribery will stop. The senate will function only in the name of Roman justice. And all of you who have acquired position dishonestly will be replaced by men who love Rome better than their purses. I will break everything rotten in this senate like an old dry twig! On that basis only will I become your emperor.

It is an eloquent speech, with more than a touch of epic presence as it shows a man rising to fulfil a destiny thrust upon him. Alongside his scenes with Peter Ustinov in *Spartacus*, the rescued chunks of *I, Claudius* contain Laughton's finest acting of all his historical films, and some of the best of his entire career.

There is only a handful of films which do not rely on the aforementioned easy contrast between degenerate Rome and redeeming Christianity. Victor Saville's *The Silver Chalice* (1954) is a brave attempt to examine the conflict between paganism and early Christianity within a Palestinian background (only the last few reels of the film are set in Neronian Rome), and it almost succeeds. The film opens in Antioch, twenty years after the Crucifixion, and the point is well made that Christianity was still distinctly unimportant in the mid-first century AD ('To the men of the first century, as in our century, it was business as usual, no more so than in the Street of the Silversmiths'). The central character, Basil (Paul Newman), is adopted as a child by a wealthy, childless Greek, sold into slavery as an adult by his adoptive uncle, is chosen by the Christian Luke to fashion a chalice for the portraits of Christ and his disciples, becomes enamoured of Luke's grand-daughter Deborra (Pier Angeli), and finally chooses her over his childhood love Helena (a very young and blonde Natalie Wood grown into Virginia Mayo), who has joined up with the pagan magician Simon (Jack Palance).

The story is full of refreshing detail. Basil, the convertee, is Greek rather than Roman and converts to Christianity not in sudden repentance for past behaviour but over a long period in which he rejects the (pagan) love of Helena for the (Christian) love of Deborra. Though on the same side of the social fence as the Christians (in that he is discredited) and fighting for his freedom, Basil does not feel any automatic solidarity with them. His gradual conversion to Christianity is charted by his ability to sculpt a head of Christ for the chalice. And Jerusalem in the sixties is shown to be a complex mixture of faiths – Orthodox Jews, Christians, pagans, and a secret non-Christian society called the Sicarii ('assassins') dedicated to

expelling the Romans. Only the structure of the plot shows a failure to work out satisfactorily all these lines: Basil's revenge on his adoptive uncle is left hanging, his love for the grown Helena seems more like infatuation, and the role of Simon is ill-defined *vis-à-vis* Basil. Yet the idea of taking the characters to Rome for the resolution of their destinies is laudable; the stage expands, Basil meets Peter, and Simon undertakes his most audacious trick before a star audience.

What chiefly lets *The Silver Chalice* down, however, is its script – a feeble and embarrassing collection of clichés woodenly interpreted by (then newcomer) Paul Newman, and only given a token overlay of sincerity and life by Pier Angeli and Jack Palance. Instead, the undoubted achievement of *The Silver Chalice* lies in its production design (Rolf Gerard) and art direction (Boris Leven) – the conscious simplicity and stylisation of Mankiewicz's *Julius Caesar* (1953) reinterpreted in Warnercolor and CinemaScope. Ignatius' house in Antioch has spartan, almost abstract interiors like a museum; the walls of the Roman garrison where Simon and Helena entertain the officers are cardboard-like; the rooftops across which Basil and Deborra flee, the Inn of the Rock at Rome, the stunning first shot of Jerusalem through the arches of a viaduct, and the house of Joseph of Arimathea in Jerusalem (like a poorer version of Ignatius') – all sport clean, model-like lines which establish an unreal atmosphere equally adaptable to the frailty of early Christianity or the theatricality of pagan magic. Franz Waxman's generally lean, though multi-thematic score mirrors the visual simplicity; there is a great deal of music in the film (ninety-five minutes for a running-time of almost two and a half hours) but harmonised in archaic, anti-romantic language and only in the use of the eighteenth-century Dresden Amen for the chalice (cf. Wagner's Grail motif in *Parsifal*) ever really arousing the emotions. Like the art direction the score may be admired on its own terms but emphasises the film's overall lack of cohesion.

The Silver Chalice is important in that the protagonists work out their destinies in non-Roman terms. Two films which show the confrontation of barbarism with a Christian Empire also avoid the lions-and-martyrs clichés, treating Rome as a concept of civilisation itself rather than a barrier to it. Both deal with Attila's challenge to Rome in the mid-fifth century AD, and are re-

67 (*opposite above*) Silent homage: Federico Fellini's *Roma*

68 (*above*) Roman ruthlessness: the Praetorian Guard in *Messalina* (1960)

69 (*opposite below*) Model design: the rooftop flight by Basil (Paul Newman) and Deborra (Pier Angeli) in *The Silver Chalice*

70 (*right*) Roman power structures: Honoria (Sophia Loren) and Aetius (Henri Vidal) in *Attila the Hun*

markably similar thematically. Douglas Sirk's *Sign of the Pagan* (1954) shows an Attila (Jack Palance) driven by sheer power-lust to rule the whole earth, not just the Roman Empire, his simple destiny progressively complicated by the encroachments of Christianity. His daughter falls for Constantinople and the Roman officer Marcian (Jeff Chandler) and, while raping and pillaging his way towards Rome, Attila is repelled from a church by a priest carrying a crucifix. His death comes not from the hands of Marcian, as epic convention would demand, but from the slave Ildico (Allison Hayes), her sword forming a convenient cross-like shadow on the ground.

Pietro Francisci's *Attila the Hun* (*Attila*, 1955) lacks the visual richness of Sirk's film but shows greater panache and a clearer idea of the opportunities for reinterpreting the period. Attila's rise to prominence in European history was sudden and transitory: he had to be bought off when he invaded Italy in 452 but the fall of the Hun empire was due simply to its overextension, lack of organisation and the loss of Attila's unifying personality when he died prematurely in the winter of 452/3. Francisci's film sketches the confusion of the age better and sets its action in the Western rather than the Eastern Empire, at the 'court of extravagant splendour' of Valentinian III in Ravenna. His sister Honoria (Sophia Loren), described variously as 'bloodthirsty, determined, ruthless' and 'the embodiment of treachery, iniquity and corruption', is united with Attila in a typical peplum relationship, obligingly dropping her cloak on their first meeting to reveal her statuesque attractions. 'I came to you expecting to find only a conqueror, yet I discovered a man – who has conquered me,' croons Honoria next morning.

The relationship is a charismatic transformation of history (Honoria actually offered herself to Attila, but by letter and while banished to Constantinople for an earlier infidelity) but is hardly given a chance to realise its potential. 'I know that my destiny is to reign at the side of the conqueror of the world', drools Honoria, as Attila nervously chews a drumstick; but by next day she is dead in battle and the earlier prophecy of Attila's woman Grune (Irene Papas) that the relationship would bring doom is unsatisfactorily left hanging. Yet *Attila* is ultimately a richer work than *Sign of the Pagan*, thanks to its unusually careful delineation of the two sides' power struc-

tures. The early scenes, as Roman emissary Aetius (Henri Vidal) journeys to Attila's camp to propose a peaceful settlement, sport some fine dialogue between the pair as they chew the cud of old friendship (attested by history) and the pros and cons of peace vs war. In Anthony Quinn's flamboyant but in fact very subtle performance, Attila becomes a proponent of might-equals-right more from his perception of past history than from any blood-lust *per se*.

This chimes well with Francisci's portrait of the fickle, crazed Valentinian and the scheming Ravenna court. Hun and Roman parallel each other: the ambitious, pragmatic Attila and Honoria vs the peace-loving, idealistic Bleda (Attila's brother) and Aetius. The summary deaths of Honoria and Aetius in the final battle (the latter was actually murdered by a jealous Valentinian a couple of years later) unbalance the structure and rob the plot of a satisfactory conclusion on its own terms. The script is explicit on the weaknesses of the Western Empire: 'These are the proud Romans, sons of Caesar and Augustus, conquerors of Gaul and Carthage. Look at them now,' Attila tells his son. 'Nothing but bones and blood. This was their army.' But this is later revealed as a ground-clearing operation for the introduction of the final *deus ex machina*, Attila's repulse by the massed Christian forces of Leo the Great.

The theme of conflicting religions is insufficiently developed for this finale to gain much epic resonance ('You have one, we have many' is all Attila offers) but Quinn's inflected performance at least makes his final retreat more convincing than Palance's in *Sign of the Pagan*, in which the meeting takes place at night and relies more on atmosphere than character development. Francisci's film goes the whole hog, with massed raised crucifixes, a mid-stream meeting between Leo and Attila, and a triumphant choral ending and superimposed cross as the barbarian rides back over the horizon with a defiant shake of his sword. Attila's retreat is still something of a historical mystery; he was probably bought off, with the added inducement of Honoria as a bride. The script ducks the problem, with the camera respectfully withdrawing for most of Leo's speech and a pompous narrator papering over the cracks: 'What further words spoke the vicar of Christ to the man of war in the attempt to placate the merciless and barbaric leader no one will ever know. History records it as one of the greatest mysteries of all time. Perhaps there is no mystery. Pope Leo need only have quoted the simple words of the scriptures, words so easily understood by all men of goodwill, great or small, Roman or barbarian, master or slave – for all are equal in God's sight.'

Much of the same self-righteousness pervades Boris Sagal's *The Antagonists* (1981), which deals with the two-year siege (70–72) by the Romans of the fortress of Masada, whither a small band of Jewish zealots fled after the fall of Jerusalem. The film's self-righteousness is entirely on the side of the Jews, portrayed as immaculate, god-guided martyrs; the Romans, in contrast, are a sweaty, down-to-earth bunch. The film does, however, have a curious ambivalence, considering the story's easy potential for set-my-people-free Zionist propaganda. Beneath the formulary surface lie some subtler characterisations: the Jews (played by American actors) are portrayed as bickering fanatics, united only when faced with a common enemy; the Romans (played by British actors) emerge as tough pragmatists, only concerned with getting the job done and going home. The script pits the Jewish leader Eleazar (Peter Strauss) against the Roman commander Flavius Silva (Peter O'Toole) and constructs an uneasy relationship between the two, partly founded on mutual respect. Unfortunately the picture suffers from having been edited down from a six-hour TV film (*Masada*, 1980) to scarcely a third its original length: the original has a genuinely spacious, long-breathed tempo, with characters properly developed (even if mostly on the Roman side) and much fascinating minutiae of Roman legionary life never before shown with such fidelity. It also boasts a rare cinematic appearance by the emperor Vespasian (Timothy West in fine no-nonsense form), surely one of history's most neglected characters – if only because of his lack of the 'traditional' Roman imperial attributes of megalomania and cruelty. Despite all, however, O'Toole's magnificent performance as the weary, not unsympathetic Silva shines through, completely eclipsing Strauss' pallid, one-dimensional performance as Eleazar.

*   *   *

As mentioned earlier, the cinema has been more concerned with pagan than with Christian Rome, the clichés inbreeding with an alarming regularity. The remainder of the works under consideration all feature Christianity as a redeeming force in an otherwise corrupt society; the method of and passage towards the redemption may differ, and the extent to which Rome is censured may vary, but the underlying theme remains the same. Alfonso Brescia's *Poppea, una prostituta al servizio dell'impero* (1972), with its floating morality, picaresque leads, arena scenes, convenient baptism and final miracle, satirises the popular aspects of the genre, while Steno's *Mio figlio Nerone* (1956), an Alberto Sordi farce notably only for the curious teaming of Gloria Swanson, Vittorio De Sica and a young Brigitte Bardot, chastely revels in the opportunities thrown up by *Quo vadis*. The sheer adaptability of the format is remarkable. Lionello De Felice's *Constantine the Great* (*Costantino il grande*, 1961), with Cornel Wilde as the emperor and Belinda Lee the hapless prey of wild beasts, resurrects Eusebius' story of the leader converted to the faith by the sight of a cross glowing in the sky; Antonio Margheriti's *Rome in Flames* (*Il crollo di Roma*, 1963) fixes on the interesting period just following the death of Constantine when sporadic persecution was still being carried out; while Mario Caiano's *Maciste and the Hundred Gladiators* (*Maciste, gladiatore di Sparta*, 1965) unites the muscleman genre (Mark Forest fighting a giant gorilla and restraining a team of horses) with the Christian cycle in Vitellian Rome, *en passant* using footage from *Constantine the Great*.

Mario Bonnard's *The Last Days of Pompeii* (*Gli ultimi giorni di Pompeii*, 1959), the latest of several Italian adaptations of Bulwer Lytton's turgid novel, is more successful than the Maciste films in uniting the muscleman and Christian themes, thanks to spectacular art direction by Augusto Lega and sparkling colour photography by Antonio López Ballesteros. The script, written by a team numbering such luminaries as Ennio De Concini, Sergio Leone and Sergio Corbucci, has Glaucus (Steve Reeves) bending prison bars, fighting crocodiles, and strangling a lion in the arena, and makes up for its leaden characterisation with the sheer *brio* of the action scenes – matched by Carmine Gallone and Amleto Palermi's version (1926), which skimps on the eruption (much smoke but precious little else) but has otherwise impres-

71 (*opposite above*) Hapless prey: Fausta (Belinda Lee) in *Constantine the Great*

72 (*opposite below*) Christian fodder: Ione (Christine Kaufmann – foreground, third from right) in *The Last Days of Pompeii* (1959)

73 (*above*) Pathetic poignancy: the final minutes of Nero (Peter Ustinov) in *Quo vadis* (1951)

sive sets, notably one for a chariot race.

Ernest B. Schoedsack's *The Last Days of Pompeii* (1935) almost totally throws the original novel overboard, to concentrate instead on a moral tale of an honest, hard-working blacksmith (Preston Foster) who becomes embittered after the death of his wife and child and turns to a Roman equivalent of thirties American gangsterism ('I've been a fool all my life. One has to kill to get money'), working in the arena and then as a slave-trader ('behind the scenes, where the action is'). The plot hiccups its way to Judaea in order to embrace its Christian message – Marcus drawing his sword to help Christ while carrying the cross, but at the last moment choosing to defend his gold instead – and after a lacuna of about forty years features a curious epilogue of Christ appearing to the white-haired Marcus after the eruption, just before he dies. Schoedsack and producer Merian C. Cooper (makers of *King Kong*) present some realistic pictures of Roman life and architecture (apart from the Pompeii arena) and a convincing eruption, but the *Little Caesar* story is impossible.

As in *Rome in Flames* and the various *Last Days of Pompeii* films, Gianfranco Parolini's *Anno 79 – distruzione Ercolano* (1963) also uses the *deus ex machina* of a final conflagration (here of Herculaneum) to resolve an otherwise convoluted plot. Only Mario Bonnard's *Slave Women of Corinth* (*Afrodite dea dell'amore*, 1958), set in first-century AD Corinth, has any subtler ambitions, with the sculptor Demetrius (Antonio De Teffè), faced with a commission to provide the city with a new statue of the goddess and having to choose between two female models – Diala (Irène Tunc), the Phoenician courtesan, and Lerna (Isabelle Corey), the Christian slave.

Given the historical facts of Nero's reign, it is not surprising that there should be a sizeable body of works which play on the Imperial vs Christian conflict, taking their cue from the persecution following the Great Fire of Rome in AD 64. This broke out near the Circus Maximus on the night of 18 July and was not completely extinguished for nine days; ten of Rome's fourteen districts were either gutted or completely destroyed. Stories that Nero played the lyre while watching the flames or deliberately planned the conflagration, though originating from rumours of the actual period, may be dismissed as romantic fiction, but later story-tellers (Henryk Sienkiewicz particularly) have

naturally seized on this folklore. The persecution of the Christians as a direct consequence of the fire is only attested by one source of the period, strangely enough; more important, we know that there was a tradition among the early Christians that direct persecution began during Nero's reign.

Everything else pales besides Sienkiewicz's mammoth treatment. We have already seen how *Quo vadis* is the *fons et origo* of much of the historical epic's base matter. It has none of the hysteria of Cecil B. DeMille's *The Sign of the Cross* (1933) which, though indebted to Sienkiewicz for its dissolute Nero (Charles Laughton) and love between a Roman soldier (Fredric March) and sweet Christian (Elissa Landi), goes way overboard both ways: the scenes with the pagan Poppaea (Claudette Colbert), all baths of asses' milk and smouldering seduction, prophesy DeMille's forthcoming *Cleopatra* (1934) with the same actress, and the film's Christian fervour is akin to that of the early apologists such as Tertullian. Even thirty years later Guido Malatesta's *Revenge of the Gladiators* (*L'incendio di Roma*, 1968), which sports a highly realistic Nero and refreshing use of familiar sets, goes wildly overboard on every other historical detail, even to the extent of placing the fire during the winter (to judge by the distracting condensation which appears every time an actor breathes).

Sienkiewicz's novel, first published in 1895, had already been seized upon by film-makers a mere six years after appearing, its popularity and potential for large-scale effects guaranteeing directors an audience. In 1912 Sienkiewicz officially sold the film rights to Italian spectacle-king Enrico Guazzoni, who had already made *Agrippina* (1910) and *Brutus* (1910) and was to go on to make *Marcoantonio e Cleopatra* (1913), *Caio Giulio Cesare* (1914), *Fabiola* (1917) and *The Fall of an Empress* (*Messalina*, 1924) before the silent Italian craze played itself out. Guazzoni's *Quo vadis* (1912), running for more than an hour and a half, boasted the biggest sets and cast of any film made up to that time; it enjoyed spectacular international success, playing with full orchestral accompaniment in major cities. The film follows Sienkiewicz's original quite closely, placing the central story of Marcus Vinicius' redemption through his love for the Christian Lygia within an impressive array of characters: Petronius, the cynical 'arbiter of elegance' who later rebels against Nero's savagery; Aulus Plautius, representative of wealthy Roman society, at whose house Lygia serves; Chilon Chilonides, the soothsayer who aids Marcus and stirs the mob against Nero; Ursus, Lygia's devoted companion; Eunice, Petronius' dedicated slave; and the apostle Peter. As a director who trained as an artist and designer, Guazzoni makes the most of his sets with splendid compositions and use of movement in depth; the latter compensates for his static camera, which is only allowed a few isolated pans in the arena scenes.

By the time of George Jacoby and Gabriele D'Annunzio's *Quo vadis* (1924) one can already see the dramatic fabric expanding. The character of Petronius is enlarged (notably his objection to Tigellinus' idea of choosing the Christians as scapegoats for the fire); Chilon becomes Linus, a Christian priest who comforts Lygia in her love for Marcus and acts as go-between when Marcus swears he will study Christianity if Lygia marries him; and Aulus Plautius and his wife Pomponia are fleshed out, astonished and troubled by Lygia's arrival in Rome. The film's more fluid visual style renders the two set-pieces of the fire and the games very impressive, especially the latter with chariot races and gladiatorial fights leading up to the main event. Only occasionally, as when Lygia is tied to the back of a rearing bull, does the film overspill into the ridiculous – a fault also afflicting some of D'Annunzio's captions ('Rising from the Catacombs, a triumphant Christianity relentlessly sweeps through Europe'). Most important, one can already see the cinema attempting to examine the epic potential in the seemingly impossible conflict of the philosophies of Marcus and Lygia.

By the time of Mervyn LeRoy's *Quo vadis* (1951) spectacle is working hand-in-hand with an intelligent script. First and foremost, LeRoy's film is beautifully structured, its gallery of characters making it a paradigm for the historical epic genre. There is a fluidity and symmetry to its construction which on repeated viewings transcends the often hammy acting (Robert Taylor, Peter Ustinov, Patricia Laffan). The triangle of Marcus/Lygia, Petronius/Eunice and Nero/Acte shows varying shades of male redemption through female love: from Marcus' fully fledged embrace of Christianity, through Petronius' atonement for his cynical past through the noble Roman act of suicide ('It is not enough to live well. One must die well'), to Nero's

cowardly embrace of death ('Is this, then, the end of Nero? To be lord of the earth in my own execution?').

The two Roman deaths function as bizarre mirror-images of each other – Petronius' noble and self-sought among friends, Nero's cowardly and unwilling amid civil anarchy. Where Petronius' is prefaced by the loving suicide of Eunice, Nero's death follows his calculated murder of Poppaea. The *deus ex machina* appearance of Acte (Rosalie Crutchley), like an Angel of Death, gives Nero's death a pathetic poignancy ('You have lived like a monster. Now die like an emperor – by your own hand'). Yet just as Nero only realises the depth of Acte's love at the very moment of his death, so even Petronius is unaware of the love of his Spanish slave Eunice (Marina Berti). In the 1912 *Quo vadis*, Petronius was wont to give Eunice fifty lashes for her devotion; in LeRoy's version this is reduced to five ('Apply the lash carefully now. Don't damage her skin') and thanks to Leo Genn's superbly modulated performance and Miklós Rózsa's emotive love theme, their relationship attains a genuine poignancy. Genn is the living incarnation of the real-life Petronius pictured by Tacitus in his *Annals* (16, 18–20), and in LeRoy's film his final, barbed letter to Nero (actually a detailed list of the emperor's crimes and lovers) is transfigured into a great anti-McCarthy speech for fifties America:

To Nero, Emperor of Rome, Master of the World, Divine Pontiff. I know that my death will be a disappointment to you, since you wished to render me this service yourself. To be born in your reign is a miscalculation; but to die in it is a joy. I can forgive you for murdering your wife and your mother, for burning our beloved Rome, for befouling our fair country with the stench of your crimes. But one thing I cannot forgive – the boredom of having to listen to your verses, your second-rate songs, your mediocre performances. Adhere to your special gifts, Nero – murder and arson, betrayal and terror. Mutilate your subjects if you must; but with my last breath I beg you – *do not mutilate the arts*. Fare well but compose no more music. Brutalise the people but do not bore them, as you have bored to death your friend, the late Gaius Petronius.

The death of the two Romans throws into relief the life-giving quality of the central relationship of

Marcus (Robert Taylor) and Lygia (Deborah Kerr). This starts with some edgy dialogue establishing their yang and yin roles: 'Conquest! But what's conquest? It's the only method of uniting and civilising the world under one power. I have to spill a little blood to do it . . .' 'No! There's a gentler and more powerful way of doing that, without bloodshed and war, without slaves and captives bound in chains to your triumphal chariots, commander.' Yet despite his conversion near the end, Marcus still achieves Nero's downfall by force of arms, still retains his soldier's post rather than opting for a pacifist life. As Marcus (Robert Taylor) and Fabius (Norman Wooland) watch Galba's army arriving, their exchange has a very early fifties Red-alert toughness:

M: Galba has a tough task ahead of him –
    rebuild Rome and bring back Roman justice.
F: I fear the glory that was Rome will never fully
    be reached again, Marcus.
M: Babylon, Egypt, Greece, Rome . . . What
    follows?
F: A more permanent world, I hope. Or a more
    permanent faith.
M: One is not possible without the other.

Quo vadis has a very real sense of history on the move, of events in flux, of a watershed approaching. The film opens in the early summer of AD 64 and goes up to the death of Nero (i.e. the end of the Julio-Claudians) and the Year of the Four Emperors (AD 68/9), from the turmoil of which the new Flavian dynasty emerges. At the beginning there is rebellion in the provinces – Marcus has just returned from quashing a revolt in Britain, a piece of information which also type-casts him as an instrument of Roman power – and during Part 2 both Marcus and Petronius are part of a plan to install as emperor Galba, who, we later hear, is already 'marching from the north'. This theme, besides mirroring the Romans' very real elation at the possibility of a fresh start to the Imperial concept, also mirrors in Roman terms the Christian hope for a new world.

This background gives the main story a distinct edge – of destinies (including Nero's) worked out against a crucial segment of history. The relative balance between the Roman and Christian messages tends to be forgotten in the face of *Quo vadis*'s spectacular arena scenes and final trium-

phant revelation to Peter on the Via Appia. In fact, the religious theme only enters strongly near the end of Part 1 with the long monologue by Peter (Finlay Currie) which gives a quick résumé of Christ and his teachings, and establishes the basis for Marcus and Lygia's love: 'Endure all things in his name, that you may dwell in blessedness.' That love runs the traditional gamut of hostility, forced separation and final reunion, but such is the film's carefully structured atmosphere that the story of the two lovers easily assumes an epic identity – if more because of the subsidiary characters than Robert Taylor's or Deborah Kerr's uninflected performances.

John Huston's original script (never filmed) played down the story's religious, uplifting angle in favour of dwelling more on Nero's evil character. LeRoy's *Quo vadis* lacks only a satisfactory examination of this central character, this wielder of men's destinies at a historical crossroads, and as such the narrator's opening speech about the individual being at the mercy of the state is trivialised more than necessary. Even Miklós Rózsa's impressively developed score, his first for a historical picture, cannot quite paper over the fundamental cracks in the film's structure: thanks to disgracefully bad dubbing, the many moods and finer details of the music (from the use of the liturgical main theme, through the delicate love and court music, to the more grandly operatic sequences) are often rendered dramatically impotent.

Henry Koster's *The Robe* (1953) was Fox's answer to M-G-M's emormous box-office success and the first film in its new process of Cinema-Scope, which immediately gave it a visual advantage over *Quo vadis*, despite early problems of warping at the edges and a creative hesitancy in realising the new shape's possibilities. The film uses a Lloyd Douglas story which constructs a story around the Roman soldier at the Crucifixion who gives away Christ's robe to his Greek slave Demetrius (Victor Mature). *The Robe* is no advance thematically, merely a retrenchment. It is the eighteenth year of Tiberius' reign, a time when, as the opening narration by the tribune Gallio (Richard Burton) tells us, 'The people of thirty lands send us tribute and their proudest sons to be our slaves. We have reached the point where there are more slaves in Rome than citizens.' *The Robe* mostly settles for an uncomplicated slave

74 (*above*) Symbolic
overlay: Gallio (Richard
Burton) and Junia (Dawn
Addams) in *The Robe*

75 (*right*) Still Christian
grace: Lavinia (Jean
Simmons) in *Androcles
and the Lion*

vs Roman argument ('To be a slave in this household is an honour', 'To be a slave anywhere is to be
a dog') with a somewhat forced symbolic overlay of
the magical qualities of Christ's robe. There are
vague parallels with Saville's *The Silver Chalice*,
made a year later, in that Gallio's obsession with
regaining the robe which has destroyed his peace
of mind is used to accumulate dramatic tension
throughout the film – in the same way as Basil's
inability to sculpt a head of Christ.

However, *The Robe* settles for plain statement
rather than any intrinsic development of Gallio's
conversion ('It changed my life. In time it will
change the world'). Despite a fine, authoritative
performance from Michael Rennie as Peter, and a
still, graceful Diana from Jean Simmons (much in
the mould of her Lavinia in Chester Erskine's
Androcles and the Lion, the year before) the most
impressive moments are not in the dialogue scenes
but in the visual *coups* throughout the film. The
Crucifixion and post-Crucifixion events feature the
thrilling use of Alfred Newman's rising chordal
theme as Demetrius first sees Christ; the thunder-
clap as Judas says his name to Gallio; the nailing
of Christ to the cross which forms the basis of
Gallio's nightmare on the ship home; and
Demetrius' condemnation of Gallio in the driving
rain, accompanied by Newman's powerful music.
And the convincingly metallic swordfight between
Gallio and Paulus (Jeff Morrow), in which Gallio
finds himself fighting a fellow-Roman, climaxes
with his casually hurled sword forming a cross as it
lands in a tree.

Yet these are insufficient treats to sustain
almost two and a half hours of ponderous story-
telling, especially when the first real action (the
swordfight) does not occur until some hundred
minutes in. None of these faults trouble the sequel,
Delmer Daves' *Demetrius and the Gladiators*
(1954), which was shot virtually simultaneously
with *The Robe* but shares none of its religious
pomposity. Aided by a busy Franz Waxman score
and Daves' tight, fast-moving direction, the film is
more interested in the court intrigue of Caligula,
Messalina and Claudius than in Demetrius'
spiritual elevation through the robe, and shows the
Greek slave dallying awhile with Messalina
(Susan Hayward) as the demented Caligula (Jay
Robinson, also from *The Robe*) steps up his search
for the magic piece of apparel. *Demetrius* aspires
lower than *The Robe*, and is certainly no epic, but

on its own level as a historical thriller it is
considerably more successful – and more fun.

From showing a central character on a passage
of faith *towards* Christ, as virtually all the religious Imperial films do, it is but a small thematic
step sideways to showing a character *reliving*
aspects of Christ's own passage. Both *Barabbas*
and *Ben-Hur*, the final two works to be considered
in this chapter, substantially enrich their redemption stories by trading off the mystique of Christ in
a way which totally escapes *The Robe*, the one by
direct parallels, the other by subtler allusions. Pär
Lagerkvist's novel *Barabbas* was first published in
October 1951, and within the space of just over ten
years two major film versions of it were released.
Lagerkvist's original is an imaginative fabrica-
tions. Ulf Palme's curiously bearded Barabbas is a
about the extent to which a robber/revolutionary
would have been affected by the experience of
Christ dying on his behalf. It is a difficult work to
translate into visual terms, since, like Howard
Fast's *Spartacus*, there is a great deal of interior
monologue, but both film versions preserve intact
the novel's main theme of a man struggling
upwards to reach the light.

Alf Sjöberg's *Barabbas* (1953), as one might
expect from the director of *Only a Mother* (*Bara en
more*, 1949), *Miss Julie* (*Fröken Julie*, 1951), or
Karin Månsdotter (1954), is a thoroughly theatrical interpretation, told in Sjöberg's acquired style
of dramatic chiaroscuro and pregnant compositions. Ulf Palme's curiously bearded Barabbas is a
glowering, guilt-ridden animal, pushed from pillar
to post by all levels of society, the victim of a
destiny he does not fully comprehend. The film is
largely studio-shot, and then much in the dark
recesses of underground passages, and Sjöberg's
limited use of exteriors (as in Barabbas being
hauled up from the sulphur mines into the bright
Mediterranean light, or the visually spare Crucifixion) is always to good point.

Richard Fleischer's *Barabbas* (*Barabba*, 1962) is
much more approachable, not because of the added
benefits of colour photography and spectacle but
because of its greater naturalism. The story of
Barabbas, though concerned with moral regeneration, is pitched throughout on a very physical level
– Barabbas, a creature of instinct, a man of
physical action, is confronted with feelings he
cannot, like Sjöberg's character, properly understand – and the complete *mise-en-scène* of

Fleischer's film, from the casting of the superbly equipped Anthony Quinn (producer De Laurentiis had envisaged him in the role from *La strada* days, and had also originally wanted Fellini to direct) to Mario Chiari's thoroughly convincing art direction, works towards this end. Fleischer brings the same *film noir* devices to a Roman subject that one finds in his earlier *Compulsion* (1959) or a plantation picture like *Mandingo* (1975), and an intensity and compassion fully equal, as we shall see in the next chapter, to that of *The Vikings* (1958). Mario Chiari's visual design again and again strikes home to support this approach with realistic detail: the painted capitals on the Jerusalem praetorium and the authentic cluster of buildings in the background, the catacombs and sulphur mines, and the circus spectacle at Rome. (It is worth noting that, apart from the error of portraying an all-stone amphitheatre some years before one was introduced at Rome, the circus sequences are the most authentic so far shown on film.)

Within such an ambience, Christopher Fry's script charts Barabbas' *Doppelgänger* existence with a sure sense of measure. The very opening shots introduce the light/darkness motif, as Pontius Pilate (Arthur Kennedy) walks before the people, the camera panning to reveal the large square before the praetorium, and the credits unroll over shots of Barabbas languishing in the gloom of an underground prison. 'I'm not used to the light; it plays tricks,' he complains as he sees Christ standing against the bright sun – and here his journey starts. It is enough to enumerate the instances at which the screenplay and the film's visual design play upon this light/darkness motif to recognise how thoroughly it permeates the story: the eclipse at Christ's crucifixion (a genuine eclipse, in fact, filmed on 15 February 1961); the words of Peter (Harry Andrews) about Christ drawing people 'out of the dark sea into the light'; Barabbas drawn up from the sulphur mines in Sicily after twenty years below ground (this sequence, paralleling the opening, ends Part 1 on a perfect cadence, preparing us for the transformation process in Part 2); the brilliance of the arena against the gloom of the amphitheatre's corridors; and Barabbas' descent into the catacombs and his emergence to face the blazing Fire of Rome. This design is subtly enmeshed with a recurring net motif – Peter as a fisher of men, Barabbas swept along, fish-like, by the movements of people and

history – which is triumphantly resolved in the climactic arena battle between Barabbas and Torvald (Jack Palance), the latter appropriately wielding a net.

Side by side with this physical expression of Barabbas' dilemma, Fry gives voice to his growing mental anguish as he rejoins his robber companions, apparently unchanged ('What's done is done; I remember the way'), but becomes aghast that he seemingly cannot be killed by the Romans ('He meant me to live. He's taken my death'). Suspended thus between life and death – a state which Lazarus (Michael Gwynn) had earlier been unable to describe, just as life cannot be explained to an unborn child – Barabbas meets the Christian Sahak (Vittorio Gassman) in the Sicilian sulphur mines, and the unease of Part 1 is gradually resolved in Part 2 through an almost parallel structure. Barabbas is again 'released' and finds himself in a physical occupation with which he can identify – as a gladiator ('I'll take this life; a man can understand this') – but again, even against the demoniacal Torvald, he proves as indestructible as in the sulphur mines, and is given his freedom once more. Yet the death of Sahak (a splendidly dramatic and gruesome affair in an empty, rain-soaked arena) compromises this freedom with more uncertainty – to which Barabbas can only respond by bowing to the inevitable and identifying himself with the Christians by fire-raising ('God, you won't find me failing this time'). His crucifixion at the end, in a field full of Christian martyrs, is all the more tragic for his (still only vague) comprehension of his destiny: 'I give myself up into your keeping . . . It is Barabbas.'

Such incomprehension is only reserved for Barabbas himself; we, the audience, are made aware of his destiny, and invited to watch his rebirth as some grotesque parody of episodes from Christ's own life. The mock crowning of a King of the Jews in a tavern and a Last Supper with Lazarus and Barabbas; the stoning of Rachela, Barabbas' woman (Silvana Mangano), like a brutal inversion of the Mary Magdalene episode; Barabbas' partial denial, *à la* Peter, of seeing Christ; his conveying of Sahak's body to the catacombs, like some disciple – all lead to Peter's final assertion to Barabbas in prison that 'Because you were farthest from him, you were nearest.' Fleischer's film writes the fate of this man large, the spectacular set-pieces (the two crucifixions, the sulphur mines, the arena battles) working especially well thanks to their thorough integration into the story. In many ways *Barabbas* breaks with epic film convention: there is no parallel love-story, no female redemptive yin to Barabbas' yang, and a deep strain of pessimism akin to that in *Spartacus*. But its message *is* one of hope – that no one is beyond redemption, even if it may be an unknowing and camel-and-needle affair – and to its great credit the film works out the tragic destiny of its central character in an atmosphere in which Roman civilisation appears the norm.

Such is also the case with *Ben-Hur*, which, while strongly condemning certain Roman attitudes and practices, remains sufficiently non-denominational (in the sense that the Zionist messages are not the work's *sine qua non*) for it to transcend the formulary suffering-Jew-and-oppressive-Roman clichés. *Ben-Hur* boasts a story which thoroughly integrates itself into its period – life under a Roman yoke but in a totally Roman world which does not apologise for itself – and is more concerned with broader emotions than stereotyped posturings. Much of this is built into the basic (original) plot: Judah Ben-Hur, at least at the start, is no downtrodden figure, but a wealthy, privileged trader, the head of one of Jerusalem's most noble families; only after being unfairly discredited and punished does he align himself uncompromisingly with anti-Roman factions, expunging the guilt of his former friendship with the Roman Messala through love for the Jewish/ Christian Esther.

In essence Ben-Hur is the rich man passing through the eye of the needle, the Roman centurion finding grace through God – New Testament parallels every part as relevant as the more obvious one of his life running adjacent to (and eventually coinciding with) Christ's. As a true epic figure, Ben-Hur is measured by and redeems himself through his actions, and is guided throughout by a sense of his own destiny. The film versions are among the very few historical pictures not featuring a land battle or gladiatorial fight; Rome does not topple; Ben-Hur does not lead an army into the fray. Instead, his destiny is worked out *per res Romanas* – in the galleys, in the circus, in Rome itself – and the basic issues are personalised into a meditation on friendship, filial duty, and love.

Lew Wallace's original novel, first published in 1880, enjoyed consistent popularity during its early years. When Wallace eventually gave permission for theatrical production, in 1899, it was an immediate success (the first staging featured later film stars William Farnum and William S. Hart as Ben-Hur and Messala) and the cinema naturally seized early upon the work. Sidney Olcott's 1907 version was the first, billed as 'Sixteen Magnificent Scenes with Illustrated Titles, Positively the Most Superb Motion-Picture Ever Made' but actually composed of a few interior scenes and a chariot race based on one staged for a local firework display. Kalem Company was sued in 1912 for breach of copyright (and lost), but by 1919 it became clear that Wallace's son was prepared to sanction an official film version. After several years of complex and expensive manoeuvring, the rights passed to the Goldwyn company, which by the time the disaster-prone production opened on 30 December 1925, had become Metro-Goldwyn-Mayer. The final director of the picture was Fred Niblo, with B. Reaves Eason credited with the chariot race. In 1931 the film was reissued in a shortened sound version, but this was not successful and promptly vanished from sight. Over a quarter of a century later M-G-M decided on a remake (in customary Hollywood style making sure that no prints of the 1925 version were in circulation); William Wyler, who had only just finished *The Big Country*, directed, and Andrew Marton was in charge of the chariot race. The dialogue, credited to sole scriptwriter Karl Tunberg, was in fact substantially revised throughout filming in Rome by Christopher Fry; Maxwell Anderson, S. N. Behrman and Gore Vidal also made uncredited contributions, the latter deepening the friendship (and later hate) of Ben-Hur and Messala; Stephen Boyd himself did much to reshape the latter role.

I have spent more time than usual sketching the production histories because the two major versions are of vital importance for their remarkable transformations of a verbose, ill-arranged and generally uncharismatic original novel. Sidney Olcott's *Ben-Hur* (1907), scripted by Kalem actress and assistant director Gene Gauntier, is only of marginal interest, but at least it established the main dramatic framework in its choice of sixteen scenes – including the House of Hur, the wounding of the Roman commander, the transport of Ben-Hur to the galleys, Ben-Hur's rescue of the commander Quintus Arrius, the challenge to Messala, the chariot race, and Ben-Hur's victory. It is Fred Niblo's *Ben-Hur: A Tale of the Christ* (1925) that properly fleshes out Olcott's bony skeleton into a fully fledged dramatic work. The opening, in a Jaffa peopled by arrogant Romans, establishes the theme of inter-racial antagonism before sketching the Nativity with beautiful simplicity (as the shepherds watch a star which brightens over Bethlehem and pulsates gently). With the appearance of the main characters, one first begins to sense the film reworking the novel as it knits the trio together into a tragic destiny: Ben-Hur is shown rescuing Esther's dove in an Antioch street, where he then meets his childhood friend Messala. Unlike the book, in which the pair (still, incidentally, in their late teens) quarrel almost immediately, Niblo's film takes pains to fill in their friendship: first in the street, where the haughty Messala does not at first recognise Ben-Hur, and later at Ben-Hur's home, where the Roman is introduced to the Jew's mother and sister.

Niblo's film then follows the structure of the book reasonably closely, only tightening up the action as it goes along – Ben-Hur's arrest for throwing a tile at the new Roman governor (actually dislodged by his sister), the scene at Nazareth where he is given water by Christ, the sea battle and Ben-Hur's rescue of Arrius, his adoption by Arrius and success as a charioteer in Rome, and his return to Judaea to find his mother and sister. It is in the later stages that the film begins to tidy up the novel's discursive ending: Messala is killed in the chariot race at Antioch (instead of being crippled and later engineering a murder attempt on Ben-Hur's life) and the figure of the Egyptian temptress Iras is briefly disposed of in a welter of straight twenties vamping. The film rightly homes in, after the death of Messala, on the Crucifixion: Ben-Hur, with all his moral debts paid, now embraces the philosophy of Christ, with whom his life has run parallel and whose suffering effects a miraculous cure on his leprous mother and sister (as Christ passes them on the way to Calvary). After a theatrical Crucifixion (lightning, panic in the city, the Senate building collapsing), the film closes with Ben-Hur, the Compleat Christian, telling his womenfolk: 'He is not dead. He will live forever in the hearts of men.'

Niblo's *Ben-Hur* is most remarkable for its dramatic shaping, playing up the spectacle of the key events (the galleys, the chariot race), homing in on the central relationship of Ben-Hur and Messala, and drastically simplifying the wearisome second half of Wallace's novel (which ends with a postscript in AD 64 which suggests that Ben-Hur was crucified by Nero after the Fire of Rome). The acting is variable, no less so than in the two leads: Ramon Novarro is a weak, unconvincing Ben-Hur and Francis X. Bushman a posturing, histrionic Messala. Only the action scenes really impress: a thrilling seven-minute chariot race (fully the equal of that in the 1959 version), some remarkably graphic detail in the sea battle, and a memorable Crucifixion. When freed of straight dialogue scenes, Niblo effects some acute touches: the water scene in Nazareth is touchingly and realistically handled; when rescued from the sea with Arrius, Ben-Hur is momentarily frozen in his tracks by the sight of a haggard face peering out from below-decks; and the sequence of his leprous mother and sister being released from their dungeon is handled with a murky horror (the gaoler using his torch to cleanse his hand). Only the mannered acting, and a lack of any true sense of period in costumes and interiors, lets down the careful dramatic design.

William Wyler's *Ben-Hur* (1959) is little more than a refinement of Niblo's structure – but with all the added resources of 70mm colour photography, stereo sound, sensitive acting in depth, a perceptive score by Miklós Rózsa, and dialogue by Christopher Fry which hits exactly the right note of elevated simplicity. Wyler, one of many assistant directors on the 1925 version's chariot race, resurrects many famous sequences almost shot for shot – the Nazareth water scene, details of the chariot race (bucking horses at the start, wreckage being cleared later on), Sheik Ilderim bringing his horses into his tent to show Ben-Hur, the hidden agony of mother and sister as Ben-Hur returns to his house in Antioch. Yet at every step Wyler deepens the tragedy, points up themes barely articulated in the novel or the 1925 version. Wyler stated that it was the theme of Jews fighting for their freedom that chiefly impressed him, but the film shows none of the Zionist fervour of works like *Spartacus* or *King of Kings* from the same period. Its one moment of overt propagandising is when the light catches Ben-Hur's Star of David as he leans triumphantly over the mangled Messala (Stephen Boyd). However, the latter's dying boast

76 (*below*) Epic *noir*: Sahak (Vittorio Gassman) and Barabbas
(Anthony Quinn) in *Barabbas*

77 (*opposite below*) Heroic posturing: Messala (Francis X. Bushman)
and Ben-Hur (Ramon Novarro) in *Ben-Hur: A Tale of the Christ*
(1925)

78 (*opposite above*) Judaean hearth and home: Tirzah (Cathy
O'Donnell), Esther (Haya Harareet), Miriam (Martha Scott),
Simonides (Sam Jaffe) and Ben-Hur (Charlton Heston) in *Ben-Hur*
(1959)

of 'It goes on, Judah . . . The race is not over . . . ,' and the fact that it is an Arab, Sheik Ilderim (Hugh Griffith), who asks Ben-Hur (Charlton Heston) to wear the star ('to shine out for your people and my people together and blind the eyes of Rome'), shows the film pleading for a general Middle East solidarity and an end to foreign interference rather than Zionism as a solution to the Jewish problem.

In this respect, it aligns itself more with Wallace's multi-racial original. Yet, once its nod to the original novel is out of the way (the main title followed, rather than integrated, with 'A Tale of the Christ by General Lew Wallace'), Wyler's film pursues its own course. The main theme of *Ben-Hur*, the source of all its epic resonances, is signalled in the very background to those titles – a slow dolly-in on the almost touching, but forever apart, fingers of Man and God in Michelangelo's Sistine Chapel fresco *The Creation of Adam*. Beyond the immediate theme of Ben-Hur's painful passage to embrace the Christ ('There are many paths to God, my son. I hope yours will not be too difficult'), the film time and again stresses the barriers to *human* contact: the enmity of the Roman Messala and Jew Ben-Hur ('Is there anything so sad as unrequited love?' observes Messala cynically); the separation of Ben-Hur from his mother and sister (two of the most moving scenes show each grieving over the other, but hidden from direct sight); the separation of Ben-Hur from his homeland (to return to which he has to reject the friendship of Arrius); and the separation of Ben-Hur and Esther.

This last relationship has often been seen by critics as unnecessary, using the argument that the Ben-Hur/Messala relationship is the film's driving force. This is true inasmuch as it is the most closely detailed – especially given the film's amplification of the early scenes of comradeship, tearfully recalling a carefree youth when problems of nationality were immaterial – but Esther is vitally important for her representation of the Judaeo-Christian cause which Ben-Hur must ultimately embrace. The great strength of Wyler's *Ben-Hur* lies in its complicated emotional tug-of-war: Ben-Hur's struggle against the *Doppelgänger* figure of Messala (a struggle that is finally played out in a Roman circus, and ends in violence and unforgivingness); his emotional attachment to both Esther (hearth and home, Judaeo-Christian-

ity) and Arrius (Mammon, Roman ideals); and his interior struggle between unchristian hatred and Christian love ('It's almost as if you have become Messala,' hisses Esther as Ben-Hur expresses his desire for revenge).

Ben-Hur weaves together several symbolic threads which discreetly underline these themes. The prolixity of crosses throughout the film (in the opening title 'Anno Domini XXVI', the cross-beams in the hall of Messala's citadel, Ben-Hur's prayer before the chariot race, and the final Crucifixion tableau) is an obvious device; more subtle are the ring and water motifs. An early scene (written by Christopher Fry) in which Esther gives Ben-Hur her slave's ring to wear as a token of her love is later paralleled in Rome when Arrius (in typically grandiose style compared with the simplicity of the Esther scene) gives Ben-Hur his ring of Roman adoption. Only when Ben-Hur has beaten Messala in the chariot race and discovered that his mother and sister are still alive does he finally reject Roman citizenship by the symbolic act of returning Arrius' ring to Pontius Pilate – a crucial scene, interpreted with a nice balance of friendliness and hard pragmatism by Frank Thring ('I crossed this floor in friendship, as I would speak to Arrius. But when I go up those stairs I become the hand of Caesar, ready to crush all those who challenge his authority. If you stay here you will find yourself part of this tragedy').

In its portrait of Ben-Hur's journey to self-awareness, the film makes consistent use of water as an agent of renewal: the drink offered by Christ at Nazareth; the water offered by Arrius after being rescued from the sea; the stream below the Sermon on the Mount; the water Ben-Hur in his turn gives to Christ on the way to Calvary. It is entirely fitting that, when Ben-Hur returns to his home at Antioch, its courtyard fountain is shown to be dry, in contrast to its luxuriance at the beginning of the film, and that the miraculous cure of his mother and sister comes with the liberating rains which accompany Christ's ascent to Heaven.

From being a man who had boasted to old Balthasar (Finlay Currie) 'I don't believe in miracles,' Ben-Hur finally learns the ultimate humility of Christianity. It is a transformation that is convincing in both personal and epic terms, thanks to the richness of the screenplay, the conviction of the acting (especially Stephen Boyd's Messala, who is only on screen for some 25 of the film's 211 minutes but whose presence lingers), and the resonant musical score of Miklós Rózsa. In *Ben-Hur* the music is a major ingredient of the film rather than simply an accompaniment to the action. Excluding overtures, the score runs to 110 minutes, and there is scarcely a moment when its presence does not enhance the drama, commenting on the relationships, binding scenes into unified sequences and expressing characters' emotions in passages without dialogue. As in previous historical scores, Rózsa uses such devices as fourths, fifths and inversions to summon up an archaic, heroic atmosphere, and his adaptation of original folk material (such as the emotive theme symbolising 'A Mother's Love') is seamlessly woven into the score's fabric. From the gentle Nativity music, through the great B flat major tutti which announces the main title, to the famous marches (the first of which is lifted from his earlier *Quo vadis*), the music carries the audience along in a stream of melody and counter-melody, its absence (as in the nine-minute chariot race and scenes like the reunion of Ben-Hur and Esther) as potent as its presence. Side by side with this runs Wyler's perceptive use of small detail to enhance the period setting: charioteers preparing for the race backstage, deserted streets on the day of the Crucifixion, a fan running into the circus to grab the souvenir of Messala's helmet, the doctor's surgery in which Messala dies, the claustrophobic horrors of galley existence, and the binding rather than the traditional and unauthentic nailing of the crucified. It is supremely ironic that a director who later claimed that *Ben-Hur* 'was never intended to be anything more or less than an adventure story with no artistic pretentiousness at all' should have given the cinema the richest, and perhaps noblest, historical epic of all.

Early Medieval: Norsemen, Saxons, and the Cid

'Can man live without honour?'

'No.'

> Rodrigo to Gormaz in *El Cid* (1961)

'Love and hate are horns on the same goat.'

> rune woman in *The Vikings* (1958)

We have now reached the last leg of the journey away from myth – the so-called Dark Ages, or early medieval period, during which Europe underwent the various social, geographical and intellectual convulsions which led to the Middle Ages, the foundation-stone of modern history. As an end-date I have chosen the end of the eleventh century, a time when, on many fronts, the Heroic Age was changing to the Age of Chivalry, when Europe was becoming recognisably reorganised into the form it held during the Middle Ages, and when a new era of exploration and intellectual consciousness was dawning. The First Crusade – the earliest prototype for the Age of Chivalry which was to spawn the swashbuckler as hero – began in 1096 and, like Attila before Leo the Great, I have refrained from crossing the magic line.

Specifically, this chapter is concerned with the feudal period and the age of the nomadic civilisations. These two ways of life were in perpetual conflict during the early medieval period, and from the friction between them much epic characterisation derives. The feudal system, a fusion of the Germanic and late Roman social systems, created new heroes and villains. The peasantry of the Roman Empire, oppressed by crippling taxes, had sold their freehold on the land to local landowners, who guaranteed them comparative safety from taxation in return for a percentage of turnover. The warring Germanic tribes who found this system after the decline of Rome – a system in some ways similar to their own, in which military obligations were owed to petty kings – settled down comparatively easily: the peasants' new German overlords now guaranteed them *military* protection as well. Thus the rule of law and money was replaced by that of the tithe and obligation – a gross simplification of the elaborate Roman system, which was to remain eclipsed until the Renaissance.

Obligation was the key factor in the life of early medieval man; and under the pyramidal structure of the feudal system, *everyone* was subject to it. In epic terms, obligation became transformed into a moral quality. It had always been a central concept in the epic form (whatever the period) but with the drastic simplification in the way of life and the abolition of personal security following the Fall of Rome, it became a central issue. Feudalism began to decline around the beginning of the eleventh century, when growing wealth led to the break-up of the local feudal units and the very real possibility emerged of some form of centralised government. For Britain, the eleventh century is a crucial watershed, since it was then that the Norman Conquest took place. In Northern Europe, the Viking Age, which had begun in the eighth century, was coming to a close. And earlier that century, the last of the Saxon line, Emperor Henry II, had left the German throne.

* * *

When the Asding Vandals, grown powerful in Tunisia by holding to ransom the Romans' corn supply, crossed to Italy and thoroughly sacked Rome in AD 455, the Western Empire, tottering for half a century, finally breathed its last. While the Eastern Empire consolidated itself, expanded later under Justinian, and finally contracted again to form the Byzantine Empire in the seventh century, Western Europe became a chaos of small kingdoms. The Franks dominated France, the Visigoths Spain, the Lombards sat at the top of Italy, and all and sundry started to raid Britain in the north.

This first section of the early medieval period has been poorly treated by the cinema, and nowhere more so than in Robert Siodmak's *Battle for Rome/The Last Roman* (*Kampf um Rom*, 1968–9), a West German/Italian co-production shot in Romania and released in Germany in two halves. Elsewhere the film was telescoped to half its length, and from the original version one can see why: it is difficult to credit the lumbering plod through sixth-century history to a director who gave the American cinema of the forties some of its most stylish and pacey thrillers. *Battle for Rome* opens with the Goth Theodoric conquering Rome and the Western Empire but failing to select an heir on his death; of his two daughters, Mathaswintha (Harriet Andersson) and Amalaswintha (Honor Blackman), the latter assumes power and banishes the former to a lonely castle. From a rich and decadent court in Constantinople, Justinian (Orson Welles) directs Belisarius (Lang Jeffries) to recapture Rome; meanwhile, Mathaswintha kills her sister, ascends the Gothic throne and tries to recapture Rome, finally giving up and retreating from Italy.

The only character who registers as a human being in Siodmak's static fresco is Mathaswintha, thanks to Harriet Andersson's sensitive playing, and the only sequence in almost three hours which has any visual style or tension is Amalaswintha's death as she bathes in her sister's castle. The exotic set, with its huge nightmarish head over the bath, and the use of yellow smoke slowly filling the flooding chamber, achieves a genuinely pagan quality, helped by Mathaswintha snarling at her drowning sister through a mask-like hole in the wall. Elsewhere, there is little of note: Riz Ortolani's music (brass and percussion for the action scenes, strings and wind for romance) is unmemorable and repetitive; most of the other sets are no better than an average peplum's; and even the battle sequences are undistinguished, despite being directed by the experienced Andrew Marton and Sergiu Nicolaescu. In this film both Justinian and Theodora (Sylva Koscina) are shadows of their real selves. Only Riccardo Freda's earlier *Theodora, Slave Empress/Theodora, Queen of Byzantium* (*Teodora, imperatrice di Bisanzio*, 1954) deals with the revival of the Eastern Empire's fortunes in any depth.

In two relatively insignificant works, Guido Malatesta's *La furia dei barbari* (1960) and Carlo Campogalliani's *Goliath and the Barbarians* (*Il terrore dei barbari*, 1959), the oppressor has been reduced to the rampaging Lombards. Both films are set in AD 568, the year of the tribe's arrival in the Italian Alps from Eastern Europe, and each is remarkable for its female lead – in the former the accomplished Rossana Podestà, in the latter the imported Cuban sexpot Chelo Alonso. Both stories trade on a revenge motif which would later become so familiar in the Viking genre – personal revenge for an outrage to family or tribe. In *Goliath and the Barbarians*, the peaceable Emilianus of Verona (Steve Reeves) avenges his father's death by dressing up in an animal skin and single-handedly slaughtering packs of Lombards ('I will have my revenge. I swear it. His murderers will have no peace'). The film also looks forward to the Viking genre in its revival of the sexual polarisation which characterised the Greek pepla. Emilianus momentarily falls in love with Landa (Chelo Alonso) and their physical attraction is first sketched in their forest encounter (delicately scored in the English-language version by Les Baxter) and later painted in bold colours when Emilianus flexes his muscles in the Test of Truth in the Lombard camp. The script never really fulfils its opening promise, but it is interesting for its peaceful resolution of the Emilianus/Landa relationship rather than fabricating a pious female partner for Emilianus and playing her attractions off against Landa's.

It is interesting, in fact, how central the Viking genre is to the whole of the early medieval period: from the Norsemen radiate most of our remaining areas of interest – the early Anglo-Saxons and the German myths. 'Viking' is thought to be a corruption of *víkingr* (raider, pirate); more properly they should be called Norsemen, i.e. Norwegians and Danes, or Varangians (Danes and Swedes). Written sources vary from the *Anglo-Saxon Chronicle*, the *Russian Primary Chronicle*, the Icelandic sagas (though most of these date from after the Viking Age), various Frankish, Islamic and Irish sources, and – by the Vikings themselves – bare runic inscriptions and a few lines of densely alliterative and metaphorical scaldic verse. The so-called Viking Age lasted from c. 780 to 1070 AD, during which time overpopulation drove them to

79 (*opposite below*) Static fresco: Theodora (Sylva Koscina) and Cethegus (Laurence Harvey) in *Battle for Rome*

80 (*opposite above*) Eastern Empire: Saidia (Irene Papas) in *Theodora, Slave Empress*

81 (*right*) Physical attraction: Landa (Chelo Alonso) and Emilianus (Steve Reeves) in *Goliath and the Barbarians*

82 (*above*) Viking showbiz: the priestesses Rama and Daja (Alice and Ellen Kessler) perform in *Erik the Conqueror*

terrorise the northern seas with swift, sudden and brutal raids for plunder. Britain, raided in the north by the Norwegians and in the south by the Danes, was first alerted to the threat by the sack of the monastery at Lindisfarne in 793.

By such incursions the Vikings naturally came into contact with other religions; their own, vague and adaptable at the best of times, centred around the mighty gods Odin, Thor and Frey, with the World Ash Tree (Yggdrasill) the source of knowledge, and the Hall of the Slain (Valhalla) the only fitting place for a hero to go after death. Little is definitely known about Norse religion of these centuries, but one thing is clear: the raids were prompted not by any antagonism against the Christian religion but merely by greed for what the Christian world (with its rich churches and monasteries) had to offer. Denmark was Christianised by the end of the tenth century, Norway by the first years of the eleventh, and Sweden, whose inhabitants had been busy penetrating into Russia at the same time, somewhat later. Iceland was converted at the turn of the millennium.

The Viking Age thus reaches out farther than one might expect, both historically and thematically embracing most of the key points of the early medieval period. The great Icelandic sagas, written down in the twelfth and thirteenth centuries AD but celebrating an age several centuries earlier, combine history, heroism and moralising in a unique blend. From the standpoint of the epic tradition they bridge the gap between works like the less historical but more mythic *Beowulf* and the later tales of chivalry like *Sir Gawain and the Green Knight*. Two of the pithiest, the *Grænlendinga saga* (written c. 1190) and *Eirik's saga* (c. 1250), both celebrate the Icelandic (i.e. Viking) colonisation of Greenland and discovery of Vínland (North America) between c. 981 and 1010. Written in spare, unadorned prose, they create epic figures from such real-life characters as Eirik the Red, his daughter Freydis, Bjarni Herjolfsson, Leif Eiriksson and Thorfinn Karlsefni. In the sagas, Vínland ('Wine-Land') is an undreamt-of source of comfort and riches, finally unattainable because of the hostility of the native Skraelings (Red Indians). Mario Caiano's film, *Vengeance of the Vikings* (*Erik, il vichingo*, 1965), takes the essential of these two sagas, garbles the history and names (Bjarni, for instance, becomes a villain), but preserves and even heightens the epic form. Erik is being tricked

of his inheritance by his brother Eyjolf; a young Viking falls for a Red Indian girl, who later sacrifices her life to save Erik; and the warriors go in search of a fabulous Mountain of Gold.

It is easy to see how the Viking could take on the character of swashbuckler rather than epic hero, with his legendary skills in seamanship, exploration and lightning raids. (The famous shallow-bottomed long ships were actually not very large, carrying on average only about a couple of dozen warriors, but with a good following wind they could do about 75-100 miles a day, far outstripping anything else on the seas at that time.) Caiano's film avoids the temptation to show Vikings as swashbucklers because the plot's main emphasis is on Erik's revenge and his moral vindication. On the other hand, the far more lavish *The Long Ships* (1964), directed by Jack Cardiff, is little more than a swashbuckler in Norse dress, despite the fact that it makes several attempts to convince the viewer otherwise. The main title and prologue, the latter designed in tapestry/silhouette style by the accomplished Maurice Binder, is impressive: after an opening storm in which a long ship is wrecked, we learn, via the traditional narrator, that a survivor was carried ashore by monks, who came to forge the great Golden Bell of St James. This Viking survivor turns out to be Rolfe (Richard Widmark), son of Krok (Oscar Homolka), who later escapes home and equips another expedition in search of the great bell. Sets and detail of Viking life (filmed, like most of the picture, on the Yugoslav coast) are impressively realistic and heightened by just the necessary degree; Dušan Radić's musical score, with its overworked but heroically aspiring main theme, is also a positive bonus.

The plot's *Odyssey*-structure, with snares like the maelstrom, the Moors' barbaric Mare of Steel and the legendary bell, invites epic comparisons. Closer examination, however, reveals that this is elaborate window-dressing. *The Long Ships* goes out of its way to be *anti*-epic in characterisation and content: Rolfe may embody the Viking spirit for plunder but that is of little consequence in epic terms. He and his brother Orm (Russ Tamblyn, perfectly authentic, despite critics' sneers, as a short Viking) are hardly selfless characters, and the script's generally light-hearted tone of buccaneering is confirmed in the final scene as, the bell safely in Viking hands and the villainous El

Mansuh (Sidney Poitier) fittingly crushed by its weight, Rolfe draws King Harald aside with the words 'Have you heard, sire, of the Three Crowns of the Saxon Kings . . . ?' The plot is further distinguished by the complete absence of any love story or blood feud which might provide emotional commitment for the central character: Rolfe's only reason for embarking on the voyage, apart from greed, is to erase the personal stigma of the first mission's failure.

Such moral devaluation is underlined when King Harald (Clifford Evans) bemoans the changing times to Krok and the decline in Viking valour and manhood. It is a very sixties slant on the Viking genre, and one that is further shown in the deliberate conflict between superstition and reality. Rolfe, as he staggers from the sea ('I've got half the fjord in my guts'), is at first mistaken for a monster by one of Orm's wenches; later, Rolfe lifts the curse clinging to a funeral ship by substituting a kid for a maiden, and the superstition itself is cast in a bad light through being exploited by the villainous Sven (Edward Judd); finally, the awesome terrors of the maelstrom are shown to be conquerable after all. With its *Thousand and One Nights* atmosphere in the second half, as Viking meets Moor in a sort of ancient Bagdad, *The Long Ships* finally confirms its swashbuckler-*manqué* status by jettisoning the epic possibilities inherent in its multi-racial cast and settling into one vast escapist romp.

Purely as a matter of record, Roger Corman's essay in titillation, *The Saga of the Viking Women and Their Voyage to the Waters of the Great Sea Serpent* (1957) – known more conveniently as *Viking Women* – also mines a similar fabulous vein. Despite a majestic score by Albert Glasser, and a portentous introduction ('In the days when the world was young, and the gods had not yet abandoned the race of men, there lived in the land of the North a great stalwart people'), the film is basically a youth exploitation picture, a beach party in animal skins, with dialogue of Mae West profundity. 'Somebody has to protect you women. It's ridiculous not to have a man along on a dangerous voyage,' declares stowaway Ottar (Jonathan Haze). 'It's ridiculous,' croons Thyra (Betsy Jones-Moreland), 'not to have a man . . .'

It is to the underlying theme of revenge that one must turn for the best works in the small but not unimpressive Viking corpus. (Don Chaffey's mis-

named *The Viking Queen* (1967) is, in fact, a romantic fantasia inspired by Boudicca's revolt against the Romans in AD 61 and, though innocuous enough and easy on the eye, has nothing to do with the Viking genre, apart from featuring a photogenic Finnish model in the title role.) Giacomo Gentilomo's *The Last of the Vikings* (*L'ultimo dei vichinghi*, 1961) sports only a token revenge formula in which Harald (Cameron Mitchell) avenges his father's murder by Sveno, King of Norway (Edmund Purdom), and re-forms the kingdom of Viken (sic). The film has a broody Wagnerian flavour to some of its scenes (such as the return to Viken and the later sequences in Sveno's oppressive, low-slung castle) but this is due mostly to the atmospheric (if unauthentic) art direction. Purdom's over-the-top performance as Sveno, a cross between Richard III and a deranged Hamlet, completely eclipses Mitchell's one-dimensional Harald, who can only stand on the ramparts after killing Sveno and cry 'Odin! Odin!'

Erik the Conquerer/Fury of the Vikings (*Gli invasori*, 1962), the first and better of two Viking films that Mario Bava made starring Cameron Mitchell (the Italian industry's resident Norseman), is far more satisfying, the complex, darkly hued plot of fraternal antagonism and Viking/British interplay heightened by Bava's predilection for rich, emotive colour photography. The plot strikingly recapitulates Richard Fleischer's earlier *The Vikings* (1958): Iron, proven leader of the Vikings, sets out against Britain to avenge the death of his father; his enemy, the Duke of Helfort, is finally revealed to be his long-lost brother Erik, though Iron is accidentally killed during their final duel. The two-sided story is nicely paralleled by a sub-plot involving twin Viking priestesses – played with equal charisma by the striking German showbiz double-act, the Kessler Twins. Bava's later *Knives of the Avenger* (*I coltelli del vendicatore*, 1966) is more simply plotted – a stranger, Rurik (Mitchell), reunites a chieftain's family by avenging the murder of his own wife and child – but it is less memorable.

Of the two masterworks of the Viking genre it is Gabriel Axel's *The Red Mantle* (*Den røde kappe*, 1967) which states the epic possibilities of the Viking ethos in the most *literary* terms. And fittingly, one might imagine, given the circumstances of its production – the first large-scale colour spectacular in the history of the Danish film industry, shot in Iceland with a mostly Danish/ Swedish cast. Its authenticity, even beyond the real locations and the nationalities of the players, is impressive; its restraint even more so. Axel finds a true cinematic equivalent for the terse, unemotional, yet pregnant prose of the Icelandic sagas, filming the tale of eleventh-century blood-feuding in razor-sharp, often brutal, images. Over scenes of the three sons of King Håmund riding out to combat, the narrator intones the customary phrases: 'Here begins the story of . . . vengeance called for vengeance . . . this was the custom.' The extreme formality of the images robs the picture of any emotional involvement on the part of the spectator, and in this respect *The Red Mantle* fails to transcend its literary origins. But this is clearly intentional: the chess metaphor which runs through the film (the formal combat on the beach; the precise hierarchy of King Sigvor's home) carries moral as well as social implications, and even extends to the Romeo-and-Juliet-like doomed young lovers, Signe and Hagbard, in whom resides some hope that the blood-feud will end.

The saga is permeated by traditional legacies: the red mantle being hoisted tells Signe (Gitte Hænning) to commit suicide (cf. the black sail in the Theseus and Ariadne myth); Hagbard (Oleg Vidov) returns disguised as a woman in the mantle and when he enters the chapel his presence is instinctively sensed by Signe (cf. Odysseus' return and his recognition by his faithful dog Argos); and the paraphernalia of judgment and combat is equal to anything in the *Iliad*. The look of the film, however, with its bleak landscapes, its stress on greys and browns, its avoidance of any warm colours like greens or reds (apart from, notably, the fateful mantle); the sound of the film, with its scant, essential dialogue ('He [our son] will have your strength, and your intrepid gaze . . . I give you my pledge: if you die, I die too' – Signe to Hagbard in bed; 'Bring him to the hall in man's apparel and we will pass judgment' – King Sigvor on discovering Hagbard) – these ingredients brand the work as unmistakably Norse, with a literary mythic overlay common to all early medieval works (*Beowulf* especially). Its moral centre – the progress of King Sigvor towards realising the futility of the blood-feud and the positive aspects of the young people's love – ignores, interestingly, any religious angles (Iceland had been officially Christianised in AD 1000) and concentrates ex-

clusively on the revenge motif, here, in contrast to the previous works, shown to be a totally negative quality.

Even the major work of the Viking corpus, Richard Fleischer's *The Vikings* (1958), carries no explicit condemnation of revenge *per se*: it simply accepts the practice as part of the obligational fabric of the period and observes it in action. *The Vikings* is the major work it is because of the depth and breadth of its thematic material – it simply covers more ground than any other Norse film. Kirk Douglas, its main star and producer, has described it as 'a big outdoor picture, a sort of Scandinavian western', and certainly the sheer physical *élan* of the film, personified by Douglas' characteristic presence, is invigorating: a great long-ship in full sail up a fjord, backed by Mario Nascimbene's main theme in full orchestral splendour; the final vertiginous duel atop a tower, with (as in the Rodrigo/Gormaz fight in *El Cid*) just the crash of steel on stone; and the heady bravado of the Viking celebrations in which Einar (Kirk Douglas) displays his skill in throwing hatchets. This physical feel is present thematically in the sexual polarisation which dominates the film, the yang element residing in the Vikings and the yin in the British.

The opening narration, read by Orson Welles against the tapestry visuals and Nascimbene's pregnant music (heavy on percussion and featuring the main Viking theme in low profile), not only presents the main thematic material but also sums up the spirit of the age:

The Vikings, in Europe of the eighth and ninth century, were dedicated to a pagan god of war, Odin. Cramped by the confines of their barren, ice-bound northlands, they exploited their skill as shipbuilders to spread a reign of terror then unequalled in violence and brutality in all the records of history. The greatest wish of every Viking was to die sword in hand and enter Valhalla where a hero's welcome awaited them from the god Odin. It was no accident that the English Book of Prayer contained this sentence: 'Protect us, O Lord, from the wrath of the Northmen.'

It is an impressive introduction, informative as well as awesome. The film's plot also has an admirable simplicity at its core: Einar, boastful

83 Icelandic saga: the beach combat in *The Red Mantle*

son of the chieftain Ragnar (Ernest Borgnine), is blinded in one eye by a falcon after taunting the slave Eric (Tony Curtis); Eric escapes with the captured Welsh princess, Morgana (Janet Leigh); Einar sets out in pursuit, unaware that Eric is really his long-lost brother.

Over this bare framework is constructed a multitude of ramifications which flesh out the work's epic stature. The epic character is unmistakably Einar, and his first appearance, from beneath a wench's mass of blonde hair, establishes his renegade qualities dear to his father (*these* are the Vikings mourned by Harald in *The Long Ships*) and his supremacy in the community. These qualities are challenged throughout the film: his sexual prowess by Morgana ('Fight!' 'A woman can't fight a man. I will not lift one finger to resist you'), his physical prowess by Eric, his religious beliefs by the Britons' Christianity, and his seamanship by the primitive compass (significantly in the shape of a fish, with its Christian overtones). In addition, his vengeance for these slights is directed, unbeknownst to him, against his own flesh and blood – a fact he learns only seconds before his death.

But Einar is surely a negative character, and undergoes no moral regeneration (a final proud cry of 'Odin!'), so whence the epic development? Precisely in the friction between Einar's single-mindedness and the pursued 'innocents', Morgana and Eric: the moral transfiguration of Einar *is* his brother Eric – the two exist side by side, and Eric's final killing of Einar is, in epic terms, a powerful metaphor for the 'civilisation' of the Viking character. The English traitor Egbert had already countered one of Einar's physical displays by a nonplussed 'I live by brains, not brawn,' and the casting generally of Americans as Vikings and Britons as themselves points up this dichotomy. But this 'civilising' theme, specifically expressed as Christianity versus Norse myth ('If I have to cross the Poisoned Sea, I'll find him. I swear it – by the sacred blood of Odin,' says Einar), is further enhanced by a complex sexual overlay. The religious aspect first surfaces at the same time as the story's romantic thread – a suitably unreal, studio-bound interlude between Eric and Morgana half-way back to England, during which Nascimbene's love theme is fully developed:

M: Do you know which of all the oceans is the widest?

E: The Poisoned Sea.

M: No. The ocean between a Christian and a Heathen.

E: Our hands can reach across it as easily as that . . .

M: But that's just a joining of the flesh.

E: What else is missing?

M: The joining of our souls.

E: If our hands are touching, our souls must be touching.

M: But your soul is heathen.

E: If my soul is content to be heathen and yours content to be Christian, let's not question flesh for wanting to remain flesh.

Einar is thus doubly slighted by the pair, and his final assault on the castle becomes a sexual metaphor of epic proportions: the penetration of the outer defences by a remarkably phallic battering-ram and, in a sublime image of religious violation following the sexual, Einar crashing through the stained-glass window of the chapel in which Morgana is praying. 'You must love me exactly as I love you', says Einar. 'I hate you; it's Eric I love', replies Morgana, and the music supports her words. There is, nonetheless, a certain attraction between Morgana and Einar (the love theme's appearance is ambiguous because it is equally Morgana's Theme, and Einar and Eric are also brothers) and the latter's lack of repentance ('If I can't have your love, I'll take your hate') prepares him for his death at the hands of Eric – fittingly introduced by a distorted version of the love theme. This is only one of the many fine touches in Nascimbene's score, which only puts a foot wrong once, when the Vikings attack the fort and the brass play an inappropriately high-spirited version of the main theme over busy string figures. *The Vikings* is one of Nascimbene's finest scores (note especially the adroit development of the main theme during the Viking raid on Morgana's ship) and redeems his other, more feeble historical scores, notably *Barabbas* and *Solomon and Sheba*.

The Vikings, then, ultimately regards its subject from a non-Norse standpoint, inasmuch as, while glorifying the Viking ethos (Einar's rhapsodic funeral is sufficient proof here), it does not find its moral code from within that civilisation. But it is thus that the film is able to reconcile the buccaneering and heroic sides of the Viking character where *The Long Ships* failed, by pitting them, unrepentantly, against more pious forces. Small details of Viking life, like the major event the homecoming of a long ship must have been, fill in the background, while the power of the runes supplies much of the mythic atmosphere. Einar is initially forbidden by the runes to kill Eric, and there is a fateful touch before the final battle when Kitala (Eileen Way) is shown casting the runes but we are not allowed to know what they predict. Characterisation is on a suitably heightened scale: Douglas predictably physical, Borgnine gleefully leaping to a grisly death, Leigh mythically pneumatic and immaculate (there is even a joke about her very fifties bodice being too tight) – only Curtis, as in *Spartacus*, lacks epic presence, despite manfully suffering the severing of his left hand. But *The Vikings* is nonetheless an impressive achievement, as rich thematically as it is pleasing on the eye, and a key work of the whole early medieval corpus. Not as polemic as Douglas' later *Spartacus* but certainly consonant with Richard Fleischer's other works in its plea for tolerance embedded in a study of the destructive mind.

*   *   *

It is but a small side-step to Anglo-Saxon Britain during the early medieval period. When the Roman garrison was withdrawn from Britain at the beginning of the fifth century, it left undefended a more cosmopolitan society than is often imagined – Latin-speaking in its upper and educated strata (though for many people Latin was not a first language) and Celtic-speaking elsewhere. Britain, to Rome, was a distant and somewhat draughty province, useful as a dumping-ground, which had long ago exhausted its material promise. This, however, did not stop the Jutes, Angles, Frisians, Saxons, Picts, Irish and Danes from raiding the country as soon as the coast was clear. Before the slow but sure Anglo-Saxon advance from the south-east, the British were driven back to the west and south-west where they became known as the Welsh ('foreigners').

By the seventh century the Anglo-Saxons, who had since imposed their own tongue on the land, were Christianised, and soon the three kingdoms

of Wessex, Mercia and Northumbria began to dominate England. In the ninth century the Vikings overran the land, and it was left to Alfred of Wessex, the only kingdom left intact, to successfully rebuff the Danes, with Kenneth MacAlpin uniting the Picts and Scots in the north against the Norwegians. And so it remained until, following a brief stab at empire (1016–35) by the Danish king, Canute, William Duke of Normandy crossed the English Channel to claim his inheritance by force, and, after dividing up the two million inhabitants among his barons, inaugurated the era – ending with Elizabeth I – during which the old world changed into the world as we recognise it today.

In considering the films about this period, one must again bemoan the absence of any adaptation of *Beowulf*, which, though set in Southern Scandinavia, is the finest product of Old English poetry. Perhaps, as in passages like the monster Grendel's arrival at Heorot or the fight in the Mere with Grendel's mother, full justice could only be done to it through elaborate effects-work, but the poem contains sufficient richness of characterisation, exciting (and often horrific) action, and opportunities for visual display, for one to regret the fact that film-makers have not adapted it to the screen.

A work of even greater proportions, culled from diverse Norse and German sagas, is Richard Wagner's music-drama *Der Ring des Nibelungen*, some sixteen hours of music divided into four operas (a prologue and trilogy). The *Ring* occupied Wagner on and off for twenty-five years and was first staged complete at Bayreuth in 1876; one of the towering achievements of mankind in any art-form, it is a massive demonstration of Wagner's belief that 'myth is true for all time, and its content, however compressed, is inexhaustible throughout the ages' due simply to the 'suggestive value of the mythological symbols' as they are shown by the artist to contain a 'deep and hidden truth'. The basic theme of the *Ring* is the loss of innocence, expressed through the character of Siegfried, around whom Wagner weaves a complex web of intrigue and ambition which develops into a meditation on power itself and the fatal consequences when the all-redeeming force of love is rejected. (The interpretation of Siegfried as a blond *Übermensch* is a twentieth-century invention quite foreign to Wagner's conception. Such is the ambiguity of symbols.)

The cinema's lack of interest in the *Ring* is particularly galling when one considers that it is surely the only medium which can fully realise the composer's vision – the long-awaited *Gesamtkunst* for which this *Gesamtkunstwerk* was designed, and which has the necessary visual and sonic prowess to eliminate the problems of staging met in the opera house. The *fantastique* elements – as Bava's *Hercules in the Centre of the Earth* (1962) and Cottafavi's *Hercules Conquers Atlantis* (1961) have shown – would be the more convincing and dramatic; problems of sound balance would be overcome; and the difficulties of reconciling singing and acting skills eliminated by dubbing. Only the inordinate length of each opera would create a problem with cinema audiences – though this did not deter Leopold Lindtberg with his four-hour-plus version of *Die Meistersinger von Nürnberg* (1970), one of several filmed German productions.

If Wagner's *Ring* has been ignored, at least one of its literary sources has not – *Das Nibelungenlied*, Germany's major heroic epic composed by an unnamed poet c. AD 1200 but reaching back in spirit to the fifth and sixth centuries. Leaving aside a particularly strenuous example of German erotica entitled *The Long Swift Sword of Siegfried/ The Erotic Adventures of Siegfried* (*Siegfried und das sagenhafte Liebesleben der Nibelungen*, 1971) the major versions are worthy transformations of the original and clearly show the many differences in historical epic film treatment over the years. Fritz Lang's *Die Nibelungen* (1924), a two-part version comprising *Siegfrieds Tod* and *Kriemhild's Revenge* (*Kriemhilds Rache*), is in fact quite free with the original, and interpolates detail from the Norse sagas which Wagner also used. The visit of Siegfried to Alberic and Nibelheim, and the slaying of the dragon – both little more than footnotes in the original – are expanded into major set-pieces, and there is an opening sequence of Siegfried forging the Perfect Sword which is solely indebted to Wagner's opera.

Lang's films have a stature which quite transcends the limitations of silent film-making. First, Lang is one of the supreme visual architects of the cinema, as he was later to show in both his crime dramas and even the fabulous two-part *The Tigress of Bengal/Journey to the Lost City* (*Das indische Grabmal*, 1958): emotion and conflict expressed not merely through acting but in lighting and composition – and composition of a strength and rigidity which seems to sit and judge the characters in their actions. Thus, such magnificent set-pieces as in the gates of Gunther's palace opening to reveal Siegfried and his vassal-kings, or Kriemhild arguing with Brunhilda on the cathedral steps, use spectacle in such a way that it becomes an inseparable component of the drama – the protagonists, as in folk-lore (to which Lang makes frequent reference), welded to their surroundings with an inexorable sense of destiny. The most terrifying expression of this *mise-en-scène* comes in *Kriemhild's Revenge* when Kriemhild, obsessed with avenging the underhand murder of her husband Siegfried, is virtually transformed into the architecture herself as she waits, transfixed like a stone pillar, outside the burning palace for Hagen, Siegfried's murderer, to be flushed out.

No such total conception informs the lavish widescreen colour version directed by Harald Reinl, *Whom the Gods Wish to Destroy* (*Die Nibelungen*, 1967), again in two parts, *Siegfried von Xanten* and *Kriemhilds Rache*. Lang had originally been asked to direct but was busy: he might not have made such impressive use of the copious Icelandic and Yugoslav locations (in a sheer physical sense), and would doubtless have questioned the cynical appraisal of what blind devotion to leadership can cause (the major reason why the Nazi administration did not make a version during their rule), but he would at least have imposed a sense of purpose, of direction, which is all that this production lacks. Only Karin Dor's Brunhild possesses the correct blend of stature and emotion.

Returning to Anglo-Saxon Britain, it is interesting that the largest body of films about this period centre on its historically vaguest figure – the legendary Arthur, a probably sixth-century British chieftain who temporarily staved off part of the Anglo-Saxon advance and who in later centuries was embroidered with an elaborate web of myth, including Lancelot du Lac, Guinevere, the castle Camelot, and the Round Table. This myth belongs more to the province of historial romance, and the cinema, in visualising these stories, has rightly played along with this by setting them in Age of Chivalry spirit and dress (it is worth remembering that it was the Normans who really invented the stone castle as Britain knows it, i.e. post-1066). These films are solidly twelfth-century and after, akin to *Ivanhoe* and the films of the Crusade cycle. (Only Terry Gilliam and Terry

Jones' satirical *Monty Python and the Holy Grail* (1975) attempts Dark Age veracity in its art direction; like the same team's *Jabberwocky* (1977) and *Monty Python's Life of Brian* (1979) it has the authentic odour of its chosen period but it does not achieve the same meld of authenticity and satire as Richard Lester's Roman romp, *A Funny Thing Happened on the Way to the Forum* (1966).)

These Age of Chivalry films have little to do with a brave and sturdy sixth-century chieftain fighting off the Anglo-Saxons – but the films are interesting nevertheless. Both Henry Hathaway's *Prince Valiant* (1954) and Richard Thorpe's *Knights of the Round Table* (1954) carry extremely good musical scores, the first by Franz Waxman (in Richard Strauss vein), the second by Miklós Rózsa (inspired by Malory rather than Thorpe's film), and these alone guarantee a measure of emotional involvement. *Knights of the Round Table* looks forward to the Crusade cycle, with Percival describing the Holy Grail: his winding, gentle theme, heard on solo clarinet on his first appearance, is generally placed in tandem with the Grail fanfare motif which evocatively juxtaposes major chords a third apart. (It is interesting to note that Percival's theme bears an uncanny resemblance to the joyful Miracle motif at the end of *Ben-Hur*, composed six years later; the Round Table theme which dominates the film contains a sizeable foretaste of El Cid's, written some eight years later.) *Prince Valiant*, in contrast, is a preposterous mixture of Viking and Arthurian legend, the latter more prominent.

In complete contrast is Robert Bresson's *Lancelot du Lac* (1974), a resolutely small-scale, anti-mythic treatment of Arthurian legend by France's most diffident director. The uncharismatic juvenile leads are further diminished by Bresson's direction: his renowned use of flat, uninflected delivery and selective close-ups (a foot, a hand or a sword more important than landscape or a figure's totality) here works against the story rather than enforcing its emotional intensity. The gauche playing and feeble action scenes (notably the final battle in the forest) seem unjustifiable on any level, and are a sad accomplishment from a director prized for his sharp and touching examinations of human faith and despair. Similarly constrained by budget but more successful in its reinterpretation of myth is Eric Rohmer's *Perceval of Wales* (*Perceval le Gallois*, 1978). One of the French cinema's greatest exponents of the written word, Rohmer here concentrates on the linguistic beauty of the original text, from his own translation of Chrétien de Troyes' twelfth-century verse romance. The Arthurian knight's adventures are set in a colourful studio-bound world of cardboard castles and cut-out trees, immaculately captured by Nestor Almendros' Eastmancolor photography in a conscious evocation of medieval tapestries. Even with such devices as a musical chorus commenting on and expanding the action, the artificiality soon palls during more than two hours' running-time; but Rohmer's attempt to evoke the spirit of the Arthurian romances is commendable, if hardly epic in scope.

Stephen Weeks' *Gawain and the Green Knight* (1973) is considerably more ambitious, even if pitched at a more commercial level. After main titles in the style of a medieval manuscript (by animator Richard Williams), a narrator thrusts us into the age of myth in true bardic fashion: 'Our tale has been sung by bards and minstrels down through the centuries – the legend of Gawain and the Green Knight. Long ago, when pagan gods haunted the world and good men longed for miracles, there towered upon a craggy cliff by a winter sea the rugged fortress of Camelot.' Yet it immediately becomes clear that *Gawain*, like other film treatments of Arthurian legend, is going to opt for a medieval rather than early medieval setting: costumes and locations (Castell Coch, and Caerphilly, Cardiff and Peckforton castles) are solidly Walter Scott-ish. As we shall see from *Camelot*, this need not necessarily dilute its epic message; but the film then starts to radically transform the original poem.

Over shots of knights assembling at the court of an aged King Arthur, the narrator continues: 'Many years had passed since founding the Round Table. War had ceased and the land secured. The knights grew slack and settled. Chivalry declined and the ideals of knighthood fell into neglect. Only Gawain, a humble squire, prayed for knightly glory and adventure.' This is far from the spirit of the original poem, which depicts a robust, young Arthur, a glorious Guinevere and a Camelot 'in splendid celebration, seemly and carefree'. The fourteenth-century alliterative poem, written in North Midland dialect by an unknown author (perhaps Hugo de Masci, a Cheshire nobleman), celebrates a single adventure of an already estab-

84 (*above*) Visual architecture: Fritz Lang's *Die Nibelungen* (1924)

lished knight in bringing further honour to the Round Table. Weeks' film ditches most of the original and shows a 'boy' becoming a 'man' through a series of semi-supernatural adventures. The original Gawain certainly passes through many adventures on the way to his appointment with the Green Knight, but the poet deliberately avoids recounting these at every step ('So many marvels did the man meet in the mountains, / It would be too tedious to tell a tenth of them'). The film instead constructs a series of encounters – with a Black Knight, Christian pilgrims, wicked nobles – and turns the unnamed 'lady' of the original into Linet, a damsel in distress he meets along the way.

It is a convincing transformation on its own terms, with the Green Knight made an agent of Gawain's passage to knighthood (and dissolving when done) rather than a tester of his established virtue. However, the conception is let down by a weak and untidy plot, uncharismatic direction, and inept playing as Gawain by Murray Head, fresh from *Sunday Bloody Sunday* (1971). Even lusty and radiant characterisation, by Nigel Green (Green Knight) and Ciaran Madden (Linet) respectively, and a warm modal score by Ron Goodwin, cannot compensate.

Only Joshua Logan's *Camelot* (1967), the film version of Lerner and Loewe's 1960 musical, completely succeeds in weaving epic conflict out of Arthurian legend. In its early stages it seems to go out of its way to be irreverent (Lancelot: 'Is there some wrong I can right, some enemy I can battle?' Arthur: 'Well, actually, there's not much going on today'), but this is later revealed as part of a grand design showing Arthur's passage from innocence to kingly wisdom. The device of framing the story as a flashback on the eve of Arthur's (Richard Harris) storming the castle where Guinevere (Vanessa Redgrave) lives with Lancelot (Franco Nero) heightens the tragedy of Arthur's dilemma, the destruction of his dream of a united and peaceful England (symbolised by the Round Table). Part 1 shows the dream taking shape, the protagonists assembling; Part 2 shows its destruction (personalised in the adultery of Lancelot and Guinevere) and the agony of a philosopher-king forced to take up arms against his best friend. The tragedy is heightened by the fact that the three protagonists are shown caught up in events that none wants to happen but which have a terrible inevitability: the

final forest meeting of the trio captures this fatalism with much pathos.

At the end, as Arthur faces the fact that he must bow to the inevitable, consolation comes with the realisation that the Round Table, and all it stood for, will not be forgotten. As Arthur meets a young boy in the forest, he finds his own life at the very point of being transformed into myth, as an inspiration for the future. Young Tom of Warwick (Garry Marsh), reared on 'the stories people tell' of brave knights, is dispatched to keep those very stories alive. As Arthur says to King Pellinore (Lionel Jeffries): 'I have won my battle. And here [the boy] is my victory. What we did will be remembered – you'll see.' Joshua Logan's long-breathed direction, Frederick Loewe's inspiring music, and convinced playing from all the cast unite in a potent, epic portrait of a mythic age.

The other great work of the Arthurian cycle, John Boorman's *Excalibur* (1981), is conceived in a similarly fairy-tale style and often attains *Camelot*'s mythic power. Its strength is that the mythic elements also make sense in human terms: Arthur's later spiritual sickness is also personal grief at the collapse of his ideals. This is important in a film which mines the wizardry of Arthurian legend deeper than *Camelot*. In *Excalibur* Dark Age magic provides more than mere interludes; it is a fully fledged companion of events. The film opens near a mystical Tintagel and provides a spectacular version of Arthur's conception – the magical seduction by Uther Pendragon (Gabriel Bryne) of Igrayne (Katrine Boorman), daughter of the Duke of Cornwall, watched by her young daughter Morgana. The sequence provides a reason for the later revenge of the grown Morgana (Helen Mirren) as she does battle with a weakening Merlin (Nicol Williamson) for Arthur's throne, reciprocating Pendragon's seduction of her mother by sleeping with Arthur in the guise of Guinevere (Cherie Lunghi) and giving birth to the evil Mordred (Robert Addie). *Excalibur* goes on to embrace the whole fabric of Arthurian legend, largely dispensing with Lancelot (Nicholas Clay) in the apocalyptic finale in which Perceval (Paul Geoffrey) discovers the Holy Grail and restores a sense of purpose to Arthur's kingdom. In the bloody battle that follows, both Arthur and Mordred die, and it is left to Perceval, on Arthur's dying instruction, to return the sword Excalibur to the Lady of the Lake.

Boorman is eminently successful in the scenes of myth and magic, raiding the visual vocabulary of Steven Spielberg's *Close Encounters of the Third Kind* for Perceval's discovery of the Grail and the style of his earlier *Zardoz* (1974) for Morgana's lair (masked characters out of Greek tragedy). The great set-pieces are stunning: the opening night battle in the forest (lights, smoke and glinting armour), the magical Lady of the Lake sequences, the final meeting of Merlin and Morgana as the latter breathes out her spirit and is reduced to a hideous hag, the final battle in the blood-red rays of the dying sun. The visual design of the film is thoroughly thought through, with consistent use of green (often reflected in characters' clothes) for the moral quality of good as exemplified by the sylvan Camelot.

Excalibur is also careful to set its magical side in perspective. Both Morgana and Merlin acquire added pathos from the fact that their kind is clearly shown to be a dying race. At the moment of Camelot's greatest glory – the wedding of Arthur and Guinevere – Merlin tells Morgana that his time is coming to an end: it is the age of men, not spirits ('one god is coming to drive out all the varied spirits'). Yet in Nicol Williamson's quirky performance, all funny accent and poor jokes, Merlin is denied the full pathos which the similar character of Ulrich (Ralph Richardson) gains in Matthew Robbins' *Dragonslayer* (1981). His presence severely weakens much of *Excalibur*'s dramatic fabric, especially the crucial sequence of Merlin's and Morgana's power struggle in the former's cave, intercut with Arthur's silent discovery of Lancelot and Guinevere making love in the forest. Williamson's performance is not, however, crucial to *Excalibur*'s success: the film survives on the wealth of other fine performances, from Nigel Terry's long-suffering Arthur to Cherie Lunghi's radiant Guinevere. They are not characterisations writ large, as in *Camelot*, but in tandem with Boorman's convinced direction and perceptive use of Wagnerian excerpts (notably the *Parsifal* and *Tristan and Isolde* preludes and *Götterdämmerung* Funeral March, the latter only heard in its full glory at the end) they attain an epic stature fully worthy of Arthurian legend.

Despite their Age of Chivalry setting, the Arthur films still comprise an impressive body of work. Their achievement seems all the greater when set against a weedy work like Nathan Juran's *Siege of the Saxons* (1963), a mish-mash of Arthurian droppings in Norman and medieval dress which pitches its anti-Saxon story on a Robin Hood/Sheriff of Nottingham level and has its hero walking around for the most part with a bow but no quiver. Similarly fanciful, but at least dispatched with glee, is Albert Pyun's *The Sword and the Sorcerer* (1982), shot in tandem with its sequel, *Tales of the Ancient Empire* (1983). Clearly hampered by the lack of suitable locations in California, the film opts for a generalised evocation of bygone days, with fantasy castles, the whole paraphernalia of sorcerers, maidens and unwashed extras, and some muddy special effects to complement the equally muddy photography. The plot pits the one-handed hero Prince Talon (Lee Horsley) against the wicked Cromwell (Richard Lynch), tyrant of the erstwhile idyllic Eh-Dan conquered with the help of the sorcerer Xusia (Richard Moll). The film's chief virtues are its unflagging energy and sense of the ridiculous (the crucified Talon even ripping his own hands free of the cross); its faults are a ludicrous script and a failure to realise its own potential. *The Sword and the Sorcerer* blends *Star Wars* swashbuckling with Bavaesque imagery redolent of sixties pepla, all propelled by a derivative but thrilling score by David Whitaker. Less sixties is the heroine Alana (Kathleen Beller), much disposed to giving villains the come-on and then promptly kneeing them in the groin.

Also reminiscent of Bava in its copious use of exotic lighting and eternal mists is Terry Marcel's *Hawk the Slayer* (1981), a similar farrago of Dark Age sorcery and futuristic elements (here a Spock-like swordsman). From its very opening the script strains for a mythic elevation: 'This is a story of Heroic Deeds and the bitter struggle for the triumph of Good over Evil and of a wondrous Sword wielded by a mighty Hero when the Legions of Darkness stalk the land.' However, it rarely attains any such thing and, thanks to its lack of proper characterisation, even wastes the opportunities afforded by its paper-thin plot of two brothers locked in a feud over the dead Eliane (Catriona MacColl). As the embodiment of Pure Evil, Voltan (Jack Palance) makes a memorable figure; unfortunately, his heroic brother Hawk (weakly played by John Terry) comes a poor second in charisma, despite being supported by Morricone-ish twiddles every time he appears. Terry Marcel's workaday direction seems unable to stir itself even for the final swordfight in the nunnery and, with Voltan's towering presence gone ('I shall wait for you at the gates of Hell'), the film can only end on the lame upbeat of a promised sequel ('The Dark One is no more,' breathes the witch woman. 'But even as we speak the wizards gather in the south. Follow your destiny. We shall meet again, bearer of the Mind Sword').

Yet at least *Hawk the Slayer* makes some attempt to place its tale in a recognisable Dark Age rather than a Maloryesque fairyland. Matthew Robbins' *Dragonslayer* (1981) goes all the way, creating a bleak, forbidding landscape in which its figures move with only sorcery or individual heroism offering avenues of escape ('no knights in shining armour, no pennants streaming in the breeze, no delicate ladies with diaphanous veils waving from turreted castles, no courtly love, no Holy Grail' in Robbins' own words). *Dragonslayer* has an authentic whiff of Dark Age violence and superstition which totally escapes most sword-and-sorcery pseudo-epics, and Robbins' careful script and direction even manage to efface the obtrusiveness of the two young leads' American accents. Galen Bradwardyn (Peter MacNicol), a sorcerer's apprentice, is shown stumbling towards an uncertain destiny as slayer of the dragon which holds the people of Urland in a grip of fear. Despite killing the dragon's offspring, he can only vanquish the creature itself with the help of his master, Ulrich (Ralph Richardson). The truly cosmic finale, atop a mountain peak, reveals Ulrich as the film's (largely unseen) epic presence, a representative of a dying creed who must sacrifice his own life in the struggle. In a pointed coda, as Galen and Valerian (Caitlin Clarke) leave for a life elsewhere, the forces of both monarchy and Christianity are shown assembling over the dragon's giant carcass to take credit for the deed; but there is no doubt where the film's sympathies lie.

Beneath its flinty surface (reinforced by Alex North's harsh, unforgiving score, all low brass, percussion and strident trumpets), *Dragonslayer* conceals a wistful elegy for a bygone age. Even the dragon, like Ulrich a being out of its time, is sensitively portrayed, now grieving over its dead litter, now towering over its underground kingdom in incredibly life-like realism. The film's ambiguity extends even to its young hero and heroine: some way into the story, Valerian surprises both Galen and the audience by revealing herself as a girl, and their low-key love scene, set among craggy rocks, is fittingly scored by North with a hard-edged oboe doing its best to fashion a romantic melody.

However, the obvious sympathy of *Dragonslayer* for a pagan age is as nothing compared to that of John Milius' *Conan the Barbarian* (1982), which positively makes love with its theme in every frame. Milius has been quite explicit: '*Conan* is a genuinely pagan film. It's not a Judaeo-Christian film at all. I think it's really rather Wagnerian. I wanted to do something that dealt in Teutonic myth. Those Nordic myths and Icelandic sagas had a primitive sophistication. If you have a Viking sense of humour it's a very funny film.' *Conan* is based on the pulp fiction hero of the Texan writer Robert E. Howard, who from 1932 to his suicide in 1936 produced a vast gallery of wandering superheroes ranging from the Atlantean King Kull to the Pictish war-chief Bran Mak Morn. Milius' script takes as its starting-point a far more exotic script by Oliver Stone based on Howard's *Black Colossus* and *A Witch Shall Be Born* but locates the action more identifiably in Howard's self-styled Hyborean Age and peppers the storyline with references to many Conan tales. Most important, Milius invents a full-scale background for Conan, showing his childhood in a peaceful Cimmerian village and supplying motivation by having the ruthless Thulsa Doom murder his parents during a raid. Milius' script is true to Howard's original spirit (the character of Valeria, for example, is based on Belit in *Queen of the Black Coast*) but in visual style models itself on the more carnal, muscular illustrations of Frank Frazetta for the sixties paperback reissues rather than any of the earlier illustrators' conceptions.

It is the final hype to a film which makes no concessions to the unbeliever. Conan is no more than the peplum mythic hero writ large, but Milius is clearly concerned to create the ultimate fantasy world – from the massive bulk of Austrian bodybuilder Arnold Schwarzenegger ('If Arnold hadn't existed, we would have had to build him') to the sensual, athletic grace of dancer Sandahl Bergman, to the massive weaponry and brutal bloodletting. The production design, by Ron Cobb, is a deliberately vague mixture of several Dark Age cultures, from Viking to Mongol, and also

85 (*left*) Nuclear Valkyrie: Brunhild (Karin Dor) in *Whom the Gods Wish to Destroy*

86 (*below left*) Kingly wisdom: Arthur (Richard Harris) marries Guinevere (Vanessa Redgrave) in *Camelot*

87 (*below right*) Kingly doubts: Alfred (David Hemmings), with Athelstan (Julian Glover), Aelhswith (Prunella Ransome), Edith (Sinead Cusack) and Asher the priest (Colin Blakely) in *Alfred the Great*

88 (*above*) Figures of destiny: the Cid (Charlton Heston),
Chimene (Sophia Loren) and a dead Count Gormaz (Andrew
Cruickshank) in *El Cid*

includes fleeting references to Greek, Roman and Aztec architecture. In essence, however, the film's heart is Viking, its mythology based solidly on the Norse/Teutonic structure.

Thematically, however, it shares little in common with the Viking corpus discussed earlier. Conan (Arnold Schwarzenegger) battles for neither national nor religious reasons, and undergoes no moral regeneration as a result of his labours. Every character in *Conan* is motivated by either personal greed or simple life-for-a-life revenge, and the script makes no attempt to transfigure their deeds into moral lessons or ethical codes of conduct. Conan's own quest for Thulsa Doom is later transformed into a mercenary commission to rescue the daughter (Valerie Quinnessen) of King Osric (Max von Sydow) who has been kidnapped by Thulsa Doom (James Earl Jones) and converted to his snake cult in the Mountain of Power. Conan's companions tag along for love or kicks: Valeria (Sandahl Bergman) is a professional thief, Subotai (Gerry Lopez) a thief and archer. The world of Conan is a loveless, violent landscape, in which companionship is a thing of the moment and might equals right.

As such, *Conan* is more a reworking of the themes of Sydney Pollack's *Jeremiah Johnson* (1972), the Milius-scripted tale of a lone mountainman, than of Milius' own *The Wind and the Lion* (1975), in which personality is raised to a national level. In *The Wind and the Lion* (see Chapter 12) Milius showed history at the very moment of being transfigured into myth, through the eyes of a young boy; in *Conan* he merely shows the basic ingredients of myth. In doing so, he draws on the whole literary and cinematic corpus of heroic romance: Conan and Subotai are Siegfried figures, heroes free of fear ('two fools who laugh at death' in Valeria's words); the scenes of Conan riding in search of the Mountain of Power recall the wandering knight of *El Cid*; the sequence of Conan making love as a captive parodies the scene in *Spartacus* where Batiatus watches the gladiator and Varinia in their cell; Conan recuperating his powers by the seaside parallels similar sequences in *Fistful of Dollars* and *One-Eyed Jacks*; the pit-fighting scenes recall *Spartacus* and *Barabbas* in their loveless brutality; Conan chained to the Wheel of Pain or nailed to the Tree of Woe evoke Samson with the Philistines and the martyred Spartacus or Christ; and the film's whole vocabu-lary (Wheel of Pain, Tree of Woe, Atlantean Sword, Giant's Cave, Riddle of Steel, Tower of Set, War Yurt, Mountain of Power, Battle of the Mounds) is pitched at a heroic level. Reinforced with a propulsive score by Basil Poledouris – all pounding ostinati, braying brass and sweeping, modal-inflected love theme – *Conan* rapes the mythology of the Dark Ages for every visceral thrill in sight. It is challenging heroic cinema but, like many pepla it recalls, it is no epic.

Neither, for that matter, is Barney Platts-Mills' *Hero* (1982), a resolutely low-budget, historically vague attempt to transpose J. F. Campbell's authentic *Tales of the Western Highlands* into cinematic form. Its greatest virtue is setting its story and characters firmly in their landscape, thanks to Adam Barker-Mill's evocative photography of the harsh greens, blues and greys of the Argyll locations, in which the colourfully garbed characters move with grim fortitude. However, the promise of the opening, in which the warrior Dermid O'Duinne (Derek McGuire) joins up with the band of Finn MacCumhail (Alastair Kenneil), only to run away with his bride Grannia (Caroline Kenneil), is never fulfilled, and the film becomes inextricably bogged down in clumsy Celtic dialogue and amateurish acting. The latter was made a positive advantage in Platts-Mills' rough-hewn portrait of modern youth, *Bronco Bullfrog* (1970), but in *Hero* it is a positive disadvantage.

* * *

For true epic treatment of early medieval Britain – treatment which is in period and whose strengths are wholly from within the age – one must turn to King Alfred, a historically definite figure from the ninth century whose exploits, apart from burning the cakes, have escaped the later romancers (strangely, for he is a crucial figure of the period). He is represented by one film of remarkable quality – Clive Donner's *Alfred the Great* (1969), a late entry in the historical cycle in a decade which had been more interested in youth pictures. Curiously, however, this was to work in the film's favour (thematically only, for the picture was sneeringly received) since Alfred could be accurately portrayed as being only in his early twenties when he rose to prominence – an opportunity by which the film-makers clearly intended to show the modern relevance of their historical material.

'I found him an extraordinary figure,' said producer Bernard Smith, 'full of the conflicts of which greatness is born. Alfred is also modern in that his central conflict is between his basic desire to be reasonable and the violence needed to defend Wessex against the invading Vikings from Denmark.' Director Donner concurred: 'I was attracted by the character of the man, especially by his affinity with young people today. I have tried to use the medium of the epic to show what went on inside Alfred himself. Guthrum [the Viking leader] makes an interesting contrast with the tormented Alfred. Guthrum knows no inhibitions. He goes after, and gets, anything he sets his heart on. His character is not unlike that of some of today's outspoken, uninhibited young men. In many respects *Alfred the Great* can be viewed in terms of current circumstances and events.'

The finished film supports these statements. At the very simplest level the script raises the moral struggles of the central epic presence (Alfred) to a national level: the conflict between the Britons' peace-loving Christian God and the Danes' war-like one ('We are the sons of Odin,' says Guthrum), developed in the discussion between Alfred (David Hemmings) and Guthrum (Michael York) which shows mastery of and subservience to passion perfectly juxtaposed. To this simple conflict are added several subtleties. At home, the fraternal discord mirrors the broader national and inter-national disunity: the paradox of Alfred be-queathed a sword and Ethelred a cross by their father, with the latter a weakling king and the former a strong neophyte priest. Alfred's transition to warrior king, his restless spirit, is subtly prepared for in an early scene in which he sees the hands of some new priests being bound, and the actual transformation is powerfully stated in a simple two-shot of him against a red background – which colour is to become a fit *leitmotif* as he is drawn, to his horror and pleasure, into the blood-shed necessary to fulfil his destiny of uniting the country.

Only in the role of egalitarian monarch are the religious and power drives able to cohabit success-fully. 'My justice will be done, without distinction to any man', says Alfred to Aethelstan (Julian Glover), and he is made to champion the underdog by stressing the need for a book of laws written in accessible Saxon ('Latin is for monks'). Raymond

Leppard's modal, 'English pastoral' score lends dignity, emotion and beauty to the proceedings, complementing David Hemmings' moody but thoughtful performance which, against expecta-tion (for Hemmings personified the sixties young anti-hero), builds into one of great stature – self-doubting and sure of only one thing, his destiny.

Clive Donner manages to set the film in authen-tic surroundings (Ireland's County Galway stand-ing in for unpastured England) without diminishing the achievement of the script – a rare accomplish-ment. There is much detail of everyday existence and a very real sense of period: authentic pre-battle noise to frighten the enemy as the Danes chant and crash their spears against their shields; bloody slapdash battles; the stomach-loosening fear prior to an attack. Even the main female role is unglamorous, played with freshness by the freckle-faced Prunella Ransome. Donner achieves sequences of tremendous sweep without ever reduc-ing the combatants to anonymity – not necessarily a requirement of epic form but an accomplishment unique to *Alfred the Great*. The magnificent final battle has some excellent aerial photography of Alfred's men forming into arrow formation against the Danes' single horizontal line, then has the forethought to show the swarthy Freda (Vivien Merchant) laying about her with the basic weapon of a stick. Though on a smaller scale, this battle is every bit as effective as the similar set-piece in Kubrick's *Spartacus*, vigour replacing massive inevitability. If *Alfred the Great* is to be faulted, it is in its lack of a fitting heroine; Aelhswith mirrors none of the conflicts of Alfred nor does she significantly aid in their workings-out. Such a female epic presence is missing, but that is all that this remarkable work lacks.

This is not the case with the remaining two works – *The War Lord* and *El Cid* – both of which fully integrate the leading male and female roles into a dramatic unity. Franklin Schaffner's *The War Lord* (1965) draws much of its intensity from the fact that it is based on a play (*The Lovers*, by Leslie Stevens, which closed quickly on Broadway), and the claustrophobia fits the subject perfectly. We are already outside the Saxon/Briton ambit, on the Norman coast in the eleventh century, but *The War Lord* in spirit looks back rather than forward. Chrysagon (Charlton Heston), the Norman knight sent by his duke to oversee a dull stretch of coast inhabited by Druids and raided by Frisians, is an embodiment of feudal obligation, his own sense of duty reflected by the loyalty of his squire Bors (Richard Boone), a loyalty earned by respect for behaviour in action over the years.

Chrysagon's code of conduct is challenged by an elemental sexual attraction towards a local wench, Bronwyn (Rosemary Forsyth), already betrothed, with whom he exerts his lordly right of *ius primae noctis* after her marriage. *The War Lord* is permeated by the kind of sexual imagery found already in *The Vikings* – the final siege of Chrysagon's tower by the locals and Frisians is a violent metaphor for the 'cuckolded' groom's need for vengeance. The two leads are also subtly handled: the first meeting establishes them as sexual stereotypes (she at a disadvantage, naked in a pool, he proud atop a horse), the second (*he* naked and at a disadvantage, about to be cauterised) confirms their mutual attraction with a near-kiss, and the third shows Bronwyn taking the measure of her lord (the river scene).

Chrysagon's moral struggle has the customary personal and political dimensions, the former concerned with his own conscience, the latter put on a national level by the strife which follows his refusal to surrender Bronwyn after the *prima nox*. If *The War Lord* were only a story of temptation, however, it would fail to exert as strong an emotional effect as it does. The authentic period setting, full of the paraphernalia of the age (from chickens to war machines), certainly provides a firm foundation for the script's designs; so, too, does Jerome Moross's glowing score, its modal *Thomas Tallis*-like love theme tinged with the same autumnal melancholy as Russell Metty's Technicolor images – images of hard, grey stone, inhospitable shorescapes, and faces bathed in amber tones. And the direction by Schaffner, a TV-trained director with a particular gift for reworking clichéd characterisation and exploring the mentality of the outsider (*The Stripper*, *Patton*), draws playing of great conviction from Heston, Forsyth, Boone and Guy Stockwell (Draco).

All this evinces the work's great craftsmanship, but the story goes beyond the obvious level of sexual temptation. Chrysagon does not constrain himself, Odysseus-like, against some Bronwyn-Siren – he drinks deep and wants more, for Bronwyn offers no false attractions, no inveigling Circe-ish wiles. This is the moving quality of *The War Lord*: the weary knight ('I've lived twenty years with that cold wife,' he says of his sword) who at last finds peace and spiritual enrichment but is unable to enjoy it, most of all because he knows he must run contrary to the laws of obligation. Through his invocation of the lord's *ius*, Chrysagon first exploits, then flaunts, the feudal code by which he lives – and this must be paid for. The love story is thus raised to an epic level, to an examination of strength and weakness with wider implications.

These implications even extend to Chrysagon's family, and time is found to include the motif of fraternal enmity which resurfaces in *El Cid*. In *The War Lord* it is merely another reflection of Chrysagon's divided nature rather than a separate strand: Draco's change of loyalty serves as a reminder of where his elder brother's real loyalties should remain, but the character is oversimplified from that point on into a straightforward villain rather than following through with Chrysagon's own development. But Draco's personality, along with the subtle evocation of superstition and mystery attaching to the locale, emphasises the pressures at work, the forces that may be conjured up, when obligation is flaunted. 'You keep it, brother,' Draco says of the place, adding cynically, 'as the Lord kept Israel.' And later Chrysagon himself admits, 'There's a strangeness in this place: I've felt it since we first came here.' In such an atmosphere, the vision of Chrysagon of 'that far place', in which both he and Bronwyn would be free of worldly cares, becomes a powerful plea for an end to the absolutes of the medieval code. Yet it is a plea which goes unanswered as the work mercilessly runs its full epic course, as Chrysagon follows his father's fate of finally 'losing all' (already signposted by 'the sign of death' – the bee on the wedding garland which stings him when he first meets Bronwyn by the pool), to a conclusion in which all debts are paid and the status quo re-established.

There is, then, nothing of chivalry in *The War Lord*; though Norman, it is grounded in the world of *Alfred the Great* and before, with the lack of any easy final redemption very much a mark of the sixties. It also shows a subtle adaptation of the epic hero in the five years since Anthony Mann's *El Cid* (1961), which stylistically belongs more to the fifties, or at least works more within the fifties heroic mould, than *The War Lord*. Like Schaffner's film, *El Cid* is set on the very borders of the dividing line laid down for this book, but despite its Crusades-like Christian/Moor conflict (and even the inclusion of a jousting sequence) it finds its strengths from the early medieval fabric rather than the Age of Chivalry.

El Cid is a pivotal work in any examination of epic form in the cinema, the very finest of the finest, and certainly the greatest product from producer Samuel Bronston's stables during the early sixties. In size, scope and solid achievement it sums up the whole medieval period, and in all departments shows the same exquisite craftsmanship as the Romano-Christian paradigm, William Wyler's *Ben-Hur* (1959), sometimes even more so. From its opening credits (mythic sketches by Maciek Piotrowski) it impresses throughout with its intelligent script and genuinely epic construction. Much of this is due to the fact that the film has a proper respect for its sources, notably the *Cantar de mio Cid*, the finest medieval literary celebration of the Spanish hero, which survives in a single manuscript of some 3,700 lines. There, as in the film, the main theme is the loss and restoration of the Cid's honour, against a complex socio-political background of warring nobility (and neo-nobility) of Castile and León. The real Cid, Rodrigo Diaz, was born in Vivar c. AD 1043, rising to prominence in his twenties under the Castilian king Sancho but finding less favour under his successor, the Leónese Alfonso VI, whom Sancho had previously expelled. Alfonso tried to patch matters up by arranging Rodrigo's marriage to the Leónese noblewoman Ximena Diaz, but Rodrigo was eventually exiled, spent time in the service of the Moorish king (not mentioned in the *Cantar*), and defended Valencia against the Almoravids, a fanatical Moroccan warrior-sect, finally dying in Valencia in 1099.

The *Cantar* is not the most accurate version of Rodrigo's life (that is the early twelfth-century Latin *Historia Roderici*) but it is the finest. The film clarifies its structure and reinterprets it in cinematic form. The first part concentrates on character-building, using smaller-scale set-pieces (like the Tournament at Calahorra) to satisfy the requirements of spectacle. Then, with conflicts and themes clearly established, the second part safely opens up for the giant Siege and Battle of Valencia. A legend in his own time and the object of a tomb-cult after his death, the Cid possesses all the qualities for epic treatment: a wronged exile (due to his liberal treatment of the enemy), a leader of men ('El Cid' derives from the Arabic 'El Seid'), an unswerving patriot (despite the whining behaviour of the young king Alfonso), and a visionary pacifist (his loyalty to God and his dream of a Moorless Spain).

The opening scenes stress his semi-divine nature: first his sword-blade, then he himself, come into view, and after brushing some arrows from a sculpted cross he carries it and a wounded priest away from a Moor-devastated church. The motif resurfaces later when the Cid helps a leper, Lazarus, during his own exile: 'Thank you, my Cid' 'How do you know my name?' 'There is only one man in Spain who could humble a king and give a leper to drink from his own pouch.' At Valencia his first 'shots' against the townspeople are not rocks from the catapults but loaves of bread. And finally there is his transfiguration from history into myth, as he leads his men into battle as a corpse strapped to his horse – a prolonged low-angle shot showing him wreathed in beams of sunlight ('And thus the Cid rode out of the gates of history into legend') and giant organ chords resounding on the soundtrack ('Heavenly father, open your arms to receive the soul of one who lived and died the purest knight of all'). In print this may sound faintly histrionic; after three hours of development on screen, it has an apt inevitability.

Like Chrysagon in *The War Lord*, the Cid has an overriding desire to live in a peaceful world, typically expressed in his relationship with Chimene (Ximena of the original). Their first meeting in the film, which is set in a circular anteroom, immediately establishes their love as a emotional metaphor for the later physical and constitutional wrangles. With Miklós Rózsa's great love theme singing beneath the exquisite visuals (the central shaft of light flooding the room and pinpointing their joining of hands), the Cid states his wish to live in peace as the pair stand alone in the still room, the babble of the wordly, quarrelling court filtering through from outside. But the Cid is a figure of destiny, and when Count Gormaz (Andrew Cruickshank) strikes Don Diego (Michael Hordern) across the face, he and Chimene react to the slight with extra-sensory perception. The Cid's destiny, in fact, is only to help towards building his idealistic world for future generations, not for himself; and as an instrument of history he is a tragic figure. Remarks throughout the film stress his removal from normal affairs: 'You did take the shortest road, my son,' says the rescued priest. 'Not to your bride but to your destiny. God sent you, my son'; 'Let me now offer myself before the highest judge,' says Rodrigo as he takes up the gauntlet; 'What kind of a man are you?' asks Alfonso after being rescued on his way to Zamora, later echoing these thoughts as he progresses to his own redemption with 'He sends me the crown. What sort of man is this?' That the Cid's efforts are on behalf of a weak and ungracious monarch makes him the more tragic and noble, and Alfonso's final reconciliation as the Cid lies dying fully complements the latter's own story:

A: Forgive me.
R: No! My king kneels to no man . . . I have not failed. Spain *has* a king . . . Chimene, I want you and my children to remember me riding with my king tomorrow.

The fusion of all these elements is in the final shots, as the cry of 'For God, the Cid and Spain', watched by Chimene and the children, unites the national, religious, family and obligational strands of the story into one.

Chimene, then, like Alfonso, is central to the Cid's conflict. The line from the original poem quoted in Chapter 2 stresses the closeness of their relationship, and Chimene's first scene in the film establishes her as an equally idealised (in her case, love-) figure as the Cid. 'You have no right to ask him. He has had enough,' she rails against the soldiers who clamour for his leadership, but this movingly human response, which enhances her epic characterisation, must be a vain plea in the face of their twin destinies – also expressed visually in a magnificent crane shot as the Cid rides away with the soldiery, Chimene in the foreground. 'Chimene, you can't save my life,' says the Cid, as she pleads for the removal of the fatal arrow at the end. 'You must help me give it up.' Such pull between the epic and the personal, the stereotyped and the human, strengthens the work's emotional power – a legacy traceable to Homer.

There are many sub-themes which reinforce the strength of the central characterisations: Alfonso's passage to maturity; the conquest, by dint of sheer will, of Count Ordóñez's in-built hate (though it is fitting that the Count should die at the hands of Ben Yussuf); the period of Chimene's wounded

hate, and the chance, expressed by the Cid in the nuptial bedroom scene, that perhaps they have wounded each other too deeply (an elemental clash of the emotions); and the theme of racial unity present in the friendship between the Cid and Moutamin (Douglas Wilmer). 'How can anyone say this is wrong?' asks Rodrigo. 'They will say so – on both sides,' replies the more cynical Moor, and their second reunion, when opposing forces face each other across a river before their leaders plunge their swords into the turf and advance to embrace, is a large-scale augmentation of this trans-racial motif.

The interaction and *resolution* of these elements, over a long period, gives *El Cid* its sense of sweep and scope. Script, acting, images and music all act in perfect harmony. Philip Yordan, who also scripted Bronston's *King of Kings* prior to *El Cid*, is generally successful in his designs, wisely eschewing over-use of archaisms or significant *mots*, and only writing a line where it is absolutely necessary. The film moves swiftly but with dignity, any bridge passages pared to a minimum if not abolished altogether and fortuitous meetings (such as that between the Cid and Chimene in exile) speeding the picture along. Only in scenes like the above reunion does the dialogue verge on the fulsome; elsewhere it is marked by an admirable sense of the phlegmatic which shows its turn-of-the-decade origins.

It is hard to imagine the film without the towering presence of Heston – surely *the* epic presence, an actor, like Olivier, who plays each role straight down the line, giving a film the necessary conviction to underline the rest of the production. *El Cid* is Heston's finest epic performance, the brief space since *Ben-Hur* having been put to good use. The Cid's visionary side provides many fine moments for Heston's particular brand of heroic intensity, none more gripping than his deathbed scenes. He is ably supported by a predominantly British cast: John Fraser, Andrew Cruickshank, Douglas Wilmer, and Michael Hordern. For the rest, Sophia Loren is totally apt as Chimene, maintaining an imperishable beauty even after months in a dungeon and particularly impressive in the touching reunion scene in the monastery, the wonder of the couple's love and the young children delicately evoked by Rózsa with the love theme on solo violin over soft guitar chords. Mann wisely accentuates her classical, statuesque qualities, and Loren has rarely looked more pneumatically regal, a believable partner for the Cid.

Mann and director of photography Robert Krasker endow the work with great visual sweep. Mann's proven ability for this, evident in his Westerns, is here enhanced by his obvious love for the country (he had married Sara Montiel and settled in Madrid some time before accepting the film), and he makes good use in the Valencia scenes (actually filmed in the fishing village of Peñiscola, some 200 kilometres along the coast) of Spanish peasant faces. Crane shots are used sparingly and to effect; above all, Mann never gives the impression that the wide screen is an embarrassment. The quietly sumptuous set dressing by the team of Veniero Colasanti and John Moore provides a comfortable frame for close portrait-work, and in sequences like the pre-nuptial tension between Rodrigo and Chimene, Mann (with Rózsa's powerful music) generates considerable power by simple cross-cutting. The claustrophobic swordfight between Count Gormaz and the Cid has an authentic steel-on-steel desperation, and here the music is sensibly held back until the latter's fiery 'Now, Count; now I am satisfied.' The Tournament at Calahorra has a similar gritty tension which is far more early medieval than chivalrous, with the mighty weaponry emphasised by close camerawork.

I have paid tribute earlier to the work of Miklós Rózsa in the epic field, but no discussion of *El Cid* can forbear to call this one of his finest scores. Much music that was composed and recorded for the film was ditched at the dubbing stage in favour of sound-effects, but one would hardly realise it, such is the fluency and dramatic aptitude of the existing score (120 minutes of music for a three-hour film – the same amount as in *Ben-Hur*, a far longer work). *El Cid* derives some of its material from the earlier *Knights of the Round Table* score (notably the essence of the Cid's theme), but the prevailing use of the Phrygian mode as a harmonic basis for the score establishes the Spanish flavour of *El Cid* clearly enough, along with the free use of mordents and grace-notes. For inspiration Rózsa studied the thirteenth-century collection of *cantigas* made by Alfonso X – themselves influenced by Moorish culture – and his own modal language completed their transformation to a sound suggesting the eleventh century to modern ears. From the bracing Overture to the more darkly-hued Prelude, from the great harmonically clashing fanfares to the gentle palace music for flute and guitar, from the boldest statements of the memorable themes to their subtlest musical development, Rózsa's score (much of it written in Madrid, whither he had again been loaned by M-G-M) is an enduring monument to this noble cinematic work.

Epic Aftertastes: Misnomers and Modern Myth

'If you strike me down, I shall become more powerful than you can possibly imagine . . .'

Ben Kenobi in *Star Wars* (1977)

'A hero can't run away from his destiny . . . Sometimes you run smack into your destiny on the very same road you take away from it.'

Nobody in *My Name Is Nobody* (1973)

'When you speak of destiny, this is something I must at last believe.'

Genghis Khan in *Genghis Khan* (1965)

This book has been specifically concerned with epic form in a pre-medieval European context – models most commonly experienced by Westerners in both literature and the cinema. Before closing, however, it would be worthwhile to consider briefly some of the works which fall outside the scope of this book but which nonetheless contain elements received from the epic legacy.

In journeying eastwards one's terms of reference become more and more confused. The various Asiatic nomadic tribes share many points, in ethos and disposition, with Norse culture; but with no surviving literature one can only guess at their codes of social conduct. Their effect on European history was minimal, their challenge to the Roman Empire, as we have seen, most acutely used by the cinema. The remaining works which concentrate more closely on the various tribes share only a confused viewpoint: the sense of obligation present in the Norse works is almost entirely missing, and the majority of films settle for a spectacular mish-mash of cruelty, aggression, and vague Oriental allusions.

Richard Thorpe's *The Tartars* (*I tartari*, 1961) shows Tartar and Viking in conflict on the Russian plains and ends with the leaders of both communities (played by Orson Welles and Victor Mature)

dead and two young lovers fleeing to a promised land. Sergio Grieco's *The Huns* (*La regina dei tartari*, 1960) is a custom-built and lip-smacking vehicle for the tempestuous Chelo Alonso. Mongol culture fares little better. André de Toth's *The Mongols* (*I mongoli*, 1961) shows the hordes threatening Eastern Europe in AD 1240 and conveniently extends the life of Temujin (alias Genghis Khan) by some twenty years. Despite exciting battle sequences directed by Riccardo Freda and spirited playing by the statuesque Jack Palance and Anita Ekberg, it never explores the monumental conflict of life-styles.

Of the two works more directly concerned with Temujin, it is difficult to know which to commend the least. Dick Powell's *The Conqueror* (1956), taking its cue from the Utah locations and John Wayne in the leading role, is little more than a Western in Asiatic dress. Although Wayne is well-matched by Susan Hayward as the unwilling object of his affections, the cowboy's lumbering performance is hardly the stuff which unites warring tribes into proud solidarity. Henry Levin's *Genghis Khan* (1965) is little improvement, thanks to thoroughly incompetent direction at every turn and the casting of the insipid Omar Sharif in the title role. The script makes several efforts to build an epic structure around Temujin, rightly concentrating on his vision of uniting the Mongol tribes into a force situated between the 'white-skinned Christians' on the one hand and the Chinese in the 'rich East' on the other.

To this end much of the film deals with a (fictional) relationship between Temujin and the Emperor of China, the former respectful of the 'vast empire built on knowledge', the latter all too aware of the weakness of the ailing Sung Dynasty beneath the splendid trappings. This theme is never developed, however, and the script only explores the division within the Mongol tribes through a strained revenge plot between Temujin and Jamuga (Stephen Boyd), the inevitable final duel culminating in the former's death. Despite much talk of Temujin's sense of destiny, it is only in the final minutes that any effort is made to expand the period's mythic atmosphere: 'I have lived to see it . . . but it is my sons who will make our nation great,' whispers the dying leader. 'Turn me around to the wind. I want the gods to see me in the face.' But this is little compensation for Sharif's total lack of stature (as Jamuga says, 'Is *this* the leader who is going to unite the Mongols?'), the jokey performances of Robert Morley and James Mason as the Chinese, and the general lack of any sense of physical exultation in the portrayal of Mongol life – accentuated by Dušan Radić's feeble, posturing score.

For genuine realisation of the period's mythic possibilities, one must turn to *The Fate of Lee Khan* (*Ying-ch'un ko chih feng-po*, 1973), directed by Peking-born, now Hong Kong based, Hu Chin-ch'üan (known in the West as King Hu). Set in 1366 at the end of the enfeebled Mongol Yüan dynasty ('the empire born in the imagination of the prince of conquerors', to quote the last words of Levin's *Genghis Khan*), it crystallises the struggles between the repressive Mongols and their Chinese subjects into a mythic confrontation at a remote inn between a group of resistance fighters and a visiting war-lord and his sister. The film is the most perfect exposition of Hu's interest in the heroic aspects of the martial arts, previously given a philosophical slant in the mammoth three-hour *A Touch of Zen* (*Hsia nü*, 1969) and here raised to a level of national importance. Hu's choreographic skills, coupled with a very musical feel for action and dramatic line, imbues the drama with a supra-realistic feel, superbly realised by Hsü Feng, Mao Ying and T'ien Feng.

There is space here only to allude to the continuing examination of the heroic ethos in a national and historical background undertaken by the Hong Kong and Taiwan industries. Hu Chin-ch'üan presents this in a manner most easily comprehended by Western audiences, his direction recalling such models as Anthony Mann and Miklós Jancsó, his editing closer to Japanese models than mainstream Hong Kong film-making. Hu's *œuvre* extends so far to half a dozen pivotal works, and his influence is discernible in countless other productions. In a less consciously artistic

vein works the prolific Chang Ch'eh, who since the mid-sixties has continued to probe aspects of heroism in well over fifty productions, the vast majority in a historical setting. His early works, while a contract director with the Shaw Brothers organisation, are marked by a visual richness and sensuality, combined with the surrealistic extremes of violence and martial skills, which attains a poetry of its own. Chang's works are never less than invigorating (in the best tradition of the Italian peplum), and his highly mobile visual style, with its rejection of the traditional Hollywood master-shot, is best seen in works like *Golden Swallow/The Girl with the Thunderbolt Kick* (*Chin yen-tzu*, 1967) with mythic super-heroes meeting in combat on other-worldly planes, *King Eagle* (*Ying wang*, 1969) drawing the loneliness of the solitary hero, *The Blood Brothers/Chinese Vengeance* (*Tz'u Ma*, 1972) showing heroic obliga-tion vs blood camaraderie, and *The Water Margin* (*Shui hu chuan*, 1971) trilogy. Since 1973 Chang's visual style has become less ornate and more reliant on the dramatic powers of the zoom, his concerns narrowing almost exclusively to the *techniques* of the martial arts rather than their broader application – and always in a masculine context. Aside from the many Shaolin films of the seventies, this is best seen in *Marco Polo* (*Ma-k'o P'o-lo*, 1975), which uses the Chinese martial arts as a symbol of resistance against the Mongol overlords – certainly a more positive mythification of the period than Hugo Fregonese's *Marco Polo* (1962), with its Japanese heroine and fake Oriental swashbucklings.

I have cited the work of Hu Chin-ch'üan and Chang Ch'eh merely as convenient representatives of the Hong Kong/Taiwan heroic genre, since any fuller discussion would occupy a space equal to this whole book. The Chinese *wu-hsia p'ien* is a synthesis of many diverse strands – the Japanese swordplay films (*chambara*), the moral propagandising of mainland Chinese production, and the Italian peplum and Western schools. Post-revolutionary Mainland Chinese production is overridingly con-cerned with heroism in a national/political context: the selfless heroine Wu Ch'ing-hsia in *Red Detach-ment of Women* (*Hung-se niang-tzu-chün*, 1970) possesses no personality beyond a selfless repre-sentation of Red political aims during the Second Civil War of 1927–37; and the spectacular *From Victory to Victory* (*Nan-cheng pei-chan*, 1970) shows, within its Hollywood-influenced visuals, how all personal emotion must be subsumed into politics – a radical interpretation of heroism but perfectly in line with current national preoccupations.

Hong Kong production, while stressing individual heroism more (as befits a capitalist rather than Communist society), falls midway between the cardboard epics of Mainland China and the introverted products of the Japanese film industry. The latter's taste for *chambara* films, which examined the ethos of the Samurai warrior, principally arose during the fifties, and is most memorably seen in the work of Akira Kurosawa and Masaki Kobayashi. Where Hong Kong production is colourful and extrovert, Japanese is contemplative and measured, though the ability of directors to give mythic dress to the Samurai figure (in reality a socially *déclassé* mercenary) is often coloured by a cynicism generally absent from the Chinese equivalents. Kurosawa's *chambara* films also sport a winking humour which places them alongside Western swashbucklers rather than historical epics, and for serious consideration of the traditional codes of conduct and honour, of obligation and personal destiny, one turns to works like Kenji Mizoguchi's *The Loyal 47 Ronin of the Genroku Era* (*Genroku chushingura*, 1941) or Masaki Kobayashi's *Rebellion* (*Joi-uchi*, 1967).

Sydney Pollack in *The Yakuza* (1975) triumphantly broadened the Japanese *yakuza* film genre (itself an updating of the Samurai ethos) into a moving study of the clash of Eastern and Western codes. And, despite Kurosawa's own scepticism, his works have been transformed by other cultures into highly mythic films. At a time when the peplum was languishing after its initial thrust, *Yojimbo* (1961) became the inspiration for Sergio Leone's *Fistful of Dollars* (*Per un pugno di dollari*, 1964), the lone Samurai becoming a lone gunfighter in a Western setting, arriving to deal death and summary justice amongst the occupants of a warring Mexican border-town. Leone's elliptical direction, combined with Ennio Morricone's emotive music, gave the definitive impetus to a fresh trend in Italian popular entertainment which lasted until the seventies, and gave a new term – 'Spaghetti Western' – to filmgoers' language.

Leone's 'Dollars Trilogy' gave mythic stature to the Western gunfighter by stripping him of his essentially American qualities, surrounding him with more absolute moral stereotypes, and wrapping the whole in a quasi-operatic, high-keyed style tailored to Morricone's music, which enhanced the Angel of Vengeance parallels with its heroic use of fourths, fifths and inversions, the trademarks of the historical epic composer. The Man With No Name (Clint Eastwood) is in direct line of descent from the wandering bodybuilders of the peplum cycle, superb gunmanship replacing superb musculature, the Man righting wrongs with a Machiavellian single-mindedness and personal unconcern. His only motivation in *Fistful of Dollars* is distinctly vague: 'Why? I knew someone like you once. There was no one then to help.' Only the cynical overlay of monetary greed and the lack of any pacifist justification for the brutality brand Leone's films and their many descendants (those by Sergio Corbucci among the best) as belonging to the sixties rather than of the preceding decade.

By the time of Tonino Valerii's *My Name Is Nobody* (*Il mio nome è Nessuno*, 1974, with Leone as producer) a subtler transformation of the genre has been reached. While never compromising its brilliant meld of jaunty comedy and operatic drama, the film slowly develops into a supreme meditation on the very metamorphosis of history into myth. As ageing gunfighter Jack Beauregard (Henry Fonda) is relentlessly steered towards a fitting destiny by the cocky young 'nameless' Nobody (Mario Girotti/Terence Hill) – 'a hero can't run away from his destiny' – the script explores the whole processes of myth-creation ('There *was* never any Good Old Days') and the cyclical progress of history with considerable perception and poetry, climaxing in a great final soliloquy by Beauregard as he lives to see his own mythification take place.

Beauregard's fate is among the more hopeful and philosophical in the Italian Western. The dictum of Benito Rojo (Antonio Prieto) to the Man in *Fistful of Dollars* that 'in these parts a man's life often depends upon a scrap of information' still holds in Valerii's film, but there is a new romanticism, a greater humanity, in the later picture which only fitfully peeps through in earlier works of the sixties like the 'Dollars' trilogy.

The Italian Western's harsh moral landscape, offering little hope of resurrection, is in direct contrast to the more cosmetic Hollywood 'original', which is for the most part unalloyedly positive and imbued with a poetry drawn from the country's landscape and the triumph of middle-class values. Its failures and virtues are exemplified in a couple of key works, all with epic characteristics. John Wayne's *The Alamo* (1960) transfers the theme of Rudolph Maté's *The 300 Spartans* to the America of 1836, as a motley group of Americans, for varying reasons, engage in a suicidal, time-saving move as they defend an old mission against the advancing Mexicans. The film's failure to realise its possibilities is not only due to Wayne's un-inspired direction and his inability to understand the requirements of epic structure, nor even to the shoddy script which never progresses beyond the 'a man's gotta do . . .' stage in explaining the motivations of the participants. Rather, it lies in the mistake of equating individual heroism with the kind indelibly rooted in a sense of national and historical consciousness, the same mistake which afflicts John Sturges' *The Magnificent Seven* (1960) – inspired by Kurosawa's *Seven Samurai* (*Shichinin no samurai*, 1954) – if it is considered in epic rather than heroic terms, a fault which not even Elmer Bernstein's triumphant score can mask.

Leone's films, with their stronger mythic overlay and passage towards spiritual regeneration (epito-mised in Morricone's use of solo trumpet, human whistle, or male chorus), disregard the national element in favour of total moral allegory; so many American Westerns, however, confuse the issue. Only in works like William Wyler's *The Big Country* (1958), made immediately prior to *Ben-Hur* (1959), can one see the qualities of the historical epic reworked in an American Western setting. Wyler shows a sure sense of balance in the slowly maturing relationships and the interweav-ing of male aggression, female redemptive love, and paternal reconciliation in an overall plea for unity and tolerance. This same sense of rooting allegorical relationships in time and place can also be glimpsed in King Vidor's *Man without a Star* (1955) – a film interested in similar themes (though not so fully worked out) and also, not by coincidence, a product of the fifties.

That heroism, in any of its many forms, is a staple ingredient of the historical epic is beyond doubt, yet it is this quality which has most dogged attempts to redefine the word 'epic'. The war film features heroism in its most contentious role, for here, it seems, heroism *is* inextricably placed in a

national context. But does this make it epic? Unless there is the historical distancing I would prefer to answer no. It merely makes the film a celebration of the human spirit, of man's capacity to survive or sacrifice himself for any number of reasons – and not necessarily moral or national or with any sense of personal destiny. Cornel Wilde's *Beach Red* (1967), one of the best of a number of films which questioned this sacrifice, is quite categorical that heroism (at least in the present century) is uncharismatic; Carl Foreman's *The Victors* (1963), Lewis Milestone's *All Quiet on the Western Front* (1930) and King Vidor's *The Big Parade* (1926) concur. More positive in celebrating the triumph of the human spirit are Vittorio De Sica's *Two Women* (*La ciociara*, 1960), Sam Wood's *For Whom the Bell Tolls* (1943), Sidney Lumet's *The Hill* (1965), Sergei Bondarchuk's *War and Peace* (*Voyna i mir*, 1965), King Vidor's *Northwest Passage* (1940), D. W. Griffith's *The Birth of a Nation* (1915), Sydney Pollack's *Jeremiah Johnson* (1972), and Fred Zinnemann's *The Men* (1950). Films like J. Lee Thompson's *The Guns of Navarone* (1961), with its unabashed plagiarism of the Greek setting, and David Lean's *The Bridge on the River Kwai* (1957), use the devices of epic journeys and structures to mirror the protagonists' own heroism.

Lean, in particular, has often been dubbed an 'epic' director. This is true in so far as he has the ability to present personal conflicts satisfactorily against large canvases: the love story of *Doctor Zhivago* (1965) against a period of national and political upheaval; a story of personal obsession transformed by chance events into a sense of destiny in *Lawrence of Arabia* (1962). These merely lack the mythic trappings of antiquity but at any event are convincing evocations of con-temporary myth, espcially the latter. Only John Milius' *The Wind and the Lion* (1975), a film which starts by undermining conventional epic characteri-sation in its central love story, equals *Lawrence of Arabia* in so evocatively observing its characters in time and place, in communicating their own sense of historical destiny, and finally fixing the lead roles in a general timelessness. Not by accident, it would seem, does Milius' film carry one of Jerry Goldsmith's – and the seventies' – finest film scores, with baying horns and singing strings in full romantic flood. The film's many elements coalesce near the end in one heart-stopping moment, when El Raisuli (Sean Connery) is transfigured before a child's (our) eyes from history into myth as he sweeps past on his horse to snatch a rifle from the boy's hands.

The additional strengths of films like *Doctor Zhivago, Lawrence of Arabia* and *The Wind and the Lion* derive from the folklore tapestries in which the characters move. Zhivago is a poet of the Russian landscape (and in Lean's direction very much a part of it), and the epic feel springs from the clash of his personal emotions against those felt as an embodiment of apolitical 'Russian-ness'. Lawrence, on the other hand, is an exile in search of a country, a martyr in search of a cause, and in this respect this film examines his attempts to *assume* a folkloric mantle rather than shrug it off. Milius' film, midway between the two, polarises these forces into two main leads rather than working them out within the one man: El Raisuli and Theodore Roosevelt (Brian Keith) never meet, yet they are as one in their sense of a destiny rooted in their own cultures, however self-conscious such mythification is shown to be.

Such self-consciousness is also found in Moustapha Akkad's *The Message* (*Al-risāla*, 1976), a dogged attempt to make the Muslim religion the prime epic subject rather than its first prophet, Muhammad. The tenets of Islam prevent the film-makers from ever showing Muhammad in person, so – subjective camera apart – his presence is reflected in and diffused by his several colleagues, all of whom lack stature and any sort of conviction beyond fanaticism. Hollywood, when treating religion in a historical setting, has always reflected that religion in a central epic presence; bereft of that, Akkad shows the development of an idea snowballing into a unifying belief – an interesting concept let down by the formulary, lightweight, American TV-style direction, singularly uncharismatic in both mass and individual groupings (a flaw which even Jack Hildyard's evocative desert photography hardly corrects). Muhammad's hegira of AD 622 (from which the Islamic calendar dates) should stand as the film's central climax, but it is virtually ignored in favour of a slow overall development to Islam in the present day. The picture's propagandist stance is clearest in an epilogue which shows Muslims worshipping in modern temples – fair enough in that it celebrates the success and strength of a people's religious consciousness but disastrous in that it destroys what little sense of myth has lingered from the

promising opening three hours earlier.

Considerably more successful in this regard is Lester James Peries' *The God King* (1975), a colourful and didactic celebration of Sri Lanka's fifth-century AD struggles between traditional monarchy and representational government. Some film-makers, on the other hand, working in countries with a strong awareness of their past culture, have separated the folkloric elements from epic form and created consciously literary tributes. Bahram Beiza'i's *The Stranger and the Fog* (*Gharibeh-va-meh*, 1975) is set in a seaside community in an undefined and unrecognisable past age of Iranian history, and charts a stranger's arrival, his acceptance into the community, and his final departure into the fog whence he came, after a bloody and desperate battle against some super-warriors who arrive to claim him for an unspecified reason. Beiza'i is much concerned with the components of primitive myth – details of worship, assembly, ritual, honour. But the central characterisation, beset by self-doubt and inner fears, lacks any moral stature or wider significance.

Where Beiza'i's film is hewn prose, two other films show folklore transmuted into poetry, cinematic tone-poems of thrilling dimensions. Tengiz Abuladze's *The Invocation* (*Molba*, 1968), shot in high-contrast monochrome scope images, traces the fortunes of a Georgian warrior in his struggle to save Truth (personified by a girl in rapturous white) from the Devil (called by his Georgian name of Matzil). The film is based on two poems by Vazha Pshavella, its structure built on a series of climaxes which culminate in the stunning set-piece of Truth undergoing a ritual hanging before the assembled forces of society and the Devil. With its elliptical, transient feel – heightened and dramatised by Nodar Gabunya's musical score, which alternates between an exquisite pastoral theme and gripping use of high string tremoli – Abuladze's film is clearly influenced by its literary origins. It has the full mythic feel of the literary epic without its narrative drive or human interest.

Erik Blomberg's *The White Reindeer* (*Valkoinen peura*, 1952) is an even more breath-taking *tour de force* of purely mythic cinema, in its sixty-seven minutes expanding the ethnic side of the Finnish rural tradition to embrace a host of folkloric traditions, not all essentially Finnish but presented within a recognisably Finnish format. The story is obliquely vampiric, with Jekyll-and-Hyde elements: a Lapp wife, Pirita (Mirjami Kuosmanen), has the power to transform herself into a white reindeer which lives off the blood of men, and becomes slowly dominated by the transformation process; finally, her husband, Aslak, forges the necessary 'cold iron' which is needed to kill her (cf. Siegfried with Nothung). Thanks to the masterly photography and use of real locations in snowy Lapland, the film sustains its initial thrust; and to complete the ethnic feel, there is a near-continuous musical score by Einar Englund, replete with the special characteristics of Scandinavian music – long, thrilling pedal-points, extended brass fanfares, chattering woodwind, and ostinato bass-lines.

Such examinations of myth pure and simple, rather than as a component of epic form, show one aspect of film-makers' search for mythic material in a modern age. The literary epic has always drawn on the past for inspiration, for there resides the distorting passage of time which converts fact to myth. Where in the twentieth century does the modern mythologer turn for subject-matter? Epic poetry was originally designed to appeal to the fears and superstitions of its audience; in the late twentieth century those fears are of the future, the extra-terrestrial, the very technology which is often an enemy of romance. Space ('the final frontier'), with its vastness and technological paraphernalia, is just as incomprehensible to the modern layman as ancient theology was in its own day.

This seam was first mined on a major scale by fifties Hollywood, whose science fiction works, obsessed by the new fears of an atomic generation, show the same constructivist attitudes as many fifties historical films. Yet none show any desire to go beyond the particular to some kind of universal theme which would reinterpret the epic legacy in Space Age terms. In the past few years, several works have welded elements of Dark Age myth to Space Age stories, using the resonances of the former to enhance the spiritual bleakness of the latter. Both George Lucas' Star Wars (1977) and Irvin Kershner's The Empire Strikes Back (1980) plunder the heroic codes of Dark Age romance (summed up in the character of Ben Kenobi) to give the adventures of the innocent, Siegfried-like Luke Skywalker (Mark Hamill) an extra dimension beyond their essentially swashbuckling nature. As Ben Kenobi (Alec Guinness) tells him,

'Your destiny lies along a different path than mine.' Flash Gordon (1980) similarly raids elements of early medieval heroism, but lacks the vital presence of a Ben Kenobi figure and the thematic complexity of the Star Wars cycle, which is like a modern Ring des Nibelungen with its talk of the Force, the Dark Side, the quest for ultimate power, and its interwoven genealogy.

These films, however, do not express modern myth in purely Space Age terms. Robert Wise's Star Trek – The Motion Picture (1979) tries very hard with its story of the alien V'ger approaching Earth in its quest for a force it calls the Creator. Like many of the episodes of the original TV series (1966–9), the finale takes off into a sublime mixture of cod philosophy and visual pyrotechnics, as two of the Enterprise's crew fuse with the alien machine in a truly cosmic coupling. The picture often has a thrilling, heroic breadth, thanks to Jerry Goldsmith's uplifting Enterprise theme, but lacks a central epic presence: both the USS Enterprise and Admiral Kirk (William Shatner) are mythologised in their ways but both are robbed of participating in the final transfiguration. At least the central character of Steven Spielberg's Close Encounters of the Third Kind (1977) is allowed to fulfil his destiny in person, as he is swallowed up at the end by the benign Mother ship and, pace the revised The Special Edition of Close Encounters of the Third Kind (1980), shown a fairyland world far removed from the threatening aliens of fifties science fantasy.

Some ten years previously Stanley Kubrick had already signposted this shift of perspective in 2001: A Space Odyssey (1968), in which the central character is reborn through the benign agency of the impressive Monolith. Kubrick moves from the particular to the universal in one giant epic statement for the Space Age portrayed on the vastness of the Cinerama screen. The film's title, with its allusions to apocalypse (2001) and early epic form (Odyssey), tidily sums up its broad scope – so broad, in fact, that the normal epic progress of the destiny of a single man or nation becomes that of mankind itself, seen first in some kind of proto-Australopithecine form and next as Homo sapiens sapiens of the Space Age. Kubrick and Arthur C. Clarke, working from the latter's flimsy short story 'The Sentinel', significantly dwell only on the essentials. There are no details of evolution or earth civilisation to distract from the central thematic core; from the opening shots everything works relentlessly towards Man's next stage of evolution into Space-Child. The impassive monolith, a cold technological equivalent of the gods of Homer and Vergil (for the Space Age is not concerned with personality), conveniently works the instant transformations which propel Man, in the form of David Bowman (Keir Dullea), towards his destiny. Instead of a goddess protecting her favourite by conjuring up a dust-cloud, the monolith projects a new stage of consciousness, a fresh sense of direction (typically, for Kubrick, the ape-man's use of weapons to kill).

Such parallels can be found throughout the film: the space 'ship' gliding silently across the wide, wide screen; HAL, the one-eyed Polyphemus, who is blinded by having his memory-banks disconnected; the laboured detail of donning one's space 'armour'; the portentous introduction (now, suitably, transformed to only visuals and music, with the resonant main title speaking for itself)... Kubrick's film is both a summation and a reinterpretation of the literary epic legacy, as oblique a statement for his own time as Vergil's prophetic Fourth Eclogue, written some two thousand years ago, was for his:

The final age of Sybilline song has now come;
the great cycle of the ages is born anew.
Now the first-born child descends from the high
  heavens.
Observe the world nodding beneath its vaulted
  weight
and the lands and tracts of the sea and lofty sky.
Begin, small boy, to greet your mother with a
  smile . . .

Filmography

The following is as complete as possible a list of films set in eras up to the end of the Dark Ages (AD 1096). As such, it is oriented to European history, excluding such genres as Arabian Nights films except where the story directly touches upon European developments.

Every effort has been made to make it comprehensive but, especially in the case of silent one- and two-reelers, I am more than aware of its shortcomings. Additions and corrections from readers will be gratefully received.

The filmography includes all films released in their country of origin up to the end of 1982. It excludes time-travel films but lists those films in which flashbacks, dream sequences or parallel stories make a significant contribution (marked [†]). Uncredited work or important 2nd Unit work is noted in brackets after the credited director's name. In the case of pepla co-productions, more than one director is often credited in official sources for quota reasons; these have been included when in doubt as to who actually did the work. Real names have been substituted for pseudonyms wherever possible.

Video titles are marked with an asterisk (*). 'English-language title' also includes reissue titles, 16mm release titles and TV titles. TV movies (TVM) are only included if they have been given a theatrical release (often in a shorter version under a different title); as such they are listed under their theatrical release title.

Film title	Director	Country	Release date	Leading players	English-language title
Actéon	Jorge Grau	Sp.	1965	Martin Lassalle, Pilar Clemens	
Adam and Eve	(Vitagraph)	USA	1912	Harry T. Morey, Leah Baird	
Adam's Rib	Cecil B. DeMille	USA	1923	Milton Sills, Pauline Garon	
Adan y Eva	Alberto Gout	Mex.	1956	Carlos Baena, Christiane Martel	Adam and Eve
Afrodite dea dell'amore	Mario Bonnard	It.	1958	Isabelle Corey, Antonio De Teffè	Slave Women of Corinth
L'agonie de Byzance	Louis Feuillade	Fr.	1913	Luitz-Morat, Bréon	

Film title	Director	Country	Release date	Leading players	English-language title
Agostino d'Ippona	Roberto Rossellini	It.	1972	Dary Berkani, Virgilio Gazzolo	Augustine of Hippo
Agrippina	Enrico Guazzoni	It.	1910	Carlo Muccioli, Walter Rinaldi	Agrippina
Aida	(Pathé)	Fr.	1911	?	
Aida	(Edison)	USA	1911	Mary Fuller, Charles Ogle	
Aida	Clemente Fracassi	It.	1954	Sophia Loren, Lois Maxwell	Aida
Alexander the Great	Robert Rossen	USA	1956	Richard Burton, Fredric March	
Alfred the Great	Clive Donner	UK	1969	David Hemmings, Michael York	
L'amante di Paride[+]	Marc Allegret	It.	1955	Hedy Lamarr, Massimo Serato	The Face That Launched a Thousand Ships/ Loves of Three Queens
Amazzoni donne d'amore e di guerra	Al Bradley	It./Sp.	1973	Lincoln Tate, Lucretia Love	Barbarian Women*
Amor di schiave	(Cines)	It.	1910	?	Love of the Slaves
Gli amori di Angelica	J. McWarriol	It./Sp.	1967	Claudie Lange, Joaquín Blanco	
Gli amori di Ercole	Carlo Ludovico Bragaglia	It./Fr.	1960	Jayne Mansfield, Mickey Hargitay	Loves of Hercules/ The Love of Hercules*
L'amour et Psyché	Romeo Bossetti	Fr.	1908	?	
Amphitryon	Reinhold Schünzel	Ger./Fr.	1935	Willy Fritsch, Kathe Gold	
Amphytrion	?Louis Feuillade	Fr.	1910	?	
Androclès	Louis Feuillade	Fr.	1912	Renée Carl, Raymond Lyon	

Title	Director	Country	Year	Cast	Alternative title
Androcles and the Lion	Chester Erskine	UK	1952	Alan Young, Jean Simmons	
Annibale	Edgar G. Ulmer, Carlo Ludovico Bragaglia	It.	1960	Victor Mature, Gabriele Ferzetti	Hannibal
Anno 79 – distruzione Ercolano	Gianfranco Parolini	It./Fr.	1963	Susan Paget, Brad Harris	
The Antagonists	Boris Sagal	USA	1981	Peter O'Toole, Peter Strauss	Masada (TVM) (1980)
Antigone	?Mario Caserini	It.	1911	?	
Antigone	Giorgos Tsavellas	Gr.	1961	Irene Papas, Manos Katrakis	Antigone
Antony and Cleopatra	Charles Kent	USA	1908	Paul Panzer, Maurice Costello	
Antony and Cleopatra*	Charlton Heston	UK/Sp./Switz	1972	Charlton Heston, Hildegard Neil	
L'apocalisse	G. M. Scotese	It.	1950	T. Carminati, Massimo Serato	
The Archer and the Sorceress*	Nicholas Corea	USA	1981	Lane Caudell, Belinda Bauer	
The Arena	Steve Carver	USA	1973	Pam Grier, Margaret Markov	
Arrivano i Titani	Duccio Tessari	It./Fr.	1962	Giuliano Gemma, Antonella Lualdi	Sons of Thunder/My Son, the Hero
L'asino d'oro: processo per fatti strani contro Lucius Apuleius cittadino romano	Sergio Spina	It./Alg.	1970	Barbara Bouchet, Sami Pavel	
L'assedio di Siracusa	Pietro Francisci	It./Fr.	1960	Rossano Brazzi, Tina Louise	Siege of Syracuse
Atlantis, the Lost Continent	George Pal	USA	1961	Anthony Hall, Joyce Taylor	

Film title	Director	Country	Release date	Leading players	English-language title
Atlas	Roger Corman	USA/Gr.	1961	Michael Forest, Frank Wolff	
Attila	Pietro Francisci	It./Fr.	1955	Anthony Quinn, Sophia Loren	Attila the Hun*
Attila, flagello di dio	Febo Mari	It.	1918	?	
Aux lions les Chrétiens	Louis Feuillade	Fr.	1911	Renée Navarre, Renée Carl	
Aux temps des premiers Chrétiens – Quo vadis?	André Calmettes	Fr.	1910	?	
Le avventure di Enea	Franco Rossi	It./Yug.	1974	Giulio Brogi, Olga Karlatos	
Le avventure di Ulisse	Franco Rossi, Mario Bava, Piero Schivazappa	It./Yug.	1968	Bekim Fehmiu, Irene Papas	from Odissea (TVM) (1968)
I baccanali di Tiberio	Giorgio Simonelli	It.	1960	Ugo Tognazzi, Walter Chiari	
Le baccanti	Giorgio Ferroni	It./Fr.	1961	Taina Elg, Pierre Brice	The Bacchantae
Barabba	Richard Fleischer	It.	1962	Anthony Quinn, Vittorio Gassman	Barabbas
Barabbas	Alf Sjöberg	Swed.	1953	Ulf Palme, Inge Waern	Barabbas
La battaglia di Maratona	Jacques Tourneur (+ Mario Bava, Bruno Vailati)	It./Fr.	1960	Steve Reeves, Mylène Demongeot	The Giant of Marathon
The Beastmaster	Don Coscarelli	USA	1982	Marc Singer, Tanya Roberts	
Ben-Hur	Sidney Olcott (+ Frank Oakes Rose)	USA	1907	?	
Ben-Hur	William Wyler (+ Andrew Marton, Richard Thorpe)	USA	1959	Charlton Heston, Stephen Boyd	

Title	Director	Country	Year	Cast	Alternative title
Christ	(+ Christy Cabanné, Ferdinand P. Earle, B. Reaves Eason)			Bushman	
La Bibbia	Pier Antonio Gariazzo, A. Vay	It.	1922	?	*After Six Days* (?)
La Bibbia	John Huston (+ Ernst Haas)	It.	1966	John Huston, George C. Scott	*The Bible in the Beginning...*
Bible	Wakefield Poole	USA	1974	Bo White, Caprice Couselle	
The Big Fisherman	Frank Borzage	USA	1959	Howard Keel, Susan Kohner	
Blade af Satans Bog†	Carl Dreyer	Den.	1919	Helge Nissen, Halvard Hoff	*Leaves from Satan's Book*
Boadicea	?	UK	1918	Ellaline Terriss	
Boadicea	Sinclair Hill	UK	1926	Phyllis Neilson-Terry, Lillian Hall-Davis	
The Boys from Syracuse	A. Edward Sutherland	USA	1940	Allan Jones, Martha Raye	
Brenno il nemico di Roma	Giacomo Gentilomo	It.	1963	Gordon Mitchell, Tony Kendall	*Battle of the Spartans*
Brute Force†	D. W. Griffith	USA	1914	Lionel Barrymore, Mae Marsh	
Brutus	Enrico Guazzoni	It.	1910	?	*Brutus*
Brutus II	Giuseppe De Liquoro	It.	1910	?	
Cabiria	Giovanni Pastrone	It.	1914	Lidia Quaranta, Bartolomeo Pagano	*Cabiria*
La caduta di Troia	Piero Fosco	It.	1910	Mme. Devesnes, Giulio Vino	*The Fall of Troy*
*Caesar and Cleopatra**	Gabriel Pascal	UK	1945	Vivien Leigh, Claude Rains	
Cain and Abel	(Vitagraph)	USA	1911	?	
Caio Giulio Cesare	Enrico Guazzoni	It.	1914	Amleto Novelli, Gianna Terribili Gonzales	*Julius Caesar*

Film title	Director	Country	Release date	Leading players	English-language title
Caio Gracco tribuno	(Latium Film)	It.	1911	?	
Le calde notti di Caligula	Roberto Bianchi Montero	It.	1977	Carlo Colombo, Gastone Pescucci	Caligula's Hot Nights
Le calde notti di Poppea	Guido Malatesta	It.	1969	Olinka Bérová, Brad Harris	Poppaea's Hot Nights
Caligula	Tinto Brass	USA/It.	1979	Malcolm McDowell, Teresa Ann Savoy	
Caligula et Messalina	Antonio Passalia	Fr.	1982	John Turner, Betty Roland	Caligula and Messalina
Camelot	Joshua Logan	USA	1967	Richard Harris, Vanessa Redgrave	
Il canto di Circe	Giuseppe De Liquoro	It.	1920	?	
Carry On Cleo	Gerald Thomas	UK	1964	Sidney James, Amanda Barrie	
Cartagine in fiamme	Carmine Gallone	It./Fr.	1960	Pierre Brasseur, Daniel Gélin	Carthage in Flames*
Catilina	Mario Caserini	It.	1910	Maria Caserini Gasperini, Amleto Novelli	Catiline
Caveman	Carl Gottlieb	USA	1981	Ringo Starr, Barbara Bach	
La chanson de Roland†	Frank Cassenti	Fr./It.	1978	Klaus Kinski, Alain Cuny	
Le Christ en croix	Louis Feuillade	Fr.	1910	Mme. Gérard Bourgeois	
The Christian Martyrs	Otis Turner	USA	1909	Hobart Bosworth, Betty Harte	
Le Christ marchant sur les eaux	Georges Méliès	Fr.	1899	?	
Christus	Giulio Antomoro	It.	1915	?	Christus

Title	Director	Country	Year	Cast	Alt. title
Il Cid	Mario Caserini	It.	1910	?	
La civilisation à travers les âges†	Georges Méliès	Fr.	1908	?	
Clash of the Titans*	Desmond Davis	UK	1981	Harry Hamlin, Laurence Olivier	
Cleopatra	Charles L. Gaskill	USA	1913	Helen Gardner, Robert Gaillord	
Cleopatra	J. Gordon Edwards	USA	1917	Theda Bara, Fritz Leiber	
Cleopatra	Cecil B. DeMille	USA	1934	Claudette Colbert, Henry Wilcoxon	
Cleopatra*	Joseph L. Mankiewicz	USA	1963	Elizabeth Taylor, Richard Burton	
Cléopatre	Georges Méliès	Fr.	1899	?	
Cléopatre	(Pathé)	Fr.	1910	?	
Cléopatre	(Film d'Art)	Fr.	1910	?	
Cléopatre	M. Marlaud	Fr.	1913	?	
Il colosso di Rodi	Sergio Leone	It./Sp./Fr.	1961	Rory Calhoun, Lea Massari	The Colossus of Rhodes
Il colosso di Roma	Giorgio Ferroni	It.	1965	Gordon Scott, Massimo Serato	Arm of Fire*
I coltelli del vendicatore	Mario Bava	It.	1966	Cameron Mitchell, Elisa Mitchell	Knives of the Avenger
Columnă	Mircea Drăgan	Rom.	1968	Richard Johnson, Antonella Lualdi	The Column
Conan the Barbarian	John Milius	USA	1982	Arnold Schwarzenegger, Sandahl Bergman	
Il conquistatore di Atlantide	Alfonso Brescia	It./Eg.	1966	Kirk Morris, Luciana Gilli	Kingdom in the Sand
Il conquistatore di Corinto	Mario Costa	It./Fr.	1962	Jacques Sernas, Geneviève Grad	

Film title	Director	Country	Release date	Leading players	English-language title
Coriolano, eroe senza patria	Giorgio Ferroni	It./Fr.	1965	Gordon Scott, Alberto Lupo	Thunder of Battle/ Coriolanus, Hero without a Country
La cortigiana di Babilonia	Carlo Ludovico Bragaglia	It.	1955	Rhonda Fleming, Roldano Lupi	Queen of Babylon
Costantino il grande	Lionello De Felice	It.	1961	Cornel Wilde, Belinda Lee	Constantine the Great/Constantine and the Cross*
Creatures the World Forgot	Don Chaffey	UK	1971	Julie Ege, Brian O'Shaughnessy	
Il crollo di Roma	Antonio Margheriti	It.	1963	Carl Möhner, Loredana Nusciak	Rome in Flames
Cupid and Psyche	Thomas Edison	USA	1897	?	
Cupid et Psyché	(Gaumont)	Fr.	1908	?	Cupid and Psyche
Cupid et Psyché	(Pathé)	Fr.	1912	?	Cupid and Psyche
Dacii	Sergiu Nicolaescu	Rom./Fr.	1967	Amza Pellea, Pierre Brice	The Dacians/The Warriors
Damon and Pythias	Otis Turner	USA	1908	Hobart Bosworth, Betty Harte	
Damon and Pythias	Otis Turner	USA	1914	William Worthington, Frank Lloyd	
The Dancer of the Nile	William S. Earle	USA	1923	Carmel Myers, Malcolm McGregor	
Daniel	Fred Thomson	USA	1913	Courtenay Foote, Charles Kent	
A Daughter of Pan	Charles L. Gaskill	USA	1913	Helen Gardner	
The Daughter of the Hills	(Famous Players)	USA	1913	Laura Sawyer, House Peters	

Title	Director	Country	Year	Cast	English Title
David	?	It.	1912	?	
David and Bathsheba	Henry King	USA	1951	Gregory Peck, Susan Hayward	
David and Goliath	Sidney Olcott	USA	1908	?	
David e Golia	(Pathé)	Fr.	1910	?	David and Goliath
David e Golia	Richard Pottier, Ferdinando Baldi	It.	1960	Orson Welles, Ivo Payer	David and Goliath*
Day of Triumph	Irving Pichel, John Coyle	USA	1954	Robert Wilson, Lee J. Cobb	
Delenda Carthago	Luigi Maggi	It.	1914	?	
The Deluge	(Vitagraph)	USA	1911	?	
Demetrius and the Gladiators*	Delmer Daves	USA	1954	Victor Mature, Susan Hayward	
Les derniers jours de Pompei	Marcel L'Herbier	Fr./It.	1948	Micheline Presle, Georges Marchal	
Didone abbandonata	(Ambrosio)	It.	1910	?	Dido Forsaken by Aeneas
I dieci gladiatori	Gianfranco Parolini	It.	1964	Roger Browne, Susan Paget	Ten Desperate Men
Distruzione di Cartagine	Mario Caserini	It.	1912	?	
La donna dei Faraoni	Victor Tourjanksy, Giorgio Rivalta	It.	1960	Linda Cristal, Pierre Brice	The Pharaohs' Woman
Les douze travaux d'Hercule	Emile Cohl	Fr.	1910	(animated)	
Dragonslayer	Matthew Chapman	USA	1981	Peter MacNicol, Ralph Richardson	
I due gladiatori	Mario Caiano	It.	1965	Richard Harrison, Moira Orfei	Fight or Die/The Two Gladiators
Due notti con Cleopatra	Mario Mattòli	It.	1954	Sophia Loren, Alberto Sordi	Two Nights with Cleopatra

Film title	Director	Country	Release date	Leading players	English-language title
Edipo re	Giuseppe De Liquoro	It.	1910	?	Oedipus Rex
Edipo re	Pier Paolo Pasolini	It.	1967	Franco Citti, Alida Valli	Oedipus Rex
E di Shaul e dei sicari sulle vie da Damasco	Gianni Toti	It.	1974	Alessandro Haber, Brizio Montinaro	
The Egyptian	Michael Curtiz	USA	1954	Edmund Purdom, Jean Simmons	
El Cid*	Anthony Mann	Sp./It.	1961	Charlton Heston, Sophia Loren	
Elektra	(Vitagraph)	USA	1910	Mary Fuller	
Elektra	Michael Cacoyannis	Gr.	1962	Irene Papas, Yannis Fertis	Electra
An Elopement in Rome	Marshall Neilan	USA	1914	Ruth Roland, John E. Brennan	
Ercole al centro della terra	Mario Bava	It.	1962	Reg Park, Leonora Ruffo	Hercules in the Centre of the Earth/Hercules in the Haunted World/The Vampires vs Hercules
Ercole alla conquista di Atlantide	Vittorio Cottafavi	It./Fr.	1961	Reg Park, Fay Spain	Hercules Conquers Atlantis/Hercules and the Captive Women
Ercole contro i figli del sole	Osvaldo Civirani	It./Sp.	1964	Mark Forest, Anna Maria Pace	Hercules against the Sons of the Sun

Italian title	Director	Country	Year	Cast	English title
Ercole contro il gigante Golia	Guido Malatesta	It.	1965	Kirk Morris, Luciana Paoli	
Ercole contro i tiranni di Babilonia	Domenico Paolella	It.	1965	Rock Stevens, Helga Liné	*Hercules and the Tyrants of Babylon*
Ercole contro Moloch	Giorgio Ferroni	It./Fr.	1964	Gordon Scott, Rosalba Neri	*Hercules Attacks/The Conquest of Moloch/Conquest of Mycenae/Hercules' Challenge**
Ercole contro Roma	Piero Pierotti	It./Fr.	1965	Alan Steel, Wandisa Guida	*Hercules against Rome/Hercules in Rome*
Ercole e la regina di Lidia	Pietro Francisci	It./Fr.	1959	Steve Reeves, Sylva Koscina	*Hercules Unchained*/Hercules and the Queen of Lidia*
Ercole l'invincibile	Alvaro Mancori	It.	1963	Dan Vadis, Ken Clark	*Hercules the Invincible*
Ercole, Sansone, Maciste e Ursus: gli invincibili	Giorgio Capitani	It./Sp./Fr.	1965	Alan Steel, Nadir Baltimor	*Hercules, Maciste, Samson and Ursus vs the Universe/Samson and the Mighty Challenge*
Ercole sfida Sansone	Pietro Francisci	It.	1964	Kirk Morris, Richard Lloyd	*Hercules, Samson and Ulysses*
Erik, il vichingo	Mario Caiano	It./Sp.	1965	Gordon Mitchell, Giuliano Gemma	*Vengeance of the Vikings*
Erode il grande	Arnaldo Genoino	It./Fr.	1959	Edmund Purdom, Sylvia López	*Herod the Great*
Erodiade	?	It.	1912	Suzanne de Labroy	

Film title	Director	Country	Release date	Leading players	English-language title
L'eroe di Babilonia	Siro Marcellini	It./Fr.	1964	Gordon Scott, Geneviève Grad	The Hero of Babylon/Goliath – King of the Slaves
Ero e Leandro	(Ambrosio)	It.	1910	?	Hero and Leander
Ester e il re	Raoul Walsh	It.	1961	Joan Collins, Richard Egan	Esther and the King
Esther	Louis Feuillade	Fr.	1910	Renée Carl	
Excalibur	John Boorman	USA	1981	Nigel Terry, Helen Mirren	
L'Exode	Louis Feuillade	Fr.	1910	Renée Carl	
Fabiola	Enrico Guazzoni	It.	1917	Elena Sangro, Amleto Novelli	Fabiola
Fabiola	Alessandro Blasetti	It./Fr.	1949	Michèle Morgan, Henri Vidal	The Fighting Gladiator/Fabiola and the Fighting Gladiator/Fabulous Fabiola
The Fall of Pompeii	(Motograph)	UK	1913	?	
The Fall of the Roman Empire*	Anthony Mann (+ Andrew Marton)	Sp./It.	1964	Alec Guinness, Stephen Boyd	
Faraon	Jerzy Kawalerowicz	Pol.	1966	Jerzy Zelnik, Barbara Brylska	Pharaoh
Le fatiche di Ercole	Pietro Francisci	It.	1958	Steve Reeves, Sylva Koscina	Hercules*
Fedra	?	It.	?	?	Phaedra
Le festin de Balthazar	Louis Feuillade	Fr.	1910	Renée Carl, Léonce Perret	
Fidelité romaine	Louis Feuillade	Fr.	1911	Jean Ayme	
Il figlio di Cleopatra	Ferdinando Baldi	It./Eg.	1965	Mark Damon, Scilla Gabel	
Il figlio di Spartacus	Sergio Corbucci	It.	1962	Steve Reeves, Jacques Sernas	The Son of Spartacus/The Slave

Original title	Director	Country	Year	Cast	English title
La fille de Jephté	Louis Feuillade	Fr.	1910	Renée Carl, Léonce Perret	Jephthah's Daughter
Il filo d'Arianna	Mario Caserini	It.	1920	?	
Il filo d'Arianna	Eugenio Perego	It.	1928	?	
Fils de la Sunamite	Louis Feuillade	Fr.	1911	Renée Carl	
Le fils de Locuste	Louis Feuillade	Fr.	1911	Renée Carl	
Flore et Zephyre	Louis Feuillade	Fr.	1911	?	
The Folly of Vanity	Henry Otto	USA	1924	?	
Frine cortigiana d'Oriente	Mario Bonnard	It.	1954	Elena Kleus, Pierre Cressoy	
From the Manger to the Cross	Sidney Olcott	USA	1913	Robert Henderson-Bland, Gene Gauntier	
A Funny Thing Happened on the Way to the Forum	Richard Lester (+ Bob Simmons)	USA	1966	Zero Mostel, Michael Crawford	
La furia dei barbari	Guido Malatesta	It.	1960	Edmund Purdom, Rossana Podestà	
La furia di Ercole	Gianfranco Parolini	It./Fr.	1962	Brad Harris, Brigitte Corey	The Fury of Hercules
Galatée	Georges Méliès	Fr.	1909	?	
Gawain and the Green Knight	Stephen Weeks	UK	1973	Murray Head, Ciaran Madden	
Gigante di Metropolis	Umberto Scarpelli	It.	1963	Gordon Mitchell, Roldano Lupi	The Giant of Metropolis
I giganti della Tessaglia	Riccardo Freda	It./Fr.	1961	Roland Carey, Massimo Girotti	The Giants of Thessaly/Jason and the Golden Fleece
I giganti di Roma	Antonio Margheriti	It./Fr.	1964	Richard Harrison, Wandisa Guida	Giants of Rome
Giuditta e Oloferne	?	It.	1906	?	Judith and Holofernes

Film title	Director	Country	Release date	Leading players	English-language title
Giuditta e Oloferne	Baldassare Negroni	It.	1928	?	
Giuditta e Oloferne	Fernando Cerchio	It./Fr.	1960	Massimo Girotti, Isabelle Corey	Head of a Tyrant
Giulio Cesare	? Enrico Guazzoni	It.	1909	?	Julius Caesar
Giulio Cesare contro i pirati	Sergio Grieco	It.	1961	Gustavo Rojo, Gordon Mitchell	
Giulio Cesare e Brutus	Giovanni Pastrone	It.	1909	?	
Giulio Cesare il conquistatore delle Gallie	Amerigo Anton	It.	1963	Cameron Mitchell, Rik Battaglia	Caesar the Conqueror
Giuseppe venduto dai fratelli	Irving Rapper, Luciano Ricci	It.	1961	Geoffrey Horne, Belinda Lee	Sold into Egypt/ Joseph and His Brothers
Il gladiatore che sfidò l'impero	Domenico Paolella	It.	1965	Rock Stevens, Walter Barnes	
Gladiatore di Messalina	Umberto Lenzi	It.	1964	Richard Harrison, Lydia Alfonsi Gasboni	Gladiator of Messalina
Il gladiatore di Roma	Mario Costa	It.	1962	Gordon Scott, Wandisa Guida	Battles of the Gladiators/The Gladiator of Rome
Il gladiatore invincibile	Antonio Momplet	It./Sp.	1961	Richard Harrison, Isabelle Corey	Invincible Gladiator
Le gladiatrici	Antonio Leonviola	It.	1963	Susy Andersen, Joe Robinson	The Amazon Women/Women Gladiators*

Title	Director	Country	Year	Cast	English Title
Das goldene Ding	Edgar Reitz, Ulla Stoeckl, Alf Brustellin, Nikos Perakis	W. Ger.	1972	Christian Reitz, Oliver Jovine	
The Golden Fleece	?	USA	1918	?	
Golgotha	Julien Duvivier	Fr.	1935	Robert le Vigan, Jean Gabin	Golgotha
Golia alla conquista di Bagdad	Domenico Paolella	It.	1966	Rock Stevens, Helga Liné	Goliath against Bagdad
Goliath contro i giganti	Guido Malatesta, Gianfranco Parolini	It./Sp.	1961	Brad Harris, Gloria Milland	Goliath against the Giants
Goliath e la schiava ribelle	Mario Caiano	It./Fr.	1964	Gordon Scott, Ombretta Colli	Arrow of the Avenger
I grandi condottieri	Marcello Baldi, Francisco Pérez Dolz	It./Sp.	1966	Anton Geesink, Rosalba Neri	The Great Leaders
The Greatest Story Ever Told	George Stevens (+ Jean Negulesco, David Lean, Charlton Heston)	USA	1965	Max von Sydow, Charlton Heston	
The Green Pastures†	Marc Connelly, William Keighley	USA	1936	Rex Ingram, Oscar Polk	
La guerra di Troia	Giorgio Ferroni	It./Fr.	1961	Steve Reeves, Juliette Mayniel	The Wooden Horse of Troy/The Trojan War*
Le guerriere dal seno nudo	Terence Young	It./Fr./Sp.	1974	Alena Johnston, Sabine Sun	The Amazons
Hawk the Slayer*	Terry Marcel	UK	1981	Jack Palance, John Terry	
Helena – der Untergang von Troja	Manfred Noa	Ger.	1924	Edy Darclea, Wladimir Gaidarow	
Helen of Troy	Robert Wise (+ Raoul Walsh)	USA	1955	Jacques Sernas, Rossana Podestà	
Hermann der Cherusker – die Schlacht im Teutoburger Wald	Ferdy Baldwin	W. Ger./It.	1977 (prod. 1965)	Hans von Borsody, Cameron Mitchell	Arminius the Terrible

Film title	Director	Country	Release date	Leading players	English-language title
Hero	Barney Platts-Mills	UK	1982	Derek McGuire, Alastair Kenneil	
The Holy City	(Eclair)	Fr.	1913	?	
Home Talent†	Mack Sennett, James E. Abbe	USA	1921	Ben Turpin, James Finlayson	
I, Claudius (unfinished)	Josef von Sternberg	UK	1937	Charles Laughton, Flora Robson	The Epic That Never Was (TV) (excerpts)
Ifigenia	Michael Cacoyannis	Gr.	1977	Tatiana Papamoskou, Irene Papas	Iphigenia
L'île de Calypso: Ulysse et Polyphème	Georges Méliès	Fr.	1905	?	Ulysses and the Giant Polyphemus
The Illiac Passion	Gregory Markopoulos	USA	1968	Richard Beauvais	
The Illumination	(Vitagraph)	USA	1912	Helen Gardner, Tom Powers	
Ilya Muromets	Aleksandr Ptushko	USSR	1956	Boris Andreyev, Natalya Medvedeva	The Epic Hero and the Beast/ Sword and the Dragon
In a Roman Garden	Mr. McDonald	USA	1913	Edwin August, Jeanie Macpherson	
L'incendio di Roma	Guido Malatesta	It.	1968 (prod. 1963)	Lang Jeffries, Cristina Gaioni	Revenge of the Gladiators
In Cupid's Realm	(Vitagraph)	USA	1908	?	
In hoc signo vinces	Nino Oxilia	It.	1914	?	The Triumph of an Emperor
INRI†	Robert Wiene	Ger.	1923	Gregor Chmara, Asta Nielsen	Crown of Thorns (1934)
Die Insel der Seligen	Max Reinhardt	Ger.	1913	?	

Title	Director	Country	Year	Cast	Alternative title
In the Days of Trajan	Lorimer Johnston	USA	1913	J. Warren Kerrigan, George Periolat	
Intolerance[+]	D. W. Griffith	USA	1916	Constance Talmadge, Howard Gaye	
Gli invasori	Mario Bava	It./Fr.	1962	Cameron Mitchell, Giorgio Ardisson	*Erik the Conqueror/Fury of the Vikings/ Viking Invaders*
Gli invincibili fratelli Maciste	Roberto Mauri	It.	1965	Richard Lloyd, Claudie Lange	*Maciste Brothers*
Gli invincibili sette	Alberto De Martino	It./Sp.	1964	Tony Russel, Gérard Tichy	*The Invincible Seven*
Gli invincibili tre	Gianfranco Parolini	It./Tun.	1965	Alan Steel, Lisa Gastoni	*The Three Avengers*
Io, Semiramide	Primo Zeglio	It.	1963	Yvonne Furneaux, John Ericson	
L'ira di Achille	Marino Girolami	It.	1962	Gordon Mitchell, Jacques Bergerac	*Achilles*
Jack the Giant Killer	Nathan Juran	USA	1962	Kerwin Mathews, Judi Meredith	
Jason and the Argonauts[*]	Don Chaffey	UK	1963	Todd Armstrong, Nancy Kovack	
Jephtah's Daughter	(Vitagraph)	USA	1909	Annette Kellerman	
Jephtah's Daughter	(Warner's Features)	USA	1913	Arthur Maude, Constance Crawley	
Jerusalem in the Time of Christ	(Kalem)	USA	1908	?	
Jésus de Nazareth	André Calmettes	Fr.	1911	?	
Jesus of Nazareth	Sidney Olcott	USA	1912	?	
Joseph in the Land of Egypt	Eugene Moore	USA	1914	James Cruze, Marguerite Snow	
Joseph vendu par ses frères	Lucien Nonguet	Fr.	1904	?	

Film title	Director	Country	Release date	Leading players	English-language title
The Judgement of Solomon	(Vitagraph)	USA	1909	William Humphries, Florence Lawrence	
Judith et Holopherne	Louis Feuillade	Fr.	1909	Renée Carl	
Judith of Bethulia	D. W. Griffith	USA	1914	Blanche Sweet, Henry B. Walthall	Her Condoned Sin (1917)
Julius Caesar	William V. Ranous	USA	1908	William Shea, Maurice Costello	
Julius Caesar	Theo Bouwmeester	?	1910	?	
Julius Caesar	F. R. Benson	UK	1911	?	
Julius Caesar	David Bradley	USA	1949	Charlton Heston, Harold Tasker	
Julius Caesar	Joseph L. Mankiewicz	USA	1953	Marlon Brando, James Mason	
Julius Caesar	Stuart Burge	UK	1970	Charlton Heston, Jason Robards	
Jupiter's Darling	George Sidney	USA	1955	Howard Keel, Esther Williams	
Kampf um Rom (I and II)	Robert Siodmak	W. Ger./It./Rom.	1968–9	Laurence Harvey, Harriet Andersson	Battle for Rome/The Last Roman*
King of Kings	Nicholas Ray	USA/Sp.	1961	Jeffrey Hunter, Ron Randell	
The King of Kings	Cecil B. DeMille (+ D. W. Griffith)	USA	1927	H. B. Warner, Dorothy Cummings	
Knights of the Round Table	Richard Thorpe	UK	1954	Robert Taylor, Ava Gardner	
Lancelot and Guinevere	Cornel Wilde	UK	1963	Cornel Wilde, Jean Wallace	Sword of Lancelot
Lancelot du Lac	Robert Bresson	Fr./It.	1974	Luc Simon, Laura Duke Condominas	
Land of the Pharaohs	Howard Hawks	USA	1955	Jack Hawkins, Joan Collins	
Last Days of Pompeii	Robert William Paul	UK	1898	?	

Title	Director	Country	Year	Cast	English Title
The Last Days of Pompeii*	Ernest B. Schoedsack	USA	1935	Preston Foster, Basil Rathbone	
La légende de Daphnée	Louis Feuillade	Fr.	1910	?	
Les légendes des Phares	Louis Feuillade	Fr.	1909	Renée Carl	
La leggenda di Enea	Giorgio Rivalta	It./Fr.	1962	Steve Reeves, Carla Marlier	War of the Trojans
Le legioni di Cleopatra	Vittorio Cottafavi	It./Sp./Fr.	1960	Linda Cristal, Georges Marchal	Legions of the Nile
Il leone di Tebe	Giorgio Ferroni	It./Fr.	1965	Mark Forest, Yvonne Furneaux	The Lion of Thebes*
The Life of Moses	J. Stuart Blackton	USA	1909-10	William Humphrey, Charles Kent	
The Long Ships	Jack Cardiff	UK/Yug.	1964	Richard Widmark, Sidney Poitier	
The Lord of the Rings	Ralph Bakshi	USA	1978	(animated)	
I Maccabei	Enrico Guazzoni	It.	1911	Gianna Terribili Gonzales, Pina Menichelli	Maccabees
Maciste contro gli uomini luna/ Maciste e la regina di Samar	Giacomo Gentilomo	It./Fr.	1964	Alan Steel, Jany Clair	Hercules against the Moon Men/ Maciste vs the Stone Men/ Hercules Fights the Moon Men
Maciste contro il vampiro	Giacomo Gentilomo, Sergio Corbucci	It.	1961	Gordon Scott, Gianna Maria Canale	Goliath and the Vampires/Goliath against the Vampires
Maciste contro i mostri	Guido Malatesta	It.	1962	Reg Lewis, Margaret Lee	Colossus of the Stone Age/Land of the Monsters
Maciste, gladiatore di Sparta	Mario Caiano	It./Fr.	1965	Mark Forest, Marilù Tolo	Maciste and the Hundred Gladiators/ Maciste, Spartan Gladiator

Film title	Director	Country	Release date	Leading players	English-language title
Maciste il gladiatore più forte del mondo	Michele Lupo	It.	1963	Mark Forest, Scilla Gabel	Death on the Arena
Maciste, l'eroe più grande del mondo	Michele Lupo	It.	1963	Mark Forest, Giuliano Gemma	Goliath and the Sins of Babylon
Maciste, l'uomo più forte del mondo	Antonio Leonviola	It.	1961	Mark Forest, Moira Orfei	The Strongest Man in the World/The Mole Men Battle the Son of Hercules
Maciste nella terra dei Ciclopi	Antonio Leonviola	It.	1961	Gordon Mitchell, Chelo Alonso	Atlas in the Land of the Cyclops/Monster from the Unknown World/The Cyclops/Atlas against the Cyclops/Maciste in the Land of the Cyclops
Maciste nella Valle dei Re	Carlo Campogalliani	It./Fr./Yug.	1960	Mark Forest, Chelo Alonso	Maciste – the Mighty/Maciste in the Valley of Kings/Son of Samson
Maciste nelle miniere di re Salomone	Piero Regnoli	It.	1964	Reg Park, Wandisa Guida	Samson in King Solomon's Mines
The Magic Sword*	Bert I. Gordon	USA	1962	Basil Rathbone, Estelle Winwood	
Il magnifico gladiatore	Alfonso Brescia	It.	1964	Mark Forest, Marilù Tolo	
Male and Female†	Cecil B. DeMille	USA	1919	Gloria Swanson, Thomas Meighan	
Man's Genesis†	D. W. Griffith	USA	1912	Mae Marsh, Wilfred Lucas	
Manslaughter†	Cecil B. DeMille	USA	1922	Leatrice Joy, Thomas Meighan	

Marc(o)antonio e Cleopatra	Enrico Guazzoni	It.	1913	Amleto Novelli, Gianna Terribili Gonzales	Antony and Cleopatra
Marcus Lycinius	?	It.	1910	?	Marcus Lycinious
Maria Magdalena	Miguel Torres	Mex.	1946	Luis Alcoriza	
Marte, dio della guerra	Marcello Baldi	It.	1963	Roger Browne, Jackie Lane	
Martire Pompeiana	Giuseppe De Liquoro	It.	1909	?	The Martyr of Pompeii
Le martyre chrétien	(Gaumont)	Fr.	1911	?	The Christian Martyr
Les martyres chrétiens	Lucien Nonguet	Fr.	1905	?	
Medea	Pier Paolo Pasolini	It./Fr./ W. Ger.	1970	Maria Callas, Giuseppe Gentile	Medea
Messalina	Mario Caserini	It.	1910	?	
Messalina	Enrico Guazzoni	It.	1924	Rina De Liguoro, Gianna Terribili Gonzales	The Fall of an Empress
Messalina	Carmine Gallone	It.	1951	Maria Félix, Georges Marchal	The Affairs of Messalina
Messalina, Messalina	Bruno Corbucci	It.	1977	Anneka Di Lorenzo, Vittorio Caprioli	Messalina, Messalina
Messalina, venere imperatrice	Vittorio Cottafavi	It.	1960	Belinda Lee, Spiros Focas	Messalina*
Messaline	Alberto Capellani	Fr.	1909	?	Messalina
Il Messia	Roberto Rossellini	It./Fr.	1975	Piedro Maria Rossi, Anna Bonasso	The Messiah
Mikres afrodhitis	Nikos Koundouros	Gr.	1963	Takis Emmanouel, Kleopatra Rota	Young Aphrodites
The Minotaur	(Vitagraph)	USA	1910	?	
Mio figlio Nerone	Stefano Vanzina	It./Fr.	1956	Alberto Sordi, Gloria Swanson	Nero's Weekend
I misteri delle catacombe	Eugenio Perego	It.	1913	?	
La moglie di Claudio	Giovanni Pastrone	It.	1918	?	

Film title	Director	Country	Release date	Leading players	English-language title
Monty Python and the Holy Grail	Terry Gilliam, Terry Jones	UK	1975	Graham Chapman, John Cleese	
Monty Python's Life of Brian	Terry Jones	UK	1979	Terry Jones, Graham Chapman	
Moses	Gianfranco De Bosio	It./UK	1976	Burt Lancaster, Anthony Quayle	Moses the Lawgiver* (TVM)
Moses et l'Exode de l'Egypte	(Pathé)	Fr.	1907	?	Moses and the Exodus from Egypt
Moses und Aron	Jean-Marie Straub, Danièle Huillet	W. Ger./Fr./It.	1975	Günter Reich, Louis Devos	Moses and Aaron
La naissance de Vénus	Maurice Caussade	Fr.	1900	?	
La Nativité	Louis Feuillade	Fr.	1910	Renée Carl	
Nefertite, regina del Nilo	Fernando Cerchio	It.	1961	Jeanne Crain, Edmund Purdom	Queen of the Nile
Nel segno di Roma	Guido Brignone, Riccardo Freda	It./Fr./W. Ger.	1959	Anita Ekberg, Georges Marchal	Sign of the Gladiator
Neptune et Amphitrite	Georges Méliès	Fr.	1899	?	
Neptune's Daughter	Herbert Brenon, Otis Turner	USA	1914	Annette Kellerman, William Welsh	
Nero	J. Gordon Edwards	USA	1922	?	
Nero and the Burning of Rome	Edwin S. Porter	USA	1908	?	
Nerone	Arrigo Frustra	It.	1909	Alberto Capozzi, Lidia De Roberti	Nero and the Burning of Rome/ Nero, or The Fall of Rome
Nerone	Roberto Omegna	It.	1910	?	

Title	Director	Country	Year	Cast	Alternative title
Nerone	Alessandro Blasetti	It.	1930	Ettore Petrolini, Grazia Del Rio	
Nerone e Agrippina	Mario Caserini	It.	1913	Vittorio Rossi Pianelli, Mario Bonnard	
Nerone e Messalina	Primo Zeglio	It.	1954	Gino Cervi, Paola Barbara	
Néron essayant des poisons sur des esclaves	A. Promio	Fr.	1896	?	
Die Nibelungen	Harald Reinl	W. Ger./Yug.	1967	Karin Dor, Uwe Beyer	*Whom the Gods Wish to Destroy*
Die Nibelungen – Ein deutsches Heldenlied (I and II)	Fritz Lang	Ger.	1924	Paul Richter, Margarete Schön	
Noah's Ark: The Story of the Deluge	Michael Curtiz	USA	1928	Dolores Costello, George O'Brien	*Noah's Ark and the Flood That Destroyed the World*
I Normanni	Giuseppe Vari	It./Fr.	1962	Cameron Mitchell, Ettore Manni	*The Normans/ Invasion of the Normans/Attack of the Normans**
The Norseman	Charles B. Pierce	USA	1978	Lee Majors, Cornel Wilde	
L'odissea d'Homero	Giuseppe De Liquoro	It.	1910	?	*The Odyssey*
Oedipe roi	André Calmettes	Fr.	1908	?	
Oedipus the King	Philip Saville	UK	1968	Christopher Plummer, Orson Welles	
O.K. Nerone	Mario Soldati	It.	1951	Silvana Pampanini, Walter Chiari	*O.K. Nero*
One Million B.C.[†]	Hal Roach, Hal Roach Jr (+ D. W. Griffith)	USA	1940	Victor Mature, Carole Landis	
One Million Years B.C.	Don Chaffey	UK	1966	John Richardson, Raquel Welch	
L'oracle de Delphes	Georges Méliès	Fr.	1903	?	

Film title	Director	Country	Release date	Leading players	English-language title
Orazi e Curiazi	Terence Young, Ferdinando Baldi	It.	1962	Alan Ladd, Franca Bettoja	Duel of Champions*
L'orgie romaine	Louis Feuillade	Fr.	1911	?	
Oro per i Cesari	André de Toth (+ Sabatino Ciuffini, Riccardo Freda)	It./Fr.	1963	Jeffrey Hunter, Mylène Demongeot	Gold for the Caesars
La Passion	? Hollaman	Fr.	1897	?	
La Passion	Ferdinand Zecca	Fr.	1902 –7	?	
La Passion	? Jasset	Fr.	1905	?	
La Passion de Horitz	(Lumière)	Fr.	1897	?	
A Passover Miracle	Sidney Olcott	USA	1914	Henri Leone, Samuel Lowett	
The Passover Plot	Michael Campus	USA/ W. Ger.	1976	Zalman King, Donald Pleasence	
I patriarchi della Bibbia	Marcello Baldi	It.	1962	John Douglas, Judy Parker	The Patriarchs of the Bible
El pecado de Adan y Eva	Miguel Zacarias	Mex.	1969	Candy Cave, Jorge Rivero	
Pelleas and Melisande	Mr. MacDonald	USA	1913	Constance Crawley, Arthur Maude	
Perceval le Gallois	Eric Rohmer	Fr.	1978	Fabrice Luchini, André Dussolier	Perceval of Wales
Perseo l'invincibile	Alberto De Martino	It./Sp.	1963	Richard Harrison, Anna Ranalli	Perseus against the Monsters
Peter Tordenskjöld	(Continental Film)	Den.	1910	?	
Phèdre	Pathé Frères	Fr./It.?	1910	?	
Philémon et Beaucis	Georges Danola	Fr.	1910	?	

Title	Director	Country	Year	Cast	English Title
Ponzio Pilato	Irving Rapper, Gian Paolo Callegari	It./Fr.	1961	Jean Marais, Jeanne Crain	Pontius Pilate
Pope Joan	Michael Anderson	UK	1972	Liv Ullmann, Keir Dullea	
Poppea ed Ottavia	(Latium Film)	It.	1911	?	
Poppea, una prostituta al servizio dell'impero	Alfonso Brescia	It.	1972	Femi Benussi, Don Backy	
I predoni della steppa	Amerigo Anton	It.	1964	Kirk Morris, Peter White	The Mighty Khan/Terror of the Steppes
La presa di Roma	? Alberini	It.	1905	?	
La prêtresse de Carthague	Louis Feuillade	Fr.	1911	?	
Princess of the Nile	Harmon Jones	USA	1954	Debra Paget, Michael Rennie	
The Private Life of Helen of Troy	Alexander Korda	UK	1928	Maria Corda, Lewis Stone	
The Prodigal	Richard Thorpe	USA	1955	Lana Turner, Edmund Purdom	
Prométhée	Louis Feuillade	Fr.	1908	?	
Promithefs dhesmotis	Dimitrios Gaziadis	Gr.	1927	?	
La prophétesse de Thèbes	Georges Méliès	Fr.	1908	?	
The Pursuit of Venus	Edwin J. Collins	USA	1914	?	
Pygmalion et Galatée	Georges Méliès	Fr.	1898	?	
Quando gli uomini armarono la clava e con le donne fecero din don	Bruno Corbucci	It.	1971	Antonio Sabato, Aldo Giuffrè	The Age Old Battle One Thing Never Changes.../When Women Played Ding Dong
Quando le donne avevano la coda	Pasquale Festa Campanile	It.	1970	Senta Berger, Frank Wolff	When Women Had Tails

Film title	Director	Country	Release date	Leading players	English-language title
Quando le donne persero la coda	Pasquale Festa Campanile	It.	1973	Senta Berger, Lando Buzzanca	When Women Lost Their Tails
The Queen of Sheba	J. Gordon Edwards	USA	1922	Betty Blythe, Fritz Leiber	
Quest for Fire	Jean-Jacques Annaud	Can./Fr.	1982	Everett McGill, Ron Perlman	
Quo vadis	Lucien Nonguet	Fr.	1901	?	
Quo vadis	Ferdinand Zecca	Fr.	1901	?	
Quo vadis	?	Fr.	1908	?	
Quo vadis	Enrico Guazzoni	It.	1912	Amleto Novelli, Gustavo Serena	Quo vadis
Quo vadis	?	USA	1913	?	
Quo vadis	(Quo Vadis Film)	?	1913	?	
Quo vadis	George Jacoby, Gabriele D'Annunzio	It./Ger.	1924	Emil Jannings, Lilian Hall Davies	Quo vadis
Quo vadis	Mervyn LeRoy	USA	1951	Robert Taylor, Deborah Kerr	
Rachel's Man	Moshe Mizrahi	Isr.	1974	Mickey Rooney, Rita Tushingham	
Rape of the Sabines	? (Pathé)	Fr.	1910	?	
Il ratto delle Sabine	Mario Bonnard	It.	1945	Totò, Clelia Matania	The Rape of the Sabines
Il ratto delle Sabine	Richard Pottier	It./Fr.	1961	Roger Moore, Mylène Demongeot	The Rape of the Sabine Women
La regina delle Amazzoni	Vittorio Sala	It.	1960	Ed Fury, Gianna Maria Canale	Love Slaves of the Amazons/Queen of the Amazons
La regina di Ninive	(Ambrosio)	It.	c. 1911	?	The Queen of Nineveh

Original title	Director	Country	Year	Cast	English title
La regina di Saba	Pietro Francisci	It.	1952	Gino Cervi, Leonora Ruffo	The Queen of Sheba
La regina di Sparta	?	It.	1931	?	The Queen of Sparta
Una regina per Cesare	Victor Tourjansky (+ Piero Pierotti)	It./Fr.	1963	Pascale Petit, Giorgio Ardisson	A Queen for Caesar
Remo e Romolo: Storia di due figli di una lupa	Mario Castellacci, Pier Francesco Pingitore	It.	1976	Enrico Montesano, Gabriella Ferri	
Le retour d'Ulysse	Charles Le Bargy, André Calmettes	Fr.	1908	Julia Barthet, Albert Lambert	
Revak, lo schiavo di Cartagine	Rudolph Maté	It./USA	1961	Jack Palance, Milly Vitale	The Barbarian*/Revak the Rebel
Al-risāla	Moustapha Akkad	Leb.	1976	Anthony Quinn, Irene Papas	The Message
Il ritorno del gladiatore più forte del mondo	Adalberto Albertini	It.	1971	Brad Harris, John Barracuda	
La rivolta degli schiavi	Nunzio Malasomma	It./Sp./W. Ger.	1961	Rhonda Fleming, Lang Jeffries	The Revolt of the Slaves
La rivolta dei barbari	Guido Malatesta	It.	1965	Ronald Carey, Grazia Maria Spina	
La rivolta dei gladiatori	Vittorio Cottafavi	It./Sp.	1958	Gianna Maria Canale, Ettore Manni	The Warrior and the Slave Girl
La rivolta dei pretoriani	Alfonso Brescia	It.	1964	Richard Harrison, Moira Orfei	
La rivolta dei sette	Alberto De Martino	It.	1965	Tony Russel, Massimo Serato	The Spartan Gladiators/The Secret Seven
The Robe*	Henry Koster	USA	1953	Richard Burton, Jean Simmons	
Den røde kappe	Gabriel Axel	Den./Ice./Swed.	1967	Oleg Vidov, Gitte Hænning	The Red Mantle/Hagbard and Signe
Le roi de Thulé	Louis Feuillade	Fr.	1910	Renée Carl	
Roma contro Roma	Giuseppe Vari	It.	1964	John Drew Barrymore, Susy Andersen	War of the Zombies

Film title	Director	Country	Release date	Leading players	English-language title
The Roman	Otis Turner	USA	1910	Hobart Bosworth, Betty Harte	
Roman Scandals[†]	Frank Tuttle	USA	1933	Eddie Cantor, Ruth Etting	
Roma o morte!	(Vera Films)	It.	1913	?	Rome or Death
Roma rivuole Cesare	Miklós Jancsó	It.	1974	Daniel Olbrychski, Hiram Keller	Rome Wants Another Caesar
Romolo e Remo	Sergio Corbucci	It.	1962	Steve Reeves, Gordon Scott	Duel of the Titans
Rosmunda e Alboino	Carlo Campogalliani	It.	1961	Jack Palance, Eleonora Rossi Drago	Sword of the Conqueror
Il sacco di Roma	Enrico Guazzoni	It.	1920	Ida Magrini, Raimondo Van Riel	
Saffo, venere di Lesbo	Pietro Francisci	It./Fr.	1960	Tina Louise, Kerwin Mathews	Sappho, Venus of Lesbos/The Warrior Empress
The Saga of the Viking Women and their Voyage to the Waters of the Great Sea Serpent	Roger Corman	USA	1957	Abbey Dalton, Susan Cabot	Viking Women
Salammbò	(Ambrosio)	It.	1911	?	Salambo
Salammbò	(Pasquali)	It.	1914	?	Salambo
Salammbò	Pierre Marodon	Fr.	1924	Jean de Balzac, Rolla Normann	
Salammbò	Sergio Grieco	It.	1961	Jeanne Valérie, Jacques Sernas	The Loves of Salammbo
Salome	Oskar Messter	Ger.	1902	?	
Salome	J. Stuart Blackton	USA	1908	Florence Lawrence, Maurice Costello	
Salomé	(Pathé)	Fr.	1910	?	
Salome	(Brockliss)	UK	1910	?	Salome

Title	Director	Country	Year	Cast	English Title
Salomé	(Itala)	It.	c. 1913	?	Salome
Salome	(Savoia)	It.	1913	Siga. Costamegno, Suzanne de Labroy	
Salome	J. Gordon Edwards	USA	1918	Theda Bara, Albert Roscoe	
Salome	Charles Bryant	USA	1922	Alla Nazimova, Nigel de Brulier	
Salome	Malcolm Strauss	USA	1922	Diana Allen, Vincent Coleman	
Salome	Robert Wiene, Ludwig Kozma, Ernö Metzner	Ger.	1922	?	
Salome	William Dieterle	USA	1953	Rita Hayworth, Stewart Granger	
Samson	(Pathé)	Fr.	1907	?	
Samson	Lorimer Johnston, G. P. Hamilton	USA	1914	J. Warren Kerrigan, Mayme Kelso	
Samson	Edgar Lewis	USA	1915	William Farnum, Maud Gilbert	
Samson and Delilah	Cecil B. DeMille	USA	1949	Victor Mature, Hedy Lamarr	
Samson et Dalila	Ferdinand Zecca	Fr.	1902	?	
Samson und Delila†	Alexander Korda (+ Michael Curtiz)	Aus.	1923	Maria Corda, Alfredo Galoar	Samson and Delilah
San Marco	Luigi Maggi	It.	1913	?	
San Paolo	Giuseppe De Liquoro	It.	1909	?	
Sansone	Gianfranco Parolini	It.	1962	Brad Harris, Brigitte Corey	Samson
Sansone e il tesoro degli Incas	Piero Pierotti	It.	1968 (prod. 1964)	Pierre Cressoy, Alan Steel	The Last Treasure of the Aztecs
Sardanopolo re d'Assiria	Giuseppe De Liquoro	It.	1910	?	Sardanopolus, King of Assyria
Satanas†	F. W. Murnau	Ger.	1920	Fritz Kortner, Sadiah Gezza	
Satiricosissimo	Mariano Laurenti	It.	1970	Franco Franchi, Ciccio Ingrassia	

Film title	Director	Country	Release date	Leading players	English-language title
Satyricon	Gianluigi Polidoro	It.	1969	Laura Antonelli, Tina Aumont	
Satyricon	Federico Fellini	It./Fr.	1969	Martin Potter, Hiram Keller	Fellini – Satyricon
Saul and David	J. Stuart Blackton	USA	1909	Maurice Costello, William Ranous	
Saul e David	Marcello Baldi	It./Sp.	1965	Norman Wooland, Gianni Garko	Saul and David
Der Schädel der Pharaonentochter[+]	Otz Tollen	Ger.	1921	Emil Jannings	
La schiava di Roma	Sergio Grieco	It.	1961	Rossana Podestà, Guy Madison	Blood of the Warriors/The Roman Slave Girl
Le schiave di Cartagine	Guido Brignone	It./Sp.	1957	Gianna Maria Canale, Jorge Mistral	
Gli schiavi più forti del mondo	Michele Lupo	It.	1964	Roger Browne, Gordon Mitchell	Seven Slaves against Rome
Lo schiavo di Cartagine	Luigi Maggi, Roberto Omegna	It.	1910	?	The Slave of Carthage
Scipione l'africano	Carmine Gallone	It.	1937	Annibale Ninchi, Carlo Lombardi	Scipio Africanus
Scipione, detto anche 'l'africano'	Luigi Magni	It./W. Ger.	1971	Marcello Mastroianni, Vittorio Gassman	
Sebastiane	Derek Jarman, Paul Humfress	UK	1976	Leonardo Treviglio, Barney James	
Il sepolcro dei re	Fernando Cerchio	It./Fr.	1961	Debra Paget, Ettore Manni	Cleopatra's Daughter
Serpent of the Nile	William Castle	USA	1953	Rhonda Fleming, Raymond Burr	The Loves of Cleopatra
I sette a Tebe	Roy Ferguson	It./Fr.	1963	André Lawrence, Burt Plesher	
Sette contro tutti	Michele Lupo	It.	1966	Roger Browne, Liz Havilland	
Le sette folgori di Assur	Silvio Amadio	It.	1962	Jackie Lane, Howard Duff	7th Thunderbolt

I sette gladiatori	Pedro Lazaga	It./Sp.	1962	Richard Harrison, Loredana Nusciak	*Gladiators 7/ Gladiators Seven*
Le sette sfide	Primo Zeglio	It.	1961	Ed Fury, Elaine Stewart	
La sfida dei giganti	Maurizio Lucidi	It.	1966	Reg Park, Audrey Amber	
Shakespeare: La mort du Jules César	Georges Méliès	Fr.	1907	?	*Scorching Sands*
Shéhérazade	Pierre Gaspard-Huit	Fr./Sp./ It./W. Ger.	1963	Anna Karina, Gérard Barray	
The Shepherd King	J. Gordon Edwards	USA	1925	Violet Mersereau, Nerio Bernardi	
Siege of the Saxons	Nathan Juran	UK	1963	Ronald Lewis, Janette Scott	
Siegfried	Mario Caserini	It.	1912	Alberto Capozzi	*Siegfried*
Siegfried und das sagenhafte Liebesleben der Nibelungen	Adrian Hoven	W. Ger./ USA	1971	Raymond Harmstorf, Sybil Danning	*The Long Swift Sword of Siegfried/The Erotic Adventures of Siegfried*
The Sign of the Cross	W. Haggar	UK	1897	?	
The Sign of the Cross	Adolph Zukor	USA	1914	Dustin Farnum, William Farnum	
The Sign of the Cross	Cecil B. DeMille	USA	1933	Fredric March, Elissa Landi	
Sign of the Pagan	Douglas Sirk	USA	1954	Jeff Chandler, Jack Palance	
The Silver Chalice	Victor Saville	USA	1954	Virginia Mayo, Paul Newman	
Sins of Jesus	Robert Frank	?	?	?	
Sins of Jezebel	Reginald Le Borg	USA	1953	Paulette Goddard	
The Siren's Necklace	Van Dyke Brooke	USA	1909	?	
Die Sklavenkönigen[+]	Michael Curtiz	Aus.	1924	Maria Corda	*Moon of Israel*
The Slave	D. W. Griffith	USA	1909	Mary Pickford, Florence Lawrence	
Sodoma e Gomorra	Robert Aldrich (+ Sergio Leone)	It./Fr.	1962	Stewart Granger, Anouk Aimée	*Sodom and Gomorrah/The Last Days of Sodom and Gomorrah*

Film title	Director	Country	Release date	Leading players	English-language title
Sodom and Gomorrah	James Mitchell, Artie Mitchell	USA	1976	Sean Brancato, Gina Fornelli	
Sodom und Gomorrah[†] (I and II)	Michael Curtiz	Aus.	1922 –3	Lucy Doraine, Erica Wagner	Queen of Sin
Soldiers of the Cross	J. H. Perry	Austral.	1900	?	
Solo contro Roma	Herbert Wise (+ Riccardo Freda)	It.	1962	Rossana Podestà, Lang Jeffries	Vengeance of the Gladiators/Alone against Rome
Solomon and Sheba	King Vidor	USA	1959	Yul Brynner, Gina Lollobrigida	
Some Fish!	Dave Aylott	USA	1914	?	
A Son of the Immortals	Otis Turner	USA	1916	?	
La spada e la croce	Carlo Ludovico Bragaglia	It.	1959	Yvonne De Carlo, Jorge Mistral	Mary Magdalene
Una spada per l'impero	Sergio Grieco	It.	1965	Lang Jeffries, José Greci	
Le spade dei barbari	Michael E. Lemick	It.	1982	Peter McCoy, Yvonne Fraschetti	The Sword of the Barbarians
Spartaco	Ernesto Pasquali	It.	1913	Mario Asconia, Christina Ruspoli	Spartacus/The Revolt of the Gladiators
Spartaco	?	It.	1918	?	
Spartaco	Riccardo Freda	It.	1953	Massimo Girotti, Ludmilla Tcherina	Spartacus the Gladiator/Sins of Rome
Spartacus*	Stanley Kubrick	USA	1960	Kirk Douglas, Laurence Olivier	
Spartacus e i dieci gladiatori	Nick Nostro	It./Sp./Fr.	1965	Dan Vadis, Helga Liné	Day of Vengeance
Spartak	Yuri Grigorovich, Vadim Derbenyov	USSR	1975	Maris Liepa, Vladimir Vasiliev	Spartacus

Title	Director	Country	Year	Cast	Alternate title
The Star of Bethlehem	(Edison)	USA	1909	?	
The Star of Bethlehem	Theodore Marston	USA	1912	William Russell, Florence LaBadie	
Lo sterminatore dei barbari	Piero Regnoli	It.	1964	?	
The Story of Cupid	Fred W. Huntley	USA	1914	Frank Newburg	
A Story of David	Robert McNaught	UK	1962	Jeff Chandler, Basil Sydney	
The Story of Diana	Fred W. Huntley	USA	1914	?	
The Story of Mankind[†]	Irwin Allen	USA	1957	Ronald Colman, Hedy Lamarr	
The Story of Ruth	Henry Koster	USA	1960	Stuart Whitman, Elana Eden	
The Story of Venus	Fred W. Huntley	USA	1914	?	
Le supplice de Tantale	Ferdinand Zecca	Fr.	1902	?	
*The Sword and the Sorcerer**	Albert Pyun	USA	1982	Lee Horsley, Kathleen Beller	
The Sword in the Stone	Wolfgang Reitherman	USA	1963	(animated)	
Taur, il re della forza bruta	Antonio Leonviola	It.	1963	Joe Robinson, Bella Cortez	
The Ten Commandments[†]	Cecil B. DeMille	USA	1923	Theodore Roberts, Charles De Roche	
The Ten Commandments	Cecil B. DeMille	USA	1956	Charlton Heston, Yul Brynner	
Teodora	(Ambrosio)	It.	c. 1913	?	*Theodora*
Teodora	Giovanni Vitrotti, Leopoldo Carlucci	It.	1919	Rita Jolivet, René Maupré	
Teodora	?	It.	1921	?	
Teodora, imperatrice di Bisanzio	Riccardo Freda	It.	1954	Gianna Maria Canale, Georges Marchal	*Theodora, Slave Empress/ Theodora, Queen of Byzantium**/ Theodora*

Film title	Director	Country	Release date	Leading players	English-language title
Il terrore dei barbari	Carlo Campogalliani	It.	1959	Steve Reeves, Chelo Alonso	Goliath and the Barbarians*
Teseo contro il minotauro	Silvio Amadio	It.	1961	Rosanna Schiaffino, Bob Mathias	Warlord of Crete/The Minotaur
Theodora	Henri Pouctal	Fr.	1912	Mlle. Sahary-Djeli	Theodora
Theodora, imperatrice di Bizancio	Ernesto Mario Pasquali	It.	1909	?	Theodora, Empress of Byzantium
Theseus and the Minotaurus	J. Stuart Blackton	USA	?	?	
Though Your Sins Be As Scarlet	(Vitagraph)	USA	1911	Charles Kent, Julia Swayne Gordon	
The Three Ages[+]	Buster Keaton, Edward Kline	USA	1923	Buster Keaton, Wallace Beery	
The 300 Spartans	Rudolph Maté	USA	1962	Richard Egan, Ralph Richardson	
Il tiranno di Siracusa	Curtis Bernhardt, Alberto Cardone	It./USA	1962	Guy Williams, Don Burnett	The Tyrant of Syracuse/Damon and Pythias(?)
Tizio, Caio e Sempronio	Vittorio Metz, Marcello Marchesi	It.	1952	Nino Taranto, Virgilio Riento	
Le tonneau des Danaides	Georges Méliès	Fr.	1900	?	
Tonnerre de Jupiter, ou La Maison des Muses	Georges Méliès	Fr.	1903	?	
Les torches humaines de Justinien	Georges Méliès	Fr.	1908	?	
Totò contro Maciste	Fernando Cerchio	It.	1961	Totò, Samson Burke	
Totò e Cleopatra	Fernando Cerchio	It.	1963	Totò, Magali Noel	

Italian Title	Director	Country	Year	Cast	English Title
I tre centurioni	Roberto Mauri, Georges Cambret	It.	1965	Roger Browne, Mimmo Palmara	
Il trionfo dei dieci gladiatori	Nick Nostro	It./Sp.	1965	Dan Vadis, Helga Liné	Triumph of the Ten Gladiators
Il trionfo di Ercole	Alberto De Martino	It./Fr.	1964	Dan Vadis, Moira Orfei	The Triumph of Hercules/Hercules vs the Giant Warriors
Il trionfo di Maciste	Amerigo Anton	It.	1961	Kirk Morris, Cathia Caro	
The Triumph of Venus	Edwin Bower Hesser	USA	1918	?	
Trois bacchantes	Georges Méliès	Fr.	1900	?	
The Trojan Women	Michael Cacoyannis	USA	1971	Katharine Hepburn, Vanessa Redgrave	
Tryton	Alfréd Deésy	Fr.	1917	?	
Ulisse	Mario Camerini	It.	1954	Kirk Douglas, Silvana Mangano	Ulysses*
Ulisse contro Ercole	Mario Caiano	It.	1962	Michael Lane, Georges Marchal	Ulysses against Hercules/Ulysses against the Son of Hercules
Gli ultimi giorni di Pompeii	Luigi Maggi	It.	1908	?	The Last Days of Pompeii
Gli ultimi giorni di Pompeii	Giovanni Vitrotti	It.	1908	?	The Last Days of Pompeii
Gli ultimi giorni di Pompeii	Enrico Vidali	It.	1913	Suzanne De Labroy, Ines Melidoni	Last Days of Pompeii/The Priest of Isis
Gli ultimi giorni di Pompeii	Mario Caserini	It.	1913	Fernanda Negri Pouget, Eugenia Tettoni	The Last Days of Pompeii
Gli ultimi giorni di Pompeii	Amleto Palermi, Carmine Gallone	It.	1926	Maria Corda, Victor Varconi	The Last Days of Pompeii

Film title	Director	Country	Release date	Leading players	English-language title
Gli ultimi giorni di Pompeii	Mario Mattòli	It.	1937	Enrico Viarisio, Camillo Pilotto	?
Gli ultimi giorni di Pompeii	Mario Bonnard	It./Sp./Monaco	1959	Steve Reeves, Christine Kaufmann	The Last Days of Pompeii
L'ultimo dei vichinghi	Giacomo Gentilomo	It./Fr.	1961	Cameron Mitchell, Edmund Purdom	The Last of the Vikings*
L'ultimo gladiatore	Umberto Lenzi	It.	1965	Richard Harrison, Lisa Gastoni	
Ursus	Carlo Campogalliani	It./Sp.	1961	Ed Fury, Moira Orfei	Ursus/Mighty Ursus
Ursus gladiatore ribelle	Domenico Paolella	It.	1963	Dan Vadis, José Greci	The Rebel Gladiators
Ursus il terrore dei Kirghisi	Antonio Margheriti	It.	1964	Reg Park, Mireille Granelli	
Ursus nella terra di fuoco	Giorgio Simonelli	It.	1964	Ed Fury, Claudia Mori	Ursus in the Land of Fire/Son of Hercules in the Land of Fire
Ursus nella valle dei leoni	Carlo Ludovico Bragaglia	It.	196 ?	Ed Fury, Moira Orfei	Ursus in the Valley of the Lions
La valle dell'eco tonante	Amerigo Anton	It.	1965	Kirk Morris, Hélène Chanel	The Valley of the Resounding Echo/Hercules of the Desert
Il vangelo secondo Matteo	Pier Paolo Pasolini	It./Fr.	1964	Enrique Irazoqui, Mario Socrate	The Gospel according to St Matthew
Il Vecchio Testamento	Gianfranco Parolini	It.	1964	Brad Harris, Margaret Taylor	
La vendetta dei barbari	Giuseppe Vari	It.	1961	Daniella Rocca, Anthony Steel	Revenge of the Barbarians*

La vendetta dei gladiatori	Luigi Capuano	It.	1964	Mickey Hargitay, José Greci	*Goliath and the Dragon/ The Vengeance of Hercules*
La vendetta di Ercole	Vittorio Cottafavi	It./Fr.	1960	Mark Forest, Broderick Crawford	
La vendetta di Spartacus	Michele Lupo	It.	1965	Roger Browne, Scilla Gabel	*The Revenge of Spartacus/ Revenge of the Gladiators*
La vendetta di Ursus	Luigi Capuano	It.	1962	Samson Burke, Wandisa Guida	*The Mighty Warrior*
La Venere di Cheronea	Fernando Cerchio, Victor Tourjansky	It./Fr.	1958	Belinda Lee, Massimo Girotti	*Aphrodite, Goddess of Love*
La vengeance de Licinius	Alberto Capellani	Fr.	1910	?	
Vénus et Adonis	Alice Guy	Fr.	1901	?	
La vergine di Babilonia	(Ambrosio)	It.	c. 1910	?	*Virgin of Babylon*
Le vergini di Roma	Vittorio Cottafavi, Carlo Ludovico Bragaglia	It./ Fr.	1961	Louis Jourdan, Sylvia Syms	*Amazons of Rome/ Warrior Women*
Una vestale	Alberto Capellani	It.	1908	?	*One Vestal Virgin*
La vida intima de Marco Antonio y Cleopatra	Roberto Gavaldón	Mex.	1946	Luis Sandrini, Maria Antonieta Pons	
La vie du Christ	(Gaumont)	Fr.	1906	?	
La vie et la Passion de Jésus-Christ	Louis Lumière	Fr.	1897	?	
La vièrge d'Argos	Louis Feuillade	Fr.	1911	Renée Carl, Yvette Andreyor	
The Viking Queen	Don Chaffey	UK	1967	Don Murray, Carita	
The Vikings	Richard Fleischer	USA	1958	Kirk Douglas, Tony Curtis	
Vitellius	Henri Pouctal	Fr.	1911	Polin	*The Life of Christ*

Film title	Director	Country	Release date	Leading players	English-language title
Le voile des nymphes	Romeo Bossetti	Fr.	1909	?	
Vulcano, figlio di Giove	Emimmo Salvi	It.	1962	Rod 'Flash' Ilush, Bella Cortez	
The Wanderer	Raoul Walsh	USA	1925	William Collier Jr, Greta Nissen	
The War Lord	Franklin J. Schaffner	USA	1965	Charlton Heston, Rosemary Forsyth	
The Way of the Cross	J. Stuart Blackton	USA	1909	Rose Tapley, Maurice Costello	
Das Weib des Pharao	Ernst Lubitsch	Ger.	1922	Emil Jannings, Dagny Servaes	The Loves of Pharaoh
When Dinosaurs Ruled the Earth	Val Guest	UK	1970	Victoria Vetri, Robin Hawdon	
The Wife of Cain	Charles L. Gaskill	USA	1913	Helen Gardner	
Yahya peygamber	Hüseyin Peyda	Turk.	1965	Yusuf Sezgin, Ayfer Feray	
Les yeux ne peuvent pas en tout temps se fermer ou peut-être qu'un jour Rome se permettra de choisir à son tour	Jean-Marie Straub	W. Ger./ It.	1970	Adriano Aprà, Anne Brumagne	Othon

Critical Bibliography

1 Books

As the number of books dealing exclusively with historical epic films is miserably small, some titles of more general interest are also included below.

Cameron, Ian, *Adventure in the Cinema* (Studio Vista, London, 1973, 152 pp.). Lavishly illustrated general study, with one chapter, 'Adventure in History', giving an intelligent overview of the major historical epics.

Cary, John, *Spectacular! The Story of Epic Films* (Hamlyn, London, 1974, 160 pp.). Lavish, extra-large-format book dealing mostly with the facts and figures of epic films in their widest sense. Useful filmography.

Codelli, Lorenzo, and Lippi, Giuseppe, *Fant'Italia 1957–1966 emergenza apoteosi e riflusso del fantastico nel cinema italiano* (La Capella Underground, Trieste, 1976, 224 pp.). Catalogue published for the XIV Festival Internazionale del Film di Fantascienza in Trieste in 1976. Contains interesting studies of select pepla and studies of directors such as Cottafavi, Tessari, Gentilomo, Caiano and Mattòli.

Edelson, Edward, *Great Movie Spectaculars* (Doubleday, New York, 1976, 150 pp.). General study of spectaculars with details of budgets, special effects, etc.

Fofi, G., *Maciste sugli schermi* (Catalogo Bolaffi del Cinema Italiano, 1967).

Hirsch, Foster, *The Hollywood Epic* (A. S. Barnes, New Jersey, 1978, 129 pp.). Good general primer, with separate chapters on foreign epics, national epics, historical epics, the epic hero, etc.

Munn, Mike, *The Stories behind the Scenes of the Great Film Epics* (Illustrated Publications/Argus Books, Watford, 1982, 191 pp.). Beautifully illustrated pot-pourri, with many unusual stills. Variable text, weedy filmography.

Rovin, Jeff, *The Fabulous Fantasy Films* (A. S. Barnes, South Brunswick and New York, 1977, 271 pp.). Includes useful chapter on mythological films.

Solomon, Jon, *The Ancient World in the Cinema* (A. S. Barnes, South Brunswick and New York, 1978, 210 pp.). The only major study of the historical epic film, accurately and intelligently researched by a classicist from a historical point of view and supported by some fine illustrations.

Spinazzola, Vittorio, *Ercole alla conquista degli schermi* (Film 1963/Edizione Feltrinelli, Milan, 1974).

Various, *Il film storico italiano e la sua influenza sugli altri paesi* (Centro Sperimentale di Cinematografia, Rome, 1963, 110 pp.). Collection of papers presented at 1963 FIAF Congress in Italian and French, with synopses in English. Highly recommended.

2 Periodicals

The list below only includes general articles on historical epic films; it does not include reviews of films or interviews and studies of directors. Major articles are marked with an asterisk.

Arroita-Jauregui, Marcelo, 'Dos peliculas "menores": Los titanes, El hijo de Espartaco', *Film Ideal*, 15 October 1963.

Brownlow, Kevin, 'The Fabulous History of the Historical Epic', *Amateur Cine World*, December 1958.

*Cano, Luis, 'La mitologia en el cine', *Filmguia*, November 1974.

*Cano, Luis, 'Roma y el cine', *Filmguia*, March 1975.

Castellani, L., 'I film colossali', *Rivista del cinematografo*, March 1961.

Cook, Page, 'The Soundtrack', *Films in Review*, December 1963.

Cutts, John, et al., 'Symposium: Epics', *Motion*, Autumn 1963.

Dorigo, F., 'Guardano al cinema i maggiorati fisici', *Rivista del cinematografo*, March 1961.

Durand, Jacques, 'La chevalerie à l'écran', *L'Avant-Scène Cinéma*, 1 February 1979.

*Durgnat, Raymond, 'Epic', *Films and Filming*, December 1963.

Durgnat, Raymond, 'Homage to Hercules', *Motion*, Autumn 1963.

Dyer, Peter John, 'Some Mighty Spectacles', *Films and Filming*, February 1958.

Everson, William K., 'Film Spectacles', *Films in Review*, November 1954.

Farber, Stephen, 'The Spectacle Film: 1967', *Film Quarterly*, Summer 1967.

Fox, Joan, 'SPQR and All That', *Films in Review*, August/September 1961, letters.

Garel, Alain, 'Le péplum', *Image et Son*, April 1976.

*Ghigi, Giuseppe, 'Come si spiegano le fortune dei "pepla" su cui sembra che si torni a puntare', *Cineforum*, December 1977.

Heston, Charlton, 'Mammoth Movies I Have Known', *Films and Filming*, April 1962.

Houston, Penelope, and Gillet, John, 'Blockbusting', *Sight and Sound*, Spring 1963.

Jenkins, Glyn, 'What Is an Epic?', *ABC Film Review*, January 1961.

Kochenrath, Hans-Peter, 'Von Quo Vadis bis Cleopatra', *Filmstudio*, March 1964.

Lane, John Francis, 'The Money in Muscles', *Films and Filming*, July 1960.

Lawson, Robb, 'Will the Spectacle Drama Die?', *Picturegoer*, 29 August 1936.

Legrand, Gérard, 'Le péplum et la cape', *Positif*, March 1963.

Mardore, Michel, 'La fascination du phénix', *Cahiers du Cinéma*, May 1962.

Moullet, Luc, 'La victoire d'Ercole', *Cahiers du Cinéma*, May 1962.

Robinson, David, 'Spectacle', *Sight and Sound*, Summer 1955.

Sichier, Jacques, 'L'âge du péplum', *Cahiers du Cinéma*, May 1962.

Spinazzola, Vittorio, 'Herkules erobert die Leinwand', *Filmkritik*, August 1964.

Spinazzola, Vittorio, 'Significato e problemi del film storico-mitologico', *Cinema Nuovo*, July/August 1965.

*Spinazzola, Vittorio, et al., 'Le carnaval des demi-dieux', *Cinéma 64*, April 1964.

Taylor, Norman, 'Which Epic?', *ABC Film Review*, May 1971.

Torok, Jean-Paul, 'Le Maciste ne passera pas', *Midi-Minuit Fantastique*, June 1963.

*Whitehall, Richard, 'Days of Strife and Nights of Orgy', *Films and Filming*, March 1963.

*Zimmer, Jacques, 'Le peplum', *Image et Son*, July 1966.

Index of Names

Italics indicates an illustration; **bold type** indicates an entry in the filmography

Abbe, James E. **182**
Abuladze, Tengiz 164
Adam, Ken 30, 64
Addams, Dawn *127*
Addie, Robert 149
Aeschylus 67
Aimée, Anouk 30, *32*, **197**
Akkad, Moustapha 164, **193**
Alberini, (?) **191**
Albertini, Adalberto **193**
Alcoriza, Luis **187**
Aldrich, Robert 26, 30, **197**
Alessandrini, Goffredo 20
Alfonsi, Lidia 55
Allegret, Marc 64, **168**
Allen, Diana **195**
Almendros, Nestor 147
Alonso, Chelo 137, *139*, 160, **186, 200**
Amadio, Silvio 31, **196, 200**
Amber, Audrey **197**
Andersen, Susy **180, 193**
Anderson, Maxwell 130
Anderson, Michael **191**
Andersson, Harriet 137, **184**
Andrews, Harry 64, 129
Andreyev, Boris **182**
Andreyor, Yvette **203**
Andronicus, Livius 11
Angeli, Pier 117,*118*
Annaud, Jean-Jacques **192**
Annis, Francesca *97*
Antomoro, Giulio 44, **172**
Anton, Amerigo **180, 191, 201, 202**
Antonelli, Laura **196**
Antonini, Gabriele 55
Apollonius of Rhodes (Apollonius Rhodius) 10, 11, 60
Appian (Appianos) 92
Aprà, Adriano **204**
Ardisson, Giorgio **183, 193**
Aristotle 13, 53
Armstrong, Todd 60, **183**
Asconia, Mario **198**
August, Edwin **182**
Augustinus, Aurelius 11
Aumont, Tina **196**
Axel, Gabriel 141, **193**

Aylott, Dave **198**
Ayme, Jean **178**

Bach, Barbara **172**
Backy, Don **191**
Baena, Carlos **167**
Baird, Leah **167**
Baker, Diane 69
Baker, Stanley 64
Bakshi, Ralph **185**
Baldi, Ferdinando 37, 79, **175, 178, 190**
Baldi, Marcello 30, 37, **181, 187, 190, 196**
Baldwin, Ferdy **181**
Ballesteros, Antonio López 121
Baltimor, Nadir **177**
Bara, Theda 93, **173, 195**
Barbara, Paola **189**
Bardot, Brigitte 121
Barker-Mill, Adam 154
Barnes, George 36
Barnes, Joanna *113*
Barnes, Walter **180**
Barracuda, John **193**
Barray, Gérard **197**
Barrie, Amanda *90*, **172**
Barrymore, John Drew 61, **193**
Barrymore, Lionel **171**
Barthet, Julia **193**
Battaglia, Rik **180**
Baudin, Henri *82*
Bauer, Belinda **169**
Bava, Mario 6, 21, 31, 55, 64, 68, 141, 146, 150, **170, 173, 176, 183**
Baxter, Anne 36
Baxter, Les 137
Bazlen, Brigid 47, 50
Beauvais, Richard **182**
Beery, Wallace **200**
Behrman, S. N. 130
Beiza'i, Bahram 164
Beller, Kathleen 150, **199**
Benoît, Pierre 59
Benson, F. R. 89, **184**
Benussi, Femi **191**
Berger, Senta **191, 192**

Bergerac, Jacques **183**
Bergman, Ingmar 108
Bergman, Sandahl 151, 154, **173**
Berkani, Dary **168**
Bernardi, Nerio **197**
Bernhardt, Curtis **200**
Bernstein, Elmer 36, 163
Bérová, Olinka **172**
Berti, Marina 125
Bettoja, Franca 190
Beyer, Uwe **189**
Binder, Maurice 140
Blackman, Honor 60, 137
Blackton, J. Stuart 43, **185, 194, 196, 200, 204**
Blakely, Colin *152*
Blanco, Joaquín **168**
Blasetti, Alessandro 20, **178, 189**
Blomberg, Erik 164
Bloom, Claire 73
Blythe, Betty 37, **192**
Boethius, Anicius 11
Bonasso, Anna **187**
Bondarchuk, Sergei 163
Bonicelli, Vittorio 35
Bonnard, Mario 58, 72, 121, 124, **167, 179, 189, 192, 202**
Boone, Richard 156
Boorman, John 149, **178**
Boorman, Katrine 149
Borgnine, Ernest 144, 145
Borzage, Frank 42, **171**
Bossetti, Romeo **168, 204**
Bosworth, Hobart **172, 174, 194**
Bouchet, Barbara **169**
Bourgeois, Mme. Gérard **172**
Bouwmeester, Theo **184**
Bowker, Judi 59
Boyd, Stephen *2*, 88, *107*, 130, 131, 134, 161, **170, 178**
Bradbury, Ray 46
Bradley, Al **168**
Bradley, David 89, 99, **184**
Bragaglia, Carlo Ludovico 31, 59, 79, **168, 169, 174, 198, 202, 203**
Brancato, Sean **198**
Brando, Marlon *100*, 102, **184**

Index of Film Titles

Italics indicates an illustration; **bold type** indicates an entry in the filmography

Whom the Gods Wish to Destroy, see
 Die Nibelungen (1967)
The Wife of Cain **204**
The Wind and the Lion 84, 154,
 163–4
Women Gladiators, see *Le gladiatrici*
The Wooden Horse of Troy, see *La
 guerra di Troia*

Yahya peygamber **204**
The Yakuza 162
*Les yeux ne peuvent pas en tout temps
 se fermer ou peut-être qu'un jour
 Rome se permettra de choisir à son
 tour* **204**
Ying wang 161
Ying-ch'un ko chih feng-po 161

Yojimbo 162
Young Aphrodites, see *Mikres
 afrodhitis*
Young Bess 47

Zardoz 150